The Collected Works of
James M. Buchanan

VOLUME 7
The Limits of Liberty

James M. Buchanan
Blacksburg, Virginia, 1977

The Collected Works of

James M. Buchanan

VOLUME 7

The Limits of Liberty

Between Anarchy and Leviathan

LIBERTY FUND

Indianapolis

Foreword © 2000 by Liberty Fund, Inc.
The Limits of Liberty © 1975 by The University of Chicago.
All rights reserved
Printed in the United States of America

C 10 9 8 7 6 5 4 3
P 10 9 8 7 6 5 4 3 2

Library of Congress Cataloging-in-Publication Data
Buchanan, James M.
The limits of liberty : between anarchy and Leviathan / James M. Buchanan.
p. cm. — (The collected works of James M. Buchanan ; v. 7)
Includes bibliographical references.
ISBN 0-86597-225-7 (hc : alk. paper). — ISBN 0-86597-226-5 (pb : alk. paper)
1. Social contract. 2. Liberty. 3. State, The. I. Title.
II. Series: Buchanan, James M. Works. 1999 ; v. 7.
JC336.B83 2000
321'.07—dc21 99-24059

LIBERTY FUND, INC.
8335 Allison Pointe Trail, Suite 300
Indianapolis, IN 46250-1684

To the memory of my colleague

Winston C. Bush

And the main, most serious problem of social order and progress is ... the problem of having the rules obeyed, or preventing cheating. As far as I can see there is no intellectual solution of that problem. No social machinery of "sanctions" will keep the game from breaking up in a quarrel, or a fight (the game of being a society can rarely just dissolve!) unless the participants have an irrational preference to having it go on even when they seem individually to get the worst of it. Or else the society must be maintained by force, from without—for a dictator is not a member of the society he rules—and then it is questionable whether it can be called a society in the moral sense.

—Frank H. Knight,
"Intellectual Confusion on Morals and Economics"

Contents

Foreword

When *The Limits of Liberty* was published in 1975, the name James M. Buchanan became widely known even among the less well informed political philosophers and political theorists.[1] The book may be seen as a contribution to at least two debates that were thriving at the time of its publication. On the one hand, it built on and contributed to the "explorations in the theory of anarchy" (as the title of a volume edited by Gordon Tullock in 1972 is called), and thus, on a debate that at the time was one of the focal interests of the Virginia School of Political Economy.[2] On the other hand, the book contributed to the debate about political contractarianism originating from John Rawls's 1971 book *A Theory of Justice*.[3] Whereas, quite regrettably, the Virginia debate about anarchy was already well beyond its peak when *The Limits of Liberty* was published, the discussion of political contractarianism among philosophers, economists, and political scientists was still on its ascent. Within this debate, besides Rawls and Robert Nozick, Buchanan holds a central place as one of the "three new contractarians."[4]

The term "new contractarians" naturally provokes the question, who were the old ones? Now, as with the new, there certainly were more than three old contractarians. Yet, clearly, the three most prominent figures in the contractarian tradition are Thomas Hobbes, John Locke, and Immanuel Kant. In the literature, Buchanan is seen to be standing on Hobbes's shoulders, Nozick on Locke's, and Rawls on Kant's. As far as Rawls and Nozick are con-

---

1. James M. Buchanan, *The Limits of Liberty: Between Anarchy and Leviathan* (Chicago: University of Chicago Press, 1975), volume 7 in the series.

2. Gordon Tullock, ed., *Explorations in the Theory of Anarchy* (Blacksburg, Va.: Center for Study of Public Choice, 1972).

3. John Rawls, *A Theory of Justice* (Cambridge: Harvard University Press, 1971).

4. Robert Nozick, *Anarchy, State, and Utopia* (New York: Basic Books, 1974).

cerned, this classification seems natural. Rawls is a self-declared Kantian, and Nozick starts explicitly from Lockean premises. Buchanan, however, would not classify himself as a Hobbesian, and rightly so. For Buchanan's deepest ethical and normative political concern is the respect for the autonomy of the individual person. This concern is Kantian, not Hobbesian.[5]

Within the corpus of Buchanan's work, *The Limits of Liberty* has presumably the strongest relationship to *The Calculus of Consent.*[6] In this regard, some additional observations deserve to be mentioned. On the one hand, the basic normative premise of the *Calculus* requires that politics be conceived as a Paretian enterprise operating to everyone's advantage. *The Limits of Liberty* is complementary and logically prior to (even though it is chronologically later than) the *Calculus* in that it characterizes the status quo from the point where Paretian politics starts and at the same time describes conceivable processes of interindividual agreement that might lead from a natural equilibrium to a political one. On the other hand, *The Calculus of Consent* is a forerunner specifically of the contractarianism of *The Limits of Liberty* and generally of post-Rawlsian "new contractarianism." In particular, Buchanan's unduly neglected appendix to the *Calculus*, "Marginal Notes on Reading Political Philosophy," foreshadowed, at a time when political philosophy was practically dead, many arguments that would later be popularized in other works, including, of course, *The Limits of Liberty*.

Hartmut Kliemt
University of Duisburg
1998

5. This somewhat down-to-earth Kantianism of Buchanan is also clearly brought out in some of the essays on constitutional political economy, volume 16 in the series, *Choice, Contract, and Constitutions;* and the philosophical essays, volume 17 in the series, *Moral Science and Moral Order*.

6. James M. Buchanan and Gordon Tullock, *The Calculus of Consent: Logical Foundations of Constitutional Democracy* (Ann Arbor: University of Michigan Press, 1962), volume 3 in the series. Hereafter referred to as the *Calculus*.

Preface

Precepts for living together are not going to be handed down from on high. Men must use their own intelligence in imposing order on chaos, intelligence not in scientific problem-solving but in the more difficult sense of finding and maintaining agreement among themselves. Anarchy is ideal for ideal men; passionate men must be reasonable. Like so many men have done before me, I examine the bases for a society of men and women who want to be free but who recognize the inherent limits that social interdependence places on them. Individual liberty cannot be unbounded, but the same forces which make some limits necessary may, if allowed to operate, restrict the range of human freedom far below that which is sustainable.

We start from here, from where we are, and not from some idealized world peopled by beings with a different history and with utopian institutions. Some appreciation of the status quo is essential before discussion can begin about prospects for improvement. Might existing institutions conceptually have emerged from contractual behavior of men? May we explain the set of rights that exist on basically contractual grounds? How and why are these rights maintained? The relationship between individual rights and the presumed distribution of natural talents must be significant for social stability. Social order, as such, implies something that resembles social contract, or quasi-contract, but it is essential that we respect the categorical distinction between the constitutional contract that delineates rights and the postconstitutional contract that involves exchanges in these rights.

Men want freedom from constraints, while at the same time they recognize the necessity of order. This paradox of being governed becomes more intense as the politicized share in life increases, as the state takes on more power over personal affairs. The state serves a double role, that of enforcing constitutional order and that of providing "public goods." This duality generates its own confusions and misunderstandings. "Law," in itself, is a "public good," with all of the familiar problems in securing voluntary compliance. Enforcement is essential, but the unwillingness of those who abide by law to punish those who violate it, and to do so effectively, must portend erosion and ultimate destruction of the order that we observe. These problems emerge in modern society even when government is ideally responsive to the demands of citizens. When government takes on an independent life of its own, when Leviathan lives and breathes, a whole set of additional control issues comes into being. "Ordered anarchy" remains the objective, but "ordered" by whom? Neither the state nor the savage is noble, and this reality must be squarely faced.

Institutions evolve, but those that survive and prosper need not be those which are "best," as evaluated by the men who live under them. Institutional evolution may place men increasingly in situations described by the dilemma made familiar in modern game theory. General escape may be possible only through genuine revolution in constitutional structure, through generalized rewriting of social contract. To expect such a revolution to take place may seem visionary, and in this respect the book may be considered quasi-utopian. Rethinking must precede action, however, and if this book causes social philosophers to think more about "getting to" the better society and less about describing their own versions of paradise once gained, my purpose will have been fulfilled.

I am fully conscious of the fact that, as a professional economist, I am straying beyond my disciplinary boundaries. I am motivated by the importance of the issues and by the conviction that contributions in many subjects may be made by outsiders looking in as well as by insiders talking among themselves. I treat here of issues discussed by learned philosophers through the ages, whose discussions have themselves been discussed by specialists. I have read some, but by no means all, of these primary and secondary works. To have done so would have required that I become a professional political philosopher at the cost of abandoning my own disciplinary base. As an economist, I am a specialist in contract, and to my fellows a contractarian approach carries its own defense once individual values are accepted as the base materials. To those scholars, early or late, who have tried to demolish contractarian constructions, my efforts will not seem responsive to their criticisms. This is not my purpose, and those who reject the contractarian approach out of hand will find little in an economist's attempts at clarification.

In this book, as in earlier works, I emphasize the necessity of distinguishing two stages of social interaction, one which involves the selection of rules and one which involves action within these rules as selected. The critical importance assigned to this distinction reflects the general influence of "my professor," Frank H. Knight, and, somewhat more directly, the outcome of discussions with my colleague Rutledge Vining during several years of my tenure at the University of Virginia.

In its specific form, this book emerged as my own interpretation, elaboration, and extension of a more recent discussion that continued over a period of two years in Blacksburg at the Center for Study of Public Choice, Virginia Polytechnic Institute and State University. This discussion involved the participation and contributions of many colleagues and students, only a few of whom can be noted here. Gordon Tullock and Winston Bush were central figures, and the influence of each man on my own thinking was substantial. Each read early drafts of this book by chapter as these were produced. After a quasi-finished draft of the book was finished, and external to the initial discussion, William Breit, Dennis Mueller, Richard Wagner, and Robert Tollison made helpful and detailed comments. At a final revision stage, Nicolaus Tideman offered highly useful suggestions.

As for Mrs. Betty Tillman Ross, only the name is slightly changed from that which appeared in several of my earlier books. Her cheerful cooperation in general and her particular assistance in getting my manuscripts processed through various stages remain essential inputs in my own production function.

Financial support for my own research at various stages of the project was provided by the National Science Foundation.

Blacksburg, Virginia
March 1974

The Limits of Liberty

1. Commencement

Those who seek specific descriptions of the "good society" will not find them here. A listing of my own private preferences would be both unproductive and uninteresting. I claim no rights to impose these preferences on others, even within the limits of persuasion. In these introductory sentences, I have by implication expressed my disagreement with those who retain a Platonic faith that there is "truth" in politics, remaining only to be discovered and, once discovered, capable of being explained to reasonable men. We live together because social organization provides the efficient means of achieving our individual objectives and not because society offers us a means of arriving at some transcendental common bliss. Politics is a process of compromising our differences, and we differ as to desired collective objectives just as we do over baskets of ordinary consumption goods. In a truth-judgment conception of politics, there might be some merit in an attempt to lay down precepts for the good society. Some professional search for quasi-objective standards might be legitimate. In sharp contrast, when we view politics as process, as means through which group differences are reconciled, any attempt to lay down standards becomes effort largely wasted at best and pernicious at worst, even for the man who qualifies himself as expert.

My approach is profoundly *individualistic*, in an ontological-methodological sense, although consistent adherence to this norm is almost as difficult as it is different. This does not imply that the approach is personal, and the methodological individualist is necessarily precluded from the projection of his own values. His role must remain more circumscribed than that of the collectivist-cum-elitist who is required to specify objectives for social action that are independent from individual values other than his own and those of his cohorts. By contrast, the individualist is forced to acknowledge the mutual existence of fellow men, who also have values, and he violates his precepts at the outset when and if he begins to assign men differential weights. He simply cannot play at being God, no matter how joyful the pretense; hubris cannot be descriptive of his attitude.

These limits offer the individualist a distinct comparative advantage in a positive analysis of social interaction. Accepting a self-imposed inability to suggest explicit criteria for social policy, the individualist tends to devote relatively more intellectual energy to analysis of what he observes and relatively less to suggestions about what might be. He cannot stop the world and get off, but the important realization that he is one among many men itself generates the humility demanded by science. The neutrality of his analytics lends credence to his predictions. The wholly detached role of social ecologist is important and praiseworthy, and perhaps there should be more rather than less analysis without commitment, analysis that accepts the morality of the scientist and shuns that of the social reformer. Thomas Hardy in *The Dynasts*, the aging Pareto in search of social uniformities—these men exemplify the attitude involved, that of the disinterested observer who watches the absurdities of men and stands bemused at the comedy made tragedy by his own necessary participation.

There is, however, something that is itself demoralizing in accepting the mantle of the cynic, the man with little hope or faith, the sayer of social doom. Despite the pessimism of prediction, should we not try responsibly to lend our efforts toward a "better" world? And must we not acknowledge this to be possible? This brings us up to snuff, however, since we have eschewed the simplistic criteria for "betterness" handed out by the omnipresent social reformers. Consistency demands that we list our private preferences as being neither more nor less significant than those held by others, and it thereby dampens our natural lapse into the cocoon of the philosopher-king.

The approach must be *democratic*, which in this sense is merely a variant of the definitional norm for individualism. Each man counts for one, and that is that. Once this basic premise is fully acknowledged, an escape route from cynicism seems to be offered. A criterion for "betterness" is suggested. A situation is judged "good" to the extent that it allows individuals to get what they want to get, whatsoever this might be, limited only by the principle of mutual agreement. Individual freedom becomes the overriding objective for social policy, not as an instrumental element in attaining economic or cultural bliss, and not as some metaphysically superior value, but much more simply as a necessary consequence of an individualist-democratic methodology. In some personal and private baring of my soul, I may not "like" the observed results of a regime that allows other men to be free, and, further, I may not even place a high subjective value on my own freedom from the coercion of others. Such possible subjective rankings may exist, but the point to be emphasized is that the dominant role of individual liberty is imposed by an acceptance of the methodology of individualism and not by the subjective valuations of this or that social philosopher.

The Anarchist Utopia

To the individualist, the ideal or utopian world is necessarily anarchistic in some basic philosophical sense. This world is peopled exclusively by persons who respect the minimal set of behavioral norms dictated by mutual tolerance and respect. Individuals remain free to "do their own things" within such limits, and cooperative ventures are exclusively voluntary. Persons retain the freedom to opt out of any sharing arrangements which they might join. No man holds coercive power over any other man, and there is no impersonal bureaucracy, military or civil, that imposes external constraint. The state does indeed wither away in this utopia, and any recrudescence of governmental forms becomes iniquitous. Essentially and emphatically, this utopia is not communist, even in an idealized meaning of this historically tortured word. There are no predetermined sharing precepts. Communes may exist, but hermits may also abound and they may or may not be misers. Cooperative relationships are necessarily contractual, and these must reflect mutual gain to all participants, at least in some *ex ante* or anticipated stage.

This is a loosely constrained utopia. It allows for much variability in the attainable levels of "desirability," even as idealized. The persons who inhabit this utopia need do no other than respect their fellows, itself a minimal behavioral limit, at least on its face. Within this constraint, wide differences in interpersonal behavior patterns may be conceptually observable. To any single observer, some of these may be "preferred" to others.

The anarchist utopia must be acknowledged to hold a lingering if ultimately spurious attractiveness. Little more than casual reflection is required, however, to suggest that the whole idea is a conceptual mirage. What are to be the defining limits on individual freedom of behavior? At the outset, allowing each man to do his own thing seems practicable. But what happens when mutual agreement on the boundaries of propriety does not exist? What if one person is disturbed by long-hairs while others choose to allow their hair to grow? Even for such a simple example, the anarchist utopia is threatened, and to shore it up something about limits must be said. At this point, a value norm may be injected to the effect that overt external interference with personal dress or hair style should not be countenanced. But this norm would require enforcement, unless there should be some natural and universal agreement on its desirability, in which case there would have arisen no need to inject it in the first place. If there is even one person who thinks it appropriate to constrain others' freedom to their own life-styles, no anarchistic order can survive in the strict sense of the term.

When forced into such discussions of practical organizational problems, however, the philosophical anarchist has other strings to his bow. He may accept the relevance of our example, but he may reject the implications for his own vision of utopia. A notion of interpersonal reciprocity may be introduced, and the argument made that the busybody might agree voluntarily to respect others' freedom. He might do so because he would recognize that, should he fail to do so, other persons would, in their own turn, impose restrictions on his own freedom of personal action. Hence, despite his presumed internal and private preference about long hair, the potential busybody might refrain from interfering because of this fear of reciprocal intrusion into his own behavior pattern.

The anticipated reciprocities may not, however, be comparable in value as among the several actors. If others in the group possess no intrinsic desire to interfere, and especially if interference itself is costly, the busybody may, without fear, continue to forestall the attainment of what will be, at best, the fragile equilibrium of this idealized world. But this particular flaw in the anarchist's vision seems to be remedied once we allow for free exchange among persons, along with agreement on some commonly valued commodity as a numeraire. Such a commodity, a "money," facilitates a comparison of values, and allows others, acting as a unit, to buy off or to bribe a single recalcitrant. The busybody may be induced to refrain from interfering with the personal behavior of others through appropriately settled compensations. Side payments in the commonly valued commodity allow those with disparate evaluations to come to terms. Once such side payments or bribes are introduced, however, a new set of issues arises. If there is potential money in it, individuals will find it to their advantage to be recalcitrant, not because this expresses their internal private preference but because it promises to yield valued returns. If the man who genuinely dislikes long-hairs so much that he is prompted to interfere in the absence of payment is "bought off" by monetary reward, others who care not one whit for hair styles may also commence interfering, motivated by the promise of monetary reward. Order in the anarchist society is not guaranteed by some agreement on a numeraire.

Anarchy as the basic organizing principle for social order begins to break down upon careful analysis even if we stay within the confines of personal behavior, narrowly considered. Its limits become more evident when we shift attention to activities that necessarily involve potential conflict among separate persons. Before introducing these, however, a more positive, if less sweeping, defense of anarchy needs to be made. Even if we acknowledge that the principle fails as a universal basis for social order, we should recognize that its essential properties can be observed to operate over large areas of human interaction. It is important to make this recognition explicitly, since the very ubiquitousness of orderly anarchy tends to draw attention only toward the boundaries where disorder threatens.

There are countless activities that require persons to adhere to fundamental rules for mutual tolerance, activities that may be observed to go on apace day by day and without formal rules. They go on because participants accept the standards of conduct that are minimally demanded for order to be established and maintained. Consider ordinary conversation in a multiperson group. Communication does take place through some generalized acceptance of the rule that only one person speaks at a time. Anarchy works. It fails to work when and if individuals refuse to accept the minimal rule for mutual tolerance. Communication on the Tower of Babel would have ceased if all men should have tried to speak at once, quite apart from the distortion in tongues. It is paradoxical to note that modern-day radicals often call themselves anarchists when their behavior in heckling speakers and in disrupting meetings insures nothing more than a collapse of what are remaining elements of viable anarchy.

This is only a single example. Was the university of the 1960s vulnerable to disruption largely because it was organized as an orderly anarchy and, as such, critically dependent on adherence to implicit rules of mutual tolerance and respect? Since the 1960s universities have become less anarchistic; they have moved toward formalized rules as the boundary limits to acceptable behavior were overstepped. To the extent that more and more human interactions exhibit conflicts at the boundaries, institutional means for resolving these will emerge, and the set of formalized rules will expand. If men abide by rules implicitly, formalization is not required. If they do not do so, formalization, implementation, and enforcement become necessary.

The emergence of new conflicts should not, however, distract too much attention away from the analytically uninteresting but comprehensive set of interactions that continue to be carried on in acceptably orderly fashion without formally defined rules for personal behavior. Men and women manage to walk along city pavements. With rare exceptions, they respect queues in supermarkets, in banks, and in airports. There does exist a sense of ordinary respect for his fellow man in the ingrained habit pattern of the average American. This can be observed empirically all around us. Whether this reflects a heritage of Christian or Kantian ethics that were once explicitly taught or whether such habit patterns are even more basic to the human psyche, their existence cannot be denied.[1] The ominous threat posed by the 1960s was the potential erosion of these habit patterns. If Americans lose mutual tolerance for each other; if they do not continue to accept "live and let live" precepts for many of their social interactions independently of governmentally determined coercive rules, the area of civilized life that is both anarchistic and orderly must shrink, with untold consequences in human suffering. As noted earlier, any equilibrium attainable under anarchy is, at best, fragile. The individualist must view any reduction in the sphere of activities *ordered* by anarchy as an unmitigated "bad." He must recognize, nonetheless, that anarchy remains tolerable only to the extent that it does produce an acceptable degree of order. The anarchistic war of each against all, where life becomes nasty, brutish, and short, will be dominated by the order that the sovereign can impose.

1. For additional examples along with a more comprehensive discussion, see Roland N. McKean, "The Economics of Trust, Altruism, and Corporate Responsibility," in *Altruism, Morality, and Economic Theory,* ed. E. S. Phelps (New York: Russell Sage Foundation, forthcoming). Also see Diane Windy Charnovitz, "The Economics of Etiquette and Customs: The Theory of Property Rights as Applied to Rules of Behavior" (M.S. thesis, University of Virginia, Charlottesville, Virginia, 1972).

One additional point should be made in this introductory discussion of ordered anarchy, a point that has been suggested earlier but one that is worthy of emphasis. What are the moral attributes of the results that will be produced through voluntary personal interactions in the absence of formalized rules? What are "good" and "bad" results here? The answer is simple, but it is extremely important. That is "good" which "tends to emerge" from the free choices of the individuals who are involved. It is impossible for an external observer to lay down criteria for "goodness" independent of the *process* through which results or outcomes are attained. The evaluation is applied to the means of attaining outcomes, not to outcomes as such. And to the extent that individuals are observed to be responding freely within the minimally required conditions of mutual tolerance and respect, any outcome that emerges merits classification as "good," regardless of its precise descriptive content. This relationship between evaluation and procedural criteria also applies when nonanarchistic principles of order are considered. Unless it is fully understood to apply in those interactions where anarchy is the organizing principle, however, the more subtle relevance of the relationship in formalized interactions may be difficult to comprehend.

The Calculus of Consent

When he recognizes that there are limits to the other-regardingness of men, and that personal conflict would be ubiquitous in anarchy, the extreme individualist is forced to acknowledge the necessity of some enforcing agent, some institutionalized means of resolving interpersonal disputes.[2] The origins of the state can be derived from an individualistic calculus in this way, at least conceptually, as we know from the writings of Thomas Hobbes as well as from earlier and later contractarians. This essentially economic methodology can be extended to provide conceptual explanations for many of the aspects of political reality that we observe. This was the framework for *The*

---

2. There are exceptions. Murray Rothbard argues that conflicts could be resolved by the protective associations or clubs that would be formed voluntarily in genuine anarchy. See his *For a New Liberty* (New York: Macmillan, 1973). His approach fails to come to grips with the problem of defining rights initially, the issue that is central to my discussion.

Calculus of Consent (1962).[3] In that book, Gordon Tullock and I indulged our fancies and deployed our professional talents in deriving a logically consistent basis for a constitutional and democratic political structure, one which seemed to possess many of the features of the polity envisaged by the Founding Fathers. We offered an understanding of the institutions that have historically emerged in America, an understanding that differs in fundamental respects from that reflected in the conventions of modern political science. The framework for analysis was necessarily contractarian, in that we tried to explain the emergence of observed institutions and to provide norms for changes in existing rules by conceptually placing persons in idealized positions from which mutual agreement might be expected.[4] *The Calculus of Consent*, as well as other works of my own, might be interpreted as an attempt to impose a "vision of order" on observed institutional and behavioral realities.

I have come to be increasingly disturbed by this basically optimistic ontology. As several of our right-wing critics have recognized, the "theory of public choice" can be used to rationalize almost any conceivable decision rule or almost any specific outcome under preselected rules. In this, the theory seems analogous to the theory of markets as that theory is used by some of the most extreme advocates of laissez-faire. In this tautological sense, the "theory" in *The Calculus of Consent* provides no agenda for state or collective action, in either procedural or operational terms. A more important source of misgivings arises from my own perceptions. Increasingly, I have found myself describing what I observe as "constitutional anarchy" rather than any institutional translation of individual values into collective outcomes. In the 1970s, much to be explained does not seem amenable to analysis that incorporates positive-sum institutional processes. Zero-sum and negative-sum analogues yield better explanatory results in many areas of modern politics, and I find myself, like Pareto, more and more tempted to introduce nonlogical

---

3. James M. Buchanan and Gordon Tullock, *The Calculus of Consent: Logical Foundations of Constitutional Democracy* (Ann Arbor: University of Michigan Press, 1962; paperback ed., 1965).

4. Although our approach was somewhat more narrowly economic, the analytical setting is closely related to that employed by Rawls in deriving principles of justice from contractual process. See John Rawls, *A Theory of Justice* (Cambridge: Harvard University Press, 1971).

models of individual behavior along with nondemocratic and nonconstitutional models of collective choice.

Yet I remain, in basic values, an individualist, a constitutionalist, a contractarian, a democrat—terms that mean essentially the same thing to me. Professionally, I remain an economist. My purpose in this book is to "explain" some of the apparent sociopolitical malaise that I observe with the professional tools of the economist and from the value position stated. In a loose usage of terms here, the approach taken in *The Calculus of Consent* might be described as the extension of the "theory of public goods," interpreted in a Wicksellian setting, to political structures and to the formation of political decision rules. In similar usage, the approach taken in this book might be described as an extension of the "theory of public bads" to explain apparent failures in political and institutional structure. In this respect, I hope that this book will be complementary to the earlier one. In a broad sense, both are contractarian. In *The Calculus of Consent*, existing and potential institutions were conceptually explained as having emerged from contractual agreements among participating and rational individuals. In this book, by contrast, existing and potential institutions as well as behavior within certain institutional constraints are explained in terms of the failures of potentially viable contractual agreements to be made or, if made, to be respected and/or enforced. Politico-legal order is a public good; disorder is a public bad. There are two sides to the coin.

The differences between this book and the earlier work should be emphasized. Any analysis of institutional failure necessarily draws attention to the absence of effective rules for social interaction, and, similarly, to an erosion and breakdown in the workings of those nominal rules and institutions that may have once been viable. Here it is essential to examine carefully the working properties of anarchy as an organizational system in the absence of the idealized individual behavior that is characteristic in the utopias of anarchy's romantic advocates. Interpersonal conflict becomes important relative to interpersonal cooperation. When mutuality of gain is emphasized, there is less need to be concerned about the initial assignment of "rights" among persons. In *The Calculus of Consent*, we did not find it necessary to go behind the assumption that individuals with more or less well-defined rights exist at the initiation of the contractual process. This neglect may have been illegitimate, even there, but when interpersonal conflict becomes more central, the whole set of issues involving the assignment of "rights" in the first place cannot be left out of account.

One additional important difference should be noted. So long as collective action is interpreted largely as the embodiment of individual behavior aimed at securing the efficiency attainable from cooperative effort, there was a natural tendency to neglect the problems that arise in controlling the self-perpetuating and self-enhancing arms of the collectivity itself. The control of government scarcely emerges as an issue when we treat collective action in strictly contractarian terms. Such control becomes a central problem when political power over and beyond plausible contractarian limits is acknowledged to exist.

The Origin of Property

Anarchy necessarily fails when there exists no "natural" or mutually acceptable dividing lines among spheres of personal individual interest. In the lifestyle examples used earlier, we might plausibly argue that the purely personal elements of behavior would normally be left alone; that this sort of dividing line would be widely observed. Upon moving beyond personal examples, however, we immediately encounter potential for conflict. Robin Hood and Little John meet squarely in the center of the one-man footbridge. What "natural" rule is there to determine who shall be entitled to proceed and who shall withdraw? This can serve as an illustration for the multifarious set of interactions where conflict rather than implicit agreement seems characteristic. Once we are outside those activities that are largely if not wholly internal to persons, strictly private in the meaningful sense of this term, there are few "natural" limits upon which general agreement might plausibly settle. The genuinely anarchistic world becomes a maze of footbridges, and conflict rather than universalized cooperation is its central feature. And unless some modicum of agreement is enforced, even those areas within which anarchy might indeed suffice to generate tolerable order would be subject to gross violations.

The issue is one of defining limits, and anarchy works only to the extent that limits among persons are either implicitly accepted by all or are imposed and enforced by some authority. In the absence of "natural" boundaries among individuals in the activities that they may undertake, there arises the need for a definitional structure, an imputation among persons, even if this structure, in and of itself, is arbitrary. The logical foundation of property lies precisely in this universal need for boundaries between "mine and thine." Escape from the world of perpetual Hobbesian conflict requires an explicit definition of the rights of persons to do things. At this point I dare not enter into the sometimes murky discussions of "theories of property," but it is useful to be specific about some matters at the outset. There has been relatively too much emphasis on the normative function of property, and the concept of property itself has been too much tied to physical-spatial dimensions, producing an overly sharp distinction between closely related sets of human actions. As used here, property rights may or may not have spatial dimensions. To return to our life-style example, a person may possess the right to let his hair grow long, which means that he can exclude others from cutting it. But even this personal right may be circumscribed; he may not possess the right to allow his head to become lice-infected. Few, if any, rights are absolute in either a positive or a negative sense. Consider the familiar right of land ownership. This normally allows the person designated as an owner to exclude others from carrying out certain activities on the land (hunting, poaching, camping, farming, and so on), but it may not extend to the exclusion of others from carrying out other activities (easements for utility companies). The ownership right may also allow the owner to carry out certain of his own desired activities on the land, but this set is itself restricted. He may be prohibited from doing just what he pleases (for example, by zoning rules, by land-use requirements) despite his legal designation as owner.[5]

The basic function of property in any social order that embodies individual liberty as a value must be clearly understood. By allocating or parcelling out "rights" among individuals in a community, the fundamental organizing principle of anarchy can be extended over wide reaches of human behavior. If Robin Hood and Little John know, and in advance, which one has the "right" to cross the bridge when potential conflict emerges, and, furthermore,

---

5. In terms of the historical controversy, my approach is more closely related to the Germanic-feudal concept of property than to the Roman. On this distinction, as well as on many other aspects relating to the theory of property, see Richard Schlatter, *Private Property: The History of an Idea* (New Brunswick: Rutgers University Press, 1951), p. 9.

if they know that this "right" will be effectively enforced, they can go about their ordinary business of life without detailed supervision and control. If Little John is given ownership rights in the footbridge, Robin Hood can use the facility only after obtaining Little John's permission through trade or otherwise. The delineation of property rights is, in effect, the instrument or means through which a "person" is initially defined.

Conceptually, we may think of locating a "person" along a spectrum.[6] At the one extreme, that of pure and complete slavery, the human being has no rights whatsoever. He is allowed to carry on no activity of any sort, anywhere, anytime, without explicit direction by someone else. At the other extreme, that of absolute dominance, we might think of a human being who is allowed to do everything possible within physical constraints. There is quite literally nothing that he is prevented from doing; no activities are forbidden, not even those relating to other members of the human species. It is, of course, mutually contradictory that more than one person in the same interaction could occupy a position at either end of this conceptual spectrum. Once we accept the presence of many persons in social interaction, it should be obvious that the set of rights granted to any one person must lie somewhere between the extremes, and that there is really no categorical distinction to be made between that set of rights normally referred to as "human" and those referred to as "property." Does A's right to speak, sometimes labelled a "human right," encompass the authority to enter a house that B owns, a "property right," and shout obscenities? A second point to be noted is that it is impossible for *any* imputation of rights to be completely equalitarian even in a conceptually idealized sense. A single footbridge exists; *either* Robin Hood *or* Little John must be granted some right of priority in its usage. Both men cannot simultaneously possess such a right, which would, of course, be equivalent to the abolition of all rights, from which the Hobbesian conflict emerges once again. And, of course, it is precisely in those situations where separate persons and groups have conflicting claims that most of the problems of social interaction arise. But enough about these later in this book.

Without some definition of boundaries or limits on the set of rights to do things and/or to exclude or prevent others from doing things, an individual,

6. For a similar discussion, see Richard Taylor, *Freedom, Anarchy, and the Law* (Englewood Cliffs: Prentice-Hall, 1973), p. 9.

as such, could hardly be said to exist. With such defined limits, however, and regardless of the sources of their derivation, an individual is clearly an entity distinct from his fellows. Equipped with this set of rights, informed about them, and similarly informed about the rights held by others, the individual is in a position to initiate agreements with other persons, to negotiate trades, or, in more general terms, to behave as a free man *in* a society of men. Robinson Crusoe is a man who is free to do more or less as he pleases, within the limits imposed by the physical environment, but, until Friday arrives, he is not free to enter into agreements and trades with other men. If a person lives in society, he is defined by his "rights" to undertake certain things at certain times and at certain places, "rights" that he may, or may not, trade with others. If Tizio is a free man and not a slave, he may work for whom he pleases; hence, he may reach agreement with Caio to exchange or to trade work for corn. To be able to carry out his part of the bargain, Caio must hold "rights" to the corn, rights which include his ability to transfer the commodity to Tizio and to implement the transfer.

Even as our simple examples suggest, "rights" will normally be different as among separate persons. If everyone should be, in fact, identical in all conceivable respects, including the precise specification of rights, mutual agreements could not emerge except in cases of increasing returns to specialized production. In a world of equals, most of the motivation for trade disappears. Exchange of rights takes place because persons are different, whether these differences are due to physical capacities, to some assignment of endowments, or to differences in tastes or preferences.

Equal Treatment for Unequals

In Chapter 2 and beyond, I shall discuss in some detail the specific assignment of rights among persons. At this point, I must examine an apparent contradiction. The approach was described earlier as democratic or individualistic, in that each person counts for one, and for as much as any other. This essentially normative foundation for the analysis must be reconciled with the positive statement that men will necessarily differ among themselves and in any assignment of rights. Individuals differ, one from another, in important and meaningful respects. They differ in physical strength, in courage, in imagination, in artistic skills and appreciation, in basic intelligence, in preferences, in attitudes toward others, in personal life-styles, in ability to deal socially with others, in Weltanschauung, in power to control others, and in command over nonhuman resources. No one can deny the elementary validity of this statement, which is of course amply supported by empirical evidence. We live in a society of *individuals*, not a society of *equals*. We can make little or no progress in analyzing the former as if it were the latter.

In Hobbesian anarchy, individual differences would manifest themselves by varying successes in the continuous struggle for survival. But our interest lies in analyzing a social order that is nonanarchistic, at least in the sense that institutional means of resolving interpersonal conflicts exist. This implies the existence of some structure of individual rights, regardless of how these may have emerged and regardless of differences among persons, as well as the existence of some collective agency, the state. It is essential that the whole set of problems involving the assignment of rights among individuals and groups in society be separated from the set of problems involving the enforcement of the assignment that exists. Monumental but understandable confusion arises and persists from a failure to keep these two problem sets distinct.

Persons are defined by the rights which they possess and are acknowledged by others to possess. If two persons undertake trades or exchanges, one with another, each party must perforce respect, and respect equally, the defined rights of the other. If this were not the case, if the claims of one party to an exchange are respected by the second, but there is no reciprocal respect by the first party for the claims of the second, there has been no escape from anarchy, and exchange in the true sense is not possible. That is to say, mutual agreement on an assignment of rights implies *equal* and *reciprocal* respect for these rights, as assigned. The assignment of rights further implies that the enforcing agent, the state, must behave neutrally in its task, that it must treat all persons *equally* in the organization and implementation of enforcement. Individuals are treated equally because their assignment of rights implies such neutrality, not because they are equals.[7] Descriptively, persons are and must remain unequals. Hence, the neutrality condition translates into equal treatment for unequals, not equals. Confusion often arises because equality in

7. Cf. J. J. Rousseau, *The Social Contract*, vol. 38, *Great Books of the Western World* (Chicago: Encyclopaedia Britannica, 1952), p. 394. See also Henry Maine, *Ancient Law* (Boston: Beacon Press, 1963), p. 89.

treatment is itself taken to be an attribute of descriptive equality. In different terms, there is often the false presumption that equality in treatment implies equality in fact in some relevant sense, or, at the least, equality as a norm for social progress. Thomas Jefferson might have avoided much confusion had his deism allowed him to make a slight variation on his statement. Had he said, "to their creator, all men are equal," rather than "all men are created equal," he might have conveyed more adequately what seems to have been his basic intent. The equal-treatment norm emerges directly from the identification and definition of persons, as persons, and neither implies equality as fact nor infers equality as a requirement for the legitimacy of equal treatment.[8]

Quis Custodiet Ipsos Custodes?

To the individualist, utopia is anarchist, but as a realist he recognizes the necessity of an enforcing agent, a collectivity, a state. As a minimal procedural norm, any such entity must treat equally all who qualify as members, as persons, even when interpersonal differences are acknowledged. "Equality before the law," "uniformity in the application of the law," "the rule of law," "rule by law and not by man," "rules, not authorities," "justice is blind"— these are but a few of the more familiar phrases that variously reflect this fundamental norm of an individualistic social order. But what is "the law"? Or, perhaps more appropriately, what are the limits of law? The necessity for an enforcing agent arises because of conflicts among individual interests, and the enforcing role for the state involves the protection of individual rights to do things, including the making and carrying out of valid contracts. In this role, the enforcing agent starts from or commences with the assignment of rights as these exist. The state has no role in setting out or in defining these rights if we stay within the dichotomy indicated.

If, however, the collectivity is empowered to enforce individual rights, how

---

8. The French Declaration of the Rights of Man, issued in 1789, is more confusing than Jefferson's statement in the Declaration of Independence. The relevant statement in the former reads: "Men are born, and remain, free and equal *in rights*." (Italics supplied.)

The fallacious implication that men must be, or must be made to be, equals in fact before they can qualify for the equality of treatment in democratic polity is one source of the modern confusion surrounding research in genetics.

is it to be prevented from going beyond these limits? What are the "rights" of the enforcing agent itself, the state? If we are able, conceptually, to discuss the enforcement of rights and of contracts involving exchanges of rights among persons apart from questions involving exogenous changes in the assignment of rights, we must also be able to specify, again conceptually, the rights of the collectivity to do things. We cannot simply move one step further back and conceive of the appointment or selection of some superior enforcing agent, one that will protect and limit the rights of both individuals and the state. The enforcement hierarchy must stop somewhere, and for our purpose it is well to restrict discussion to the first level. It is relatively easy to think of the collectivity fulfilling its role in protecting person and property from "unlawful" acts carried out by persons. It becomes much more difficult to think of means through which individuals can enforce and protect their rights from "unlawful" acts on behalf of the collectivity itself. How can Leviathan be chained? This problem has worried political philosophers of all ages, but no fully satisfactory answer has been advanced, either as an ideal to be approached or as a practical program to be experienced.

Two distinct means of limiting collective power have been proposed and tried. First, there have been various institutional devices which are designed to restrict overall collective interferences with individual rights. The Roman republic attempted to share executive power among two or more officials appointed simultaneously to the same position. Medieval Europe opposed a decentralized feudal nobility against a centralized church and, later, against the emerging nation-states. Montesquieu discussed effective division and separation of state power along procedural lines. The Swiss have used federation effectively in keeping their society more or less free for centuries.

Second, there has been the explicit promulgation of the mystique of some "higher law," one that guides the actions of sovereigns as well as ordinary men. This, too, has taken many forms. The tablets of Moses and the Book of Mormon provide ancient and modern examples of "laws" derived from God. Philosophers have searched for "natural laws" that are inherent in man himself, laws that might be applied as norms for collectivities. Scholars of the Enlightenment evoked the social contract to explain the origin as well as the limits of governmental powers. The written constitution, carrying with it a specified historical date, presumably had as its primary objective the offering of some predictable stability concerning the limitations of state power. Heritages of the institutional devices and of the sources of mystique are mixed variously in the social orders of Western collectivities. In the United States, the Founding Fathers joined Montesquieu's separation of powers to the federal principle and attempted to secure these by a written constitution which reflected both contractarian and natural law presuppositions.

Can anyone attribute success to their efforts in the perspective of the 1970s? Viable federalism, as a means of checking dominant central-government power, has scarcely existed since the horrible civil war of the 1860s. Fortuitous circumstances alone held back the growth of federal government until the 1930s. Since the Great Depression, we have witnessed continuing and accelerating growth in our own Leviathan. Descriptively, we live in what might be called "constitutional anarchy," where the range and extent of federal government influence over individual behavior depend largely on the accidental preferences of politicians in judicial, legislative, and executive positions of power. Increasingly, men feel themselves at the mercy of a faceless, irresponsible bureaucracy, subject to unpredictable twists and turns that destroy and distort personal expectations with little opportunity for redress or retribution.

The naive among us invoke man's ultimate right of revolution as the final limit on government's power. But, as Gordon Tullock has demonstrated, the genuine revolutionary threat to ongoing collective agency is, and must be, miniscule in significance.[9] Individuals, as individuals, cannot be expected to generate the "public good" that is romantic revolution, even under the most oppressive of tyrannies. The "natural distribution" of effective power must be heavily weighted in favor of existing states, qualified only by some occasional "changing of the guard," either through formal electoral processes or through more violent and less predictable coups d'etat.

The 1970s present a paradox. There are demands from all quarters for a dismantling of bureaucracy, for a reduced governmental presence, for personal relief from accelerating tax pressures. By widespread agreement, the state has become too powerful, too pervasive in its influence over private affairs. At the same time, however, demands for extensions in public control abound. We observe government on the loose but at the same time the minimal order presumably secured by collective enforcement of rights seems to

---

9. See Gordon Tullock, "The Paradox of Revolution," *Public Choice* II (Fall 1971): 89–100.

be disappearing. Is there a connection here? Has the state become too large, too powerful, too clumsy, to carry out effectively its own raison d'être? Or is the causal link reversed? Has the state presence itself generated an erosion of the ordered anarchy on which society depends? In abiding by unenforced rules for behavior in social intercourse, individuals create "public good." As these rules are violated, "public bad" emerges, but it may be folly to expect collective correction, especially when the state itself may have been a partial source for the shift. (Those who might have thought otherwise may find these statements more persuasive after Watergate.) It seems questionable whether any government, any political party, any politician, can restore the sense of community that might be required for acceptable order in the 1970s. Yet, lacking an alternative, the state responds and the paradox deepens.

Can we hope for the genuine "constitutional revolution" that might truly reorder the rights of both individuals and government? Can American constitutional democracy function when the central government is so much more extensive than those limits envisaged for it by the Founding Fathers? Can participatory democracy, interpreted as the rights of individuals to make their own collective choices, as government "by the people," exist at all when the range of governmental-political controls is so sweeping?

God, Man, and the Good Society

These and other similar questions may not greatly concern those who take the truth-judgment approach to politics. If politics and political-governmental institutions, whether or not these are democratic, exist only as means or instruments through which the true and unique nature of the "good society" is discovered and/or revealed, there is really no difference between the behavior of the bureaucrat, the federal judge, the political party leader, the congressman, or, indeed, the practitioner of civil disobedience. If "truth" exists in politics, "out there" for the finding of it, then, once found, does it really matter very much whether or not it is self-selected, chosen in a majority vote, imposed by judicial fiat, or obtained by a bureaucratic ukase?

To those of us, individualists and nonidealists, who reject the truth-judgment approach, the questions present genuine challenges of overriding importance. We cannot claim to play as God, and we can scarcely carry off the pretense that our own private preferences reflect his "truth." Our emphasis must lie in diagnosis rather than in dreams. There are features of modern American society that suggest "sickness" to many critics. One of my purposes in this book is to offer procedural diagnoses, a step that is required before we can begin to answer the larger questions. I offer one political economist's interpretation, informed by the perspective of an individualist. My analysis employs a few critical concepts, some of which have been mentioned: the assignment and enforcement of rights among persons, the limits of collective power. As these are elaborated, two somewhat more technical concepts emerge. The first is the "publicness" of law itself, law defined as rules for behavior, whether these rules be voluntarily chosen or externally imposed. The second is the capital investment characteristic of adherence to rules. The social capital that a law-abiding society of free men represents can be "eaten up." The American society of the 1970s may well be one that has allowed elements of its capital stock to be destroyed at an excessive rate.

2. The Bases for Freedom in Society

Can two walk together, except they be agreed?

—Amos 3:3

During summer months, a roadside stand outside Blacksburg displays seasonal fruits and vegetables. I can purchase watermelons in quantities that I choose at prices which, by convention, are established by the salesman. There is little or no higgling, and a transaction can be completed in seconds. Economic exchanges like this are so familiar to us, so much a part of everyday routine, that we often overlook the bases upon which such institutions rest. I do not know the fruit salesman personally, and I have no particular interest in his well-being. He reciprocates this attitude. I do not know, and have no need to know, whether he is in direst poverty, extremely wealthy, or somewhere in between. Likewise, his ignorance concerning my economic status is complete. Yet the two of us are able to complete an exchange expeditiously, an exchange that both of us accept as "just." I make no effort to seize watermelons without his consent and without payment. The vendor does not grab coins and currency from my purse.

We transact exchanges efficiently because both parties agree on the property rights relevant to them. Both of us acknowledge that the watermelons, stacked neatly by the roadside, are "owned" by the salesman, or by the person or firm for whom he acts as agent. Both of us also acknowledge that I have the rights of disposition over the money in my pockets or in my bank account. Furthermore, both of us recognize that any unilateral attempt to violate these assigned rights of exclusion will be subject to penalty through the arms and agencies of the state. In other words, both of us agree on what "the law" is that is relevant to the exchange in question.

Let us now consider a descriptively similar example, but one that is quite different in essential respects. Suppose that it is commonly known that the watermelons are grown by a farmer who stacks them alongside the road available for the taking by passersby without charge. Suppose that, under these conditions, I happen upon someone who tries to exact a money price from me. This setting is quite different behaviorally from the first. Since I do not recognize any right of ownership on the part of the person who has now expropriated the melons, I am reluctant to pay, despite the fact that my evaluation may exceed the money price asked. On the other hand, the nominal possessor of the goods is unwilling to meet my demands without a price since, in his view, a right of ownership has been established. Ordinary exchange, which seemed so simple and straightforward in the first example, is made extremely difficult here because the parties do not agree on the "law of property" in being, which means, in turn, that they are uncertain as to what action the state might take in any dispute. If I should be certain that the alleged salesman has no rights under law, I should take the watermelons, and should he try to prevent my doing so, I should call the police. But, of course, in an acknowledged absence of legal rights, he would not exert physical force to constrain me. On the other hand, should I be certain that his alleged rights were enforceable, then no matter how I might feel about the morality of his position, I should probably purchase the melons and go on my way as before.

The point illustrated by these simple examples is clear. Economic exchange among persons is facilitated by mutual agreement on defined rights. Both parts of this principle must be satisfied. Individual rights must be well defined and nonarbitrary, and, in addition, these rights must be recognized and accepted by participants. If rights are known to be well defined and nonarbitrary but if knowledge about them is available to persons only on considerable investment in information gathering, many exchanges that are otherwise mutually beneficial may never come into being. Once both parts of the principle are met, however, once the limits of each person's rights are defined by agreement, economic interchange becomes almost the archetype of ordered anarchy. Individuals can deal with one another through wholly voluntary behavior without coercion or threat. They can enter into and complete exchanges without detailed knowledge of the political persuasions, sexual attitudes, or economic statuses of their actual trading partners. The traders may be unequal in any or all of such descriptive characteristics, yet they can and do deal with one another as equals in the exchange itself. In this classic sense, economic exchange is wholly impersonal, which seems to be precisely the ideal-type interaction embodied in ordered anarchy. Each person is treated strictly as he is, and presumably as he wants to be, in such a relationship. The fruit stand operator may beat his horse, shoot dogs, and eat rats. But none of these qualities need affect my strictly economic trade with him.

Under regimes where individual rights to do things are well defined and recognized, the free market offers maximal scope for private, personal eccentricity, for individual freedom in its most elementary meaning. The failure of the romantic advocates of anarchy to recognize this feature of free markets is difficult to understand; this is one of the sources for the paradox observed in the 1970s and noted above in Chapter 1. Socialist organization, defined broadly as extended collective or state control over voluntary exchange processes, must be and can only be antithetic to anarchy, despite the surprising linkage of these two contradictory organizational norms in much of the romantic literature.[1]

Economics, the science of markets or of exchange institutions, commences with a well-defined structure or set of individual rights and offers explanatory, predictive propositions concerning the characteristics of outcomes along with conditional predictions about the effects of imposed structural changes on such outcomes.[2] Economic theory is sufficiently powerful to explain many varieties of exchange relationships. The central tradition of this theory involves analysis of two-party exchanges imbedded in and constrained by a network of interrelated potential and actual trading pairs. It is not my pur-

1. For a relatively recent book that falls within the romantic tradition, and which summarizes other works, see Daniel Guerin, *Anarchism,* intro. Noam Chomsky, trans. Mary Klopper (New York: Monthly Review Press, 1970).

There exists a variant of anarchism which is, instead, based squarely on the recognition of the free market's role in facilitating individual relationships in the absence of government. This has been called "private property anarchism" by Laurence Moss, who traces out the contributions of Americans to this variant. See Laurence S. Moss, "Private Property Anarchism: An American Variant" (Paper presented at the Southern Economic Association meeting in Washington, D.C., November 1972). Murray Rothbard is a modern expositor of this variant. See his *For a New Liberty.*

2. This is my own definition of economics. It is elaborated in some detail in my 1963 presidential address to the Southern Economic Association. See "What Should Economists Do?" *Southern Economic Journal* 30 (January 1964): 213–22. This view is at variance with those who define economics in terms of the central maximizing principle. Differences in definition here need not, however, affect the main argument of the text.

pose to summarize this theory here. As Chapter 3 will suggest, however, straightforward extension of some of the models to the many-party, complex exchanges that collective action may represent yields substantial explanatory results. In all cases, and this is my emphasis, the analysis proceeds from some initial imputation of rights among participating persons in the interchange, an imputation that is assumed to be conceptually observable and also to be recognized and respected by all parties.

Commonality and Noneconomic Interaction

The dependence of efficient trade upon a delineation and identification of individual rights is revealed most clearly in the case of fully partitionable "private" goods. It should be evident that the requirements for mutually accepted definitions of structure need not be so restricted. Consider facilities that may, due to either technological necessity or social decision, be accessible to all members of the relevant group. Mutual agreement on the behavioral limits with respect to the use of such property is, at base, no different from mutual agreement on the boundary lines for strictly private holdings. My recognition that the fruit salesman owns the watermelons is not, in concept, different from my recognition that both he and I have rights to walk along the village street, rights that both of us honor and respect, and which neither of us calls into dispute. We both utilize the common-access facility, and we do so without overt conflict only because of our mutual recognition and acceptance of these rights. If a particular road or street should be "Private"; if one of us should hold legal title to the facility which embodies rights to exclude, the other would normally respect a "No Trespassing" sign if one appears. This despite the possibility that, descriptively, the road or street facility might be identical in the two settings. Conflict emerges, or may emerge, not from any specific assignment of individual rights, but from disagreement over and uncertainty about just what the legally enforceable assignment is.

The same principle applies to many aspects of human behavior that are not normally classified as "economic" and that are not explicitly treated as exchange relationships. The reconciliation of individuals' desires to "do their own things" with the fact that they live together in society is accomplished largely by mutual agreement on spheres of allowable or tolerated activity. "Equal freedom," as a norm or rule for social intercourse, has little or no meaning until and unless individuals are first identified in terms of acknowledged limits to behavior. The acceptance of such limits is so familiar to us all, pervading wide reaches of routine behavior as well as our attitudes toward the behavior of others, that we rarely think of the structure of individual "rights" that is underneath. Our attention is turned to definition of rights only when the tolerated limits are exceeded, when previously accepted boundaries are crossed. Only at this stage do we begin to consider drawing the limits more carefully, possibly calling on enforcement agents, or thinking about recourse to personal means of redress or defense.

The set of manners, the customary modes for personal behavior, which reflects the mutual acceptance of limits, will of course vary somewhat from culture to culture, but it is relatively easy to think of examples in any setting. I do not start my power mower early on Sunday morning, and my neighbor does not play stereo music loudly after eleven at night. Both of us recognize the possibly harmful effects on the other, and we refrain from imposing costs in this manner, even at some personal sacrifice. If one of us violates this set of "live and let live" rules, the other is prompted to take specific action in redress. If my neighbor operates his stereo loudly in the wee hours, and does this repeatedly, I should be prompted to try deliberately to annoy him with my lawn mower, to get the police to enforce the antinoise or antinuisance ordinance, or, if one does not exist, to try to get the town council to enact such an ordinance. If all else fails, I might then resort to direct physical action against the neighbor's property or person.

It is in this context that some of the behavioral changes of the 1960s raise fundamental and disturbing issues for social stability. As noted, individuals have lived, one with another, under implicit behavioral rules that were respected by all, or nearly all, persons in community. But one of the instruments employed by the participants in the counterculture involved the explicit flaunting of traditional codes of conduct, the direct and open disregard for what had previously been considered to be acceptable standards for elementary "good manners." This placed stresses on the ordered anarchy that still describes much of ordinary social life in our society, stresses which were evidenced by calls for "law and order," for formalization and enforcement of rules that were previously nonexistent.

Social stability requires agreement on and enforcement of a structure of individual rights, whether these rights be over the disposition of privately partitionable goods, over the usage of common facilities, or over ordinary patterns of interpersonal behavior, and whether the enforcement be externally imposed or internally monitored. A possible source of ambiguity should be mentioned here. Mutual agreement, backed up if necessary by effective enforcement, is a necessary condition for social interchange. But this agreement may embody any one of an almost infinite variety of actual distributions and/or imputations of rights among persons, constrained by any one of an equally large number of possible sets of rules for personal behavior. Neither the specific distribution of rights among separate persons nor the general characteristic of the rights structure itself is relevant directly to the issue of mutual agreement, certainty in definition, and enforcement.[3] Physical facilities may be variously partitioned among individuals, as units of "private property." Or, alternatively, such facilities may be organized under rules that dictate common usage by large groups of persons, including the whole membership of the community. If the limits to individual behavior are well defined, voluntary social interaction can proceed in an orderly fashion under any structure. Interpersonal dealings can take place under *any* agreed-on assignment. Only at a second, and quite different, level of discourse do problems arise about the relative desirability of specific distributions of rights and/or about the relative efficiencies of different structures. The tendency or proclivity to inject either equity or efficiency norms, or both, too early has plagued the discussion of property rights throughout the ages.

It is, of course, possible to evaluate alternative distributions on personally chosen criteria of "justice" or "equity." More positively, it may be possible to array alternative structures of rights by criteria of economic efficiency. The owners of cattle and sheep on a grazing range may either (1) hold rights to the common pasture or (2) hold individually fenced-off parcels of land. The second arrangement may, on examination and analysis, prove to be more efficient than the first in some standard efficiency sense, but the relative inef-

---

3. This is emphasized clearly by David Hume; see *A Treatise of Human Nature,* ed. L. A. Selby-Bigge (Oxford: Clarendon Press, 1960), pp. 502–3. Hume's whole discussion concerning the origins of property rights and the advantages of such rights for social stability is similar in many respects to that which is developed in this book.

Hegel's basic conception of property is also similar to that developed here. See Shlomo Avineri, *Hegel's Theory of the Modern State* (Cambridge: Cambridge University Press, 1972), pp. 88f.

ficiency generated under the common-ownership arrangement is not at all comparable and indeed is different in kind from that which might emerge when mutuality of agreement on rights disappears, when there is uncertainty as to just what structure of rights will be legally enforced. The range wars in the American West in the late 1880s arose because of such uncertainties as these, and not because the structure in existence was grossly inefficient in the orthodox sense or was demonstrably "unjust" by other criteria.[4]

Rights and Contract

The argument to this point is straightforward and could scarcely be disputed. A necessary starting position for a society of free individuals, related one to another in a network of interdependence, is some agreement on a structure of rights which, in effect, defines the entities who enter negotiations. It is difficult even to imagine a relationship when such mutual agreement is wholly absent. How could two men, meeting for the first time, carry out the simplest form of interchange without implicit acceptance of some behavioral limits?

As I have noted, these bases for individual behavior in society are simply taken for granted by most of us, so much so that we rarely pause to examine the issues that are posed. As Blackstone suggested: "These inquiries, it must be owned, would be useless and even troublesome in common life. It is well if the mass of mankind will obey the laws when made."[5] Once individual rights are acknowledged, contractual negotiations become possible, and, as economists, we launch off into the interesting problems posed by the contracting or exchange process itself. We sometimes fail to recognize, or otherwise forget, that the whole institution of contract, whether this takes the

4. The "theory of property" that is implicit in my discussion here and elsewhere in the book can perhaps best be classified as some mixture of the "personality" and "utilitarian," especially as the latter is represented by the discussion of David Hume. These and other useful classifications of theories of property, along with a good general discussion, are found in Frank I. Michelman, "Property, Utility, and Fairness: Comments on the Ethical Foundations of 'Just Compensation' Law," *Harvard Law Review* 80 (April 1967), especially pp. 1202–13.

5. The citation is from Blackstone's *Commentaries on the Laws of England*, 12th ed. (London: T. Cadell, 1794), 2:2–3.

simplest form of isolated two-party trade or the more complex *n*-person agreement, rests on the possibly shaky foundations of mutual agreement on individual rights, including agreement by an enforcing agent, a state, which must also limit its own behavior. It is perhaps time that economists begin to devote more attention to the origins of contract.

The modern contributions to the "economics of property" can only be welcomed. I refer to the contributions of Alchian, Cheung, Demsetz, Furubotn, Kessel, McKean, North, Pejovich, Thomas, and others.[6] Nonetheless, the emphasis in this now burgeoning subdiscipline is on the way in which alternative property-right structures can modify individual and group behavior, with the orthodox criterion of economic efficiency implicitly at the base of the analysis. To this point, these contributions have not concentrated on explaining the emergence of property rights.[7]

---

6. A partial listing of the contributions is as follows: A. A. Alchian and R. Kessel, "Competition, Monopoly, and the Pursuit of Money," in *Aspects of Labor Economics* (New York: National Bureau of Economic Research, 1962), pp. 157–75; S. Cheung, "Private Property Rights and Sharecropping," *Journal of Political Economy* 76 (December 1968): 1107–22; Harold Demsetz, "The Exchange and Enforcement of Property Rights," *Journal of Law and Economics* 7 (October 1964): 11–26; R. McKean, "Divergences between Individual and Total Cost within Government," *American Economic Review* 54 (May 1964): 243–49; Douglass C. North and Robert Paul Thomas, *The Rise of the Western World: A New Economic History* (Cambridge: Cambridge University Press, 1973). These and other contributions are discussed by Furubotn and Pejovich in a lengthy review article, which also includes a full set of references. See Eirik Furubotn and Svetozar Pejovich, "Property Rights and Economic Theory: A Survey of Recent Literature," *Journal of Economic Literature* 10 (December 1972): 1137–62.

7. Among the modern "property rights economists," S. Pejovich is the only one who has attempted a generalized discussion of origins. He states explicitly that his aim is to show that "the creation . . . of property rights is endogenously determined" (p. 310). A careful reading of Pejovich's paper suggests, however, that the endogeneity does not refer to the exchange process. Instead, individuals are motivated by private utility-maximizing norms to invest resources in defense and predation of resource stocks, behavior which is, of course, descriptive of Hobbesian anarchy. I prefer that we limit "economic explanations" of institutional change to the contractual process. In this context, as my analysis suggests, property rights may emerge from an economic calculus that prompts the negotiation of a "constitutional contract." But this is quite different from the results emergent from the independent, utility-maximizing behavior of the parties. See S. Pejovich, "Towards an Economic Theory of the Creation and Specification of Property Rights," *Review of Social Economy* 30 (September 1972): 309–25.

This may be illustrated with reference to Harold Demsetz's discussion of private-property rights among the Canadian Indians.[8] In his interpretation of the history, the Indians of the Labrador peninsula accepted common usage of hunting grounds prior to the dramatic increase in beaver-skin prices caused by French traders. This price increase stimulated increased hunting effort; beaver skins became relatively scarce, and individual hunting tended to produce an uneconomic utilization of the common resource. As a means of internalizing the external diseconomies that this rights arrangement fostered, the Indian tribes shifted from a common-usage to a private-property structure. The historical accuracy or inaccuracy of this account need not concern us here. But note that Demsetz essentially "explains" a change in rights structure by resort to a new contractual arrangement made desirable by exogenous changes in economic data. He is employing the historical example to demonstrate the proposition or principle that there will always be a tendency for characteristics of the rights structure to be shifted toward that set which is most efficient under the conditions faced by the community. There can be no quarrel with this, and Demsetz's contribution can be acknowledged. We should not, however, make the mistake of saying that this approach explains the origin or emergence of rights among individuals or families (tribes) independent of contractual agreement, whether this be explicit or implicit. In his conceptual model, the rights of the several participants must have been mutually recognized by all participants *before* further contractual negotiations could be undertaken to change the structural characteristics.

With regard to the emergence of initial rights, we must acknowledge that any attempted economic explanation will be insufficient. How might the rights of individuals (families, tribes), rights to do things, including rights over domain, rights that are mutually respected, arise? What is the logical basis of property? To such a question, there cannot be an exclusively contractarian answer. The concept of externality may, however, prove helpful in pointing toward meaningful analysis. Demsetz argued that property rights change for the objective of "internalizing externalities." His particular discussion was directed, as noted, toward explaining how structures are shifted

8. Harold Demsetz, "Toward a Theory of Property Rights," *American Economic Review* 57 (May 1964): 347–59.

toward satisfying overall efficiency norms. He did not, at least explicitly, try to extend his thesis backward, so to speak, to examine the noncontractual elements.

This step can be taken if we introduce a sufficiently broad definition of externality. In a world without interpersonal conflict, potential or actual, there would, of course, be no need to delineate, to define, to enforce, any set of individual (family) rights, either in the ownership and use patterns of physical things or in terms of behavior with respect to other persons. I use "conflict" rather than "scarcity" here, because even if all "goods" that might be "economic" should be available in superabundance, conflict among persons might still arise. Social strife might arise in paradise. Total absence of conflict would seem to be possible only in a setting where individuals are wholly isolated one from another, or in a social setting where no goods are scarce and where all persons agree on the precise set of behavioral norms to be adopted and followed by everyone. In any world that we can imagine, potential interpersonal conflict will be present, and, hence, the need to define and enforce individual rights will exist.

The "Natural Distribution"

Consider a simple two-person world. All "goods" save one, which we shall call x, are available to each person (A and B) in superabundance. But good x is "scarce." No production is required for its enjoyment, however, and quantities of this good simply "fall down" in fixed proportions onto each of the two persons at the onset of each period of consumption. There are no property rights, no law, in this economy. Hence, we may say that the consumption or use of a unit of x by individual A imposes an "external diseconomy" on B, and similarly, that the consumption of a unit by B imposes a diseconomy on A. In an orthodox externality setting, and notably in small-number groups where transactions costs are not prohibitively high, we might predict that "trade" between the two persons would take place, accomplishing an internalization of the reciprocal externality relationship. In our example, however, regardless of the initial distribution of x, there is no surplus to be secured through a direct trading process. Nonetheless, each of the two persons will have an incentive to "internalize the externality" that the other imposes on him.

Both A and B might seek to consume all of the good x that is available. As Thomas Hobbes perceptively noted, in this state of nature each person has a "right" to everything. Each would find it advantageous to invest effort, a "bad," in order to secure the good x. Physical strength, cajolery, stealth—all these and other personal qualities might determine the relative abilities of the individuals to secure and protect for themselves quantities of x, which may be quite different from the relative quantities that were arbitrarily assigned by the initial disposition. These attributes may, but need not, include some inherent "live and let live" attitude among members of the common species. In any case, as a result of the actual or potential conflict over the relative proportions of x to be finally consumed, some "natural distribution" will come to be established.[9] This cannot properly be classified as a structure of *rights*, since no formal agreement is made, although there might well exist mutual recognition of the appropriate bounds on individual action. Nonetheless, the natural distribution may represent a conceptual equilibrium, in which each person extends his own behavior in securing (defending) shares in x to the limit where marginal benefits from further effort are equal to the marginal costs that such effort requires. In the "natural distribution," the two persons, A and B in our example, continue to impose external diseconomies on each other in the sense noted above. But now, because this distribution does offer a base from which some predictions may be made, indirect "trades" become possible that will internalize the external diseconomies.

The "natural distribution," secured upon investment of effort in attack and/or defense of consumption shares in x, serves to establish an identification, a definition, of the individual persons *from which* contractual agreements become possible. Absent such a starting point, there is simply no way of initiating meaningful contracts, actually or conceptually. But, in the natural distribution, both A and B will recognize, on rational observation, that

9. The formal characteristics of this "natural distribution" have been worked out by Winston Bush. See his "Individual Welfare in Anarchy," in *Explorations in the Theory of Anarchy*, ed. Gordon Tullock (Blacksburg, Virginia: Center for Study of Public Choice, 1972), pp. 5–18.

The notion of such a distribution is, of course, to be found in the work of several of the philosophers who have thought about the origin of property, notably in Aegidius, Hugo Grotius, and Thomas Hobbes.

much of the effort expended in securing and defending stocks of x is wasteful. Whatever might be the characteristics of this distribution, whether rough symmetry prevails or whether one participant becomes a consumption giant and the other a pygmy, and even if all of x is secured by one party, *both* parties will be made better off if agreement can be reached. Trades can be arranged in the sense of agreement on a set of behavioral limits. Mutual gains are possible in this way over a wide range of assignments of final consumption, with the particular assignment finally negotiated dependent on bargaining skills and other factors.

The Emergence of Property

It is appropriate to call this a genuine basis for the emergence of property rights.[10] Both parties agree to and accept the assignment, which carries with it the complementary agreement that they will not behave so as to violate the terms. Both parties can, therefore, reduce their private investment in attack and defense; in the limit, the full value of x can be realized without cost.[11] The agreement on rights of the two parties represents a contractual internalization of an externality relationship that existed in the precontract state of nature. Note, however, that the reversion to some sort of "natural distribution" is required in order that potential trading participants can themselves be identified. This may be illustrated by tracing an alternative conjectural history of the emergence of private property among the various Indian tribes of the Labrador peninsula. The increase in the demand for beaver converted what had previously been an abundant resource into one that was scarce. No property rights previously existed, and the new scarcity produced conflict among the separate tribes. As a result of actual or potential intertribal wars, some "natural distribution" emerged that came to be recognized by all tribes.

---

10. This conceptual explanation is variously presented by many of the social philosophers, notably those in the general contractarian tradition. Particular versions are to be found in the works of Aegidius, Bodin, Grotius, Hobbes, and Hume. For a good summary treatment, see Richard Schlatter, *Private Property*.

11. The more general theme that all investment that takes the form of protecting rights must be, in the net, socially wasteful is developed at some length by Gordon Tullock in his forthcoming book, *The Social Dilemma*.

A reassignment of territorial hunting grounds could then have taken place by mutual agreement, with each tribe finding it advantageous because of the allowable reductions in military effort.[12]

The specific distribution of rights that comes in the initial leap from anarchy is directly linked to the relative commands over goods and the relative freedom of behavior enjoyed by the separate persons in the previously existing natural state. This is a necessary consequence of contractual agreement. In Hobbes's model, there are, by inference, considerable differences among separate persons in a precontract setting. To the extent that such differences exist, postcontract inequality in property and in human rights must be predicted. For my purposes, there is no need to discuss in detail the degree of possible inequality among separate persons in the conceptual state of nature that has been used to derive the logical origin of property rights. Those who have referred to the strong enslaving the weak may well have exaggerated the differences. The romantic moderns, on the other hand, who adopt their own variants on Rousseau's noble savage may be equally off the mark in the opposing direction. To make meaningful statements here, it would be necessary to sift and to examine the available anthropological, ethological, and historical evidence, a task that lies beyond both my competence and my interest.

Nor need the analysis depend critically on the acceptance or rejection of any particular model or hypothesis about human behavior. We need not follow Hobbes and assume that men behave from narrowly defined self-interest. We could assume, equally well, that even in some state of nature men behave in accordance with self-interest tempered by regard for their fellows. Or, in the other limit, we might also assume that individuals adopt precepts for behavior that reflect the interest of the human species. The inequalities among persons that may be conceptually observed in the "natural distribution" will result both from the inherent differences in personal capacities and in the types of behavior actually adopted. If, for example, personal capacities should be widely different, but, at the same time, all persons behave nonindividualistically, the observed natural distribution might reflect considerably less in-

12. For a paper that specifically introduces the Demsetz example, but which interprets the emergence of property rights in a manner fully consistent with that which is developed here, see Charles R. Plott and Robert A. Meyer, "The Technology of Public Goods, Externalities, and the Exclusion Principle," Social Science Working Paper No. 15 (revised) (California Institute of Technology, February 1973).

equality than that which would be observed under hedonistic behavior patterns. Since all we can observe, even conceptually, is the natural distribution itself, the precise combination of inherent personal qualities and behavioral norms is not relevant. It is, however, relevant to note that there is no basis for assuming equality in the conceptually observed distribution among persons in the natural state, and, consequent on this, no basis for predicting equality in the agreed-on allocation or distribution of rights in the initial post-contract setting. There is nothing to suggest that men must enter the initial negotiating process as equals. Men enter as they are in some natural state, and this may embody significant differences.

Violations of Contract

The gains-from-trade that are potentially achievable by an agreement on rights are realized by all parties through the disinvestment in socially wasteful effort devoted to both predatory and defense activity. An agreed-on assignment will not normally be stable in one particular sense. Once reached, one or all parties may find it advantageous to renege on or to violate the terms of contract. This applies to *any* assignment that might be made; the tendency toward individual violation is not characteristic of only some subset of possible agreements. Within the setting of an agreed-on assignment of rights, the participants in social interaction find themselves in a genuine dilemma, familiarized under the "prisoners' dilemma" rubric in modern game theory. All persons will find their utility increased if all abide by the "law," as established. But for each person, there will be an advantage in breaking the law, in failing to respect the behavioral limits laid down in the contract.

This may be illustrated for our two-person model through a simple matrix, as shown in figure 2.1. In the natural distribution, in which neither party acknowledges or respects any rights to the single scarce good, the utility levels achieved are shown in Cell IV. The left-hand numbers in each cell represent utility indicators or net payoff values for A, the right-hand numbers those for B. As indicated, the utility payoffs need not be equivalent in this anarchistic "equilibrium." (We need not introduce complexities about interpersonal utility comparability at this point since it is the absence of equality that is important, not the demonstration of inequality.) Upon agreement, the utility payoffs are those shown in Cell I, where both persons are in positions

	B	
	Respects Rights	Respects No Rights
A Respects Rights	Cell I 19, 7	Cell II 3, 11
Respects No Rights	Cell III 22, 1	Cell IV 9, 2

Figure 2.1

that are superior to those achieved in Cell IV. Also, joint or combined payoffs are maximized in Cell I. (Here, again, qualifications concerning interpersonal comparability and, hence, additivity would be required for completeness.) As depicted, however, both A and B have private incentives to renege on or to violate the contractual agreement on rights provided that they can do so unilaterally. The position for individual A is improved if he can secure a shift to Cell III, while that for individual B is improved if he can somehow get to Cell II.

In the strict two-person setting, either one or both of the persons may refrain from violating the contract because he may rationally anticipate that the other's reaction would force a quick return to the precontract state of nature. In the simple game setting of figure 2.1, Cell I is in the "core," to introduce a term specific to modern game theory. No player can guarantee for himself a better outcome than that which he secures under universal adherence to the agreed-on rights assignment. No person can assure himself that breaking the law will not result in a worsening of his own position. This characteristic suggests that there are important elements of stability in a Cell I position. Such stability tends to disappear, however, as the number of participants in the interaction increases, even if the formal properties remain unmodified. Furthermore, variations in the characteristics and relationships within the payoff structures, which will be introduced in later chapters, may eliminate the stability that here is apparent.

Two-Stage Contract

To this point, the conceptual emergence of some initial assignment or imputation of individual rights has been discussed in an extremely abstract and simplified model. I have assumed that only one scarce good exists other than time itself. The model is also limited to a two-person interaction; and it is timeless, which amounts to saying that none of the elements change over time. It will be necessary to relax each of these restrictions. The treatment must be generalized to allow for scarcity in many goods, to explain the interaction of many persons; and the effects of time in modifying the contractual relationship must be incorporated directly into the analysis. In the remainder of Chapter 2, I shall make the first two extensions. The introduction of time is sufficiently complex to require additional space.

We may continue to use the two-person model but allow for more than a single scarce good. Conflict between A and B in the state of nature will now arise over the disposition of all of those goods that are not superabundant. For present purposes, we shall continue to assume that these goods are not produced, but instead that quantities of these goods simply "fall down" in some distribution between the two persons.

As in the one-good model, a natural distribution will emerge from actual or potential conflict. This distribution, which will now be many-dimensional, will be influenced by the initial disposition of the goods, and by the relative personal characteristics and behavior patterns of each person. The outcome may be described by a vector whose components represent net amounts of each of the scarce goods finally enjoyed in consumption by each person,

$$(X_A, X_B; Y_A, Y_B; \dots).$$

In attaining his share in this natural distribution, each person finds it necessary to invest effort (time and energy) in predatory and/or defense activity. There is no difference in this respect between this and the one-good model. And, as before, the natural distribution provides the base from which contractual agreements become possible. Agreement will, as before, take the form of some mutual acknowledgment of rights. Gains are secured from the reductions in predation-defense effort. This contract, which becomes the initial leap from Hobbesian anarchy, is the first stage of a two-stage contractual process. For purposes of convenience, I shall, here and later, refer to this as "constitutional contract."[13]

---

13. The position taken here is that *both* constitutional and postconstitutional rights conceptually emerge from *contract,* but that it is essential that the two stages be kept distinct. This may be compared with the position advanced by F. A. Hayek in his work *Law,*

It is the existence of two stages or levels of agreement that distinguishes the many-good from the one-good model. In the latter, the initial agreement on shares in the single scarce good represents the limit to trade. No further contracts between the two persons will offer mutual gains. The two-person group attains the Pareto-frontier through its initial agreement on rights of disposition. The many-goods model differs sharply at precisely this point. If individual tastes differ, there may be potential gains-from-trade over and beyond the initial "trade" of agreements on individual rights. The trading process at this second, or *postconstitutional*, stage is, of course, the domain of traditional economic theory. Individual participants are assumed to enter the potential trading arena with identifiable endowments and/or capacities, and their rights to these initially held endowments are assumed to be mutually accepted by all members of the community and to be enforced by the state. The two-stage contractual sequence may be depicted simply with a diagram like that of figure 2.2. The utility attained by individual A is shown on the ordinate, that attained by individual B on the abscissa. The natural distribution, that outcome which emerges as a quasi-equilibrium in the genuine state of nature, is shown at D. The initial constitutional contract, which involves nothing more than mutual agreement on some structure of rights, shifts the outcome in a general northeasterly direction, bounded as indicated by the dotted lines drawn from D. Suppose that the actual agreement shifts the utility positions to C. In the one-good model, no further trades are possible, and the utility-possibility frontier is attained for the two-man community. In the many-goods model, however, further trades in specific goods may be mutually advantageous. This will always be possible if tastes differ and if the agreed-on assignments do not correspond precisely to the preferred final-goods packages.

There seems little reason to predict such precise correspondence, although

---

Legislation, and Liberty, vol. 1, *Rules and Order* (Chicago: University of Chicago Press, 1973). If I interpret his argument correctly, Hayek suggests that "law," which is equivalent to what I have called constitutional contract, is not contractual in origin but emerges from an unpredictable evolutionary process. He advances this argument in opposition to the "constructivists," who are alleged to think of law as willed by someone. In historical fact, evolutionary elements may explain much of the emergence and development of "law." Acceptance of this does not, however, negate the application of contractual-constructivist criteria in an evaluation of that "law" which exists, and which might be willfully modified.

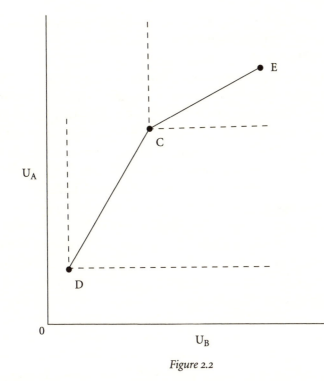

Figure 2.2

some tendency toward correspondence might be present. In the natural state, individuals will devote more effort to securing and protecting those final goods that stand relatively high in their own preference rankings. Furthermore, in the conceptual bargaining over the rights to be accepted, individuals will tend to sacrifice goods that they value relatively lower than goods which they secure in "exchange." Relative abilities to secure and defend goods, and to secure goods in conceptual bargaining, need not correspond closely with relative values placed on goods by the separate participants. Under any combination of these elements that generates an absence of precise correspondence between originally agreed endowments and optimally preferred bundles, trades can be made, and these trades will move the utility positions further in the northeasterly direction, with the bounds for postconstitutional trades indicated by the dotted lines extending from C. In some final trading equilibrium, say, E, the utility-possibility frontier is attained. The constitutional contract involves the initial shift from D to C; postconstitutional contract involves the shift from C to E. Economists have concerned themselves almost exclusively with the latter to the neglect of the former.[14]

Further classification that is more familiar to economists can be made within postconstitutional contracts or exchanges. The shift from C to E can take place through two types of process. In the first, individuals exchange goods that are rival in usage and fully partitionable or divisible among persons, both at the stage of initial rights assignments and at the stage of final consumption. If X and Y are two such goods, and individual A is initially given rights to relatively more X, he will then give up units to B in exchange for units of Y. This trade, which we may call *private-goods* trade, using conventional terminology, may be institutionalized through markets when large numbers of potential traders are interlinked.

Mutual gains may continue to exist, however, over and beyond these achievable by trades in purely partitionable goods. Joint rather than separate consumption of some goods may be relatively efficient. To illustrate, let us suppose that both goods X and Y are rival in consumption of A and B, but that good Z is potentially able to meet the demands of both persons simultaneously; there is no rivalry in consumption with respect to Z. We continue to assume that we are examining a no-production economy, with initial supplies of goods arbitrarily distributed. In this setting, some question might be raised as to why Z, defined as a purely public good, again to use conventional terminology, should be included in the "scarce" category with individual rights to its disposition assigned in an initial contract at the constitutional stage. If treated independent of all other goods, there would be no need for any such assignment; indeed one means of describing a purely collective or public good is to say that no distributional problem exists.[15] But when distributional conflict characterizes other private or partitionable goods, X and Y in this example, individuals may seek to establish rights over the distribution of Z as an indirect means of securing more X and Y in the postconstitutional trading process. This will become more relevant as we move to more

14. Note that the distinction made here need not require that any historical relevance be attributed to constitutional contract. No matter how a structure of property rights may emerge, it is useful to separate the definition of structure from the exchange of rights within this structure.

15. For an elaboration of this point, see my *Demand and Supply of Public Goods* (Chicago: Rand McNally, 1968), especially chap. 9.

complex and more realistic models later in the book. In any case, we assume here that the agreed-on assignment of rights provides net quantities of both private and potentially public goods to A and B. For illustration, suppose that this structure assigns all units of X to A, and all units of both Y and Z to B. Trade in private goods, X and Y, proceeds in the orthodox manner. For the good that is nonrival in final use, Z, individual B will agree to make some (all) of it available jointly to A upon the payment, by A, of some appropriately negotiated quantity of X, which is rival in final usage.[16] This sort of "trade" with respect to Z is different in kind from trade among persons in ordinary goods and services that are rival in consumption. The shift of a community from the position depicted by the movement from C to E in figure 2.2 is accomplished by some combination of *private-goods trade* and *public-goods trade,* both of which take place within the limits defined by constitutional contract.

From Small to Large Numbers

Before proceeding from the two-person to the *n*-person model, it is perhaps useful to summarize the conceptual schemata that has been developed. From a

1. natural distribution, a
2. constitutional contract is negotiated, from which, in turn,
3. postconstitutional contract becomes possible, through
   a. private-goods trade (goods rival in consumption) and/or
   b. public-goods trade (goods nonrival in consumption).

When we introduce a large number of participants, negotiations may take place among subgroups or coalitions contained within the larger and more inclusive community membership. A "natural distribution" may, therefore, be conceived at any one of several levels of aggregation. At one extreme, which we might call the pure natural distribution, no coalitions exist, and

16. In the elementary discussion here, I am assuming that B is able to exclude A from the use of Z without excessive cost. If nonexclusion is inherent in Z, then no property right will be initially assigned in this good in the no-production setting. If Z must be produced, however, the discussion becomes applicable, even if, once produced, Z is nonexcludable. Exclusion will, in this case, take the form of not producing.

each person acts strictly on his own in the genuine Hobbesian "warre" of each against all. From this base, however, "constitutional contracts" may be made among members of groups of any two or more persons, with internal assignments of rights, while as among the separate groups conflict continues. At such levels, the separate subgroups or coalitions (some of which may include only one member) are in a natural distribution fully analogous to that described for the two-person model. The process of contractual internalization may proceed as the subgroups become larger until some final negotiating process which incorporates all persons in the community within a single constitutional structure.

The final or ultimate constitutional contract will define the rights assigned to each person in the inclusive community. And each person will find his own position improved over that which he might have enjoyed in any one of the natural distributions noted above, because he will not have to exert or contribute effort to defense and predation, either as an individual on his own account or as a contributing member of a subset of the total community.[17] The second, or postconstitutional, stage of negotiation can commence. At this point, the shift from the two-person to the n-person model introduces other important differences in results. With respect to private-goods trade, exchanges can proceed in the orthodox manner that has been exhaustively

---

17. Complexities arise in the large-number setting which make any assignment of rights less stable than in the small-number setting. There are two reasons for this difference. In the first place, almost any imputation or assignment that is agreed on will dominate that which the individual would anticipate were he to opt out and to try to exist on his own in pure anarchy. With large-number communities, however, the set of rights assignments that will dominate, for each person, the position that he might expect to secure if *any* coalition opts out, is much more restricted, and, indeed, this set might be empty in many interactions. These aspects of interactions have been discussed in detail, formally, in modern game theory. To use the appropriate terminology, for large-number groups there may be no imputation or assignment that is in the core, and, if a core does exist, the number of imputations contained may be small. For an introductory discussion of these concepts, see Duncan Luce and Howard Raiffa, *Games and Decisions* (New York: John Wiley and Sons, 1957).

Second, even if the assignment finally arrived at should qualify for inclusion in the core in the game-theoretic sense, individuals would still find it advantageous to violate the terms if they predict an absence of response on the part of remaining members of the group. This tendency toward instability is present in both the small- and large-number groupings, but the sheer impersonality or anonymity of individuals in large groups makes strategic behavioral calculations much less likely to occur.

treated by economists. Market institutions will be formed; bargaining ranges will be restricted by the presence of multiple alternatives for each buyer and each seller of goods; outcomes will tend to be more determinate than in the small-number setting. The important point to be stressed, for my purposes, is that these exchanges in private goods still take place between separate pairs of traders, between individual buyers and individual sellers. Each exchange remains a two-party transaction, as in the simplified model, despite the addition of numbers. There is no necessity to bring all members of the community into each contract. There is nothing that might be classified as "social contract" here.

Over and beyond all such exchanges in private goods, there may exist further potentially realizable surpluses from "trades" in public or collective-consumption goods and services, those that can simultaneously meet the demands of *all* persons in the group. In reference to our simple example, suppose, as before, that Z is such a public good, which may be consumed jointly and simultaneously by all members of, say, a three-man community, A, B, and C. Assume, as before, that all of the available supply of Z is under the disposition of individual B under terms of the basic constitutional contract. "Trades" can be made which involve a transfer of privately partitionable goods from A and C to B in exchange for the latter's willingness to make available Z for joint consumption. The point to be emphasized here is that, in such trade, *all* members of the final consuming group must be brought directly into the contractual negotiations with respect to provision of the public good. It is not possible to factor down a network of economic exchange into separate two-party transactions. This feature categorically distinguishes public-goods trade from private-goods trade when large numbers are involved. With the former, with public-goods trade, something akin to "social contract" again comes into being, comparable in numbers of participants to the constitutional contract that delineates individual rights.

Before we can develop further the implications of this similarity, and the confusion that the similarity fosters, certain ambiguities must be clarified. For expository purposes, I have assumed that all scarce goods fall into either one or the other polar extreme—the purely private good or the purely public good.[18] Furthermore, I have implicitly assumed that the "range of public-

---

18. This is the same assumption that was made by Samuelson in his classic formulation of the welfare norms for public-goods provision. See Paul A. Samuelson, "The Pure The-

ness" for all goods in the public-goods classification extends precisely to the limits of the inclusive community membership. This assumption is perhaps even more restrictive than the polar classification. There may exist many goods that qualify as "public" or "collective" over differing numbers of consumers but which, at the same time, become fully rival in consumption as the number of users is increased. The size of the consuming "club" that meets efficiency criteria may be much less than the total membership of the community.[19] If such "clubs" are small, relative to the size of the total community, market institutions can emerge that will internalize the required contractual arrangements, even though the strict pairwise exchange-characteristics of pure markets are violated. For our purposes, having recognized that much of the noncollective sector may embody such small-number jointness, we can treat all "trades" that do not involve substantial fractions of the total community membership as taking place in "private goods." In somewhat more practical terms, this amounts to a neglect of local government decision-making, as such.

The analysis suggests that "social contracting," defined as those negotiations which involve *all* members of the community, may take place conceptually at two levels or tiers: at some initial stage of constitutional contract, in which agreement is reached on an assignment of individual rights, and at some postconstitutional stage in which individuals agree on quantities and cost shares of jointly consumed goods and services. Essentially the same problems emerge at each tier, problems that are created largely by the necessity to bring large numbers of persons into the same contractual arrangements. The sheer cost of getting agreement on any outcome rises sharply as numbers increase. In two-party trading, only the single buyer and the single seller need agree. This difference in numbers alone makes for major differences in costs. But the absence of alternatives exacerbates the attainment of agreement in many-party negotiations. It may not prove overwhelmingly costly for very large numbers of persons to reach agreement if each participant has available to him other avenues for securing comparable objectives. To the extent that

---

ory of Public Expenditure," *Review of Economics and Statistics* 36 (November 1954): 387–89.

19. For a more extended treatment, see my "An Economic Theory of Clubs," *Economica* 32 (February 1965): 1–14.

an individual has other opportunities, he can withdraw from participation in the large-number group if a proposed settlement does not fall within his broadly defined preferences. For the single inclusive community, however, the necessary participation of all members eliminates the prospects of effective alternatives. National states, from which out-migration can take place normally only at significant costs to an individual, rather than local governments, become the real-world organizational units to which the analysis is most directly applicable.

A final qualification must be introduced at this point in order not to give the appearance of inconsistency with the discussion in subsequent chapters. This involves the delineation or assignment of individual rights emerging from constitutional contract. It is essential that the potential variability in the specification of individuals' rights be recognized. The conceptual agreement may range from an assignment that invokes relatively little "law" in the formalized sense to an assignment that rigidly constrains individual behavior over many dimensions of adjustment. An assignment of rights is not an all-or-nothing choice. Ceteris paribus, the liberty inherent in anarchistic order without law is the most desirable state of affairs. The extent to which an individual, or the community of individuals, may be willing to trade off the liberty that remains present even in the Hobbesian jungle for the stability promised in regimes with varying degrees of formal restrictiveness will depend on the nastiness of the jungle, the value placed on order, the costs of enforcement, and on many other factors, some of which will be subsequently discussed.

3. Postconstitutional Contract
The Theory of Public Goods

In this chapter I shall discuss in more detail the 3b category in the conceptual schemata. This category includes the many-party agreements, the genuine "social contracts," that may take place after (1) individual rights are assigned in constitutional contract, and (2) all gains-from-trade in strictly private or partitionable goods are realized. The analysis may be summarized under the rubric "theory of public goods" defined in an inclusive sense. The basic analytical material is familiar to modern economists, but the setting for the discussion may be sufficiently novel as to warrant further consideration.

I have modified the logical order suggested by the schemata itself. This would place conceptual constitutional contract which embodies the definition and assignment of individual rights ahead of and prior to postconstitutional contract, which embodies trade among persons in both private and public goods after rights have been defined and mutually accepted. I have reversed the order of analysis for didactic purposes. The theory of postconstitutional contracting and exchanging, whether this be the theory of trade in private goods (the domain of orthodox microeconomic theory) or the theory of trade in public goods, is less complex than that of constitutional contract. Indeed it is largely because the complexities of the latter are ignored or assumed away that we are able to develop sophisticated and rigorous analyses of the second set of personal interactions.

Except for an introductory paragraph in the following section, I am also neglecting the most important category of postconstitutional contract itself, the exchange of private or partitionable goods and services. In part this omission stems from the familiarity of this theory. But, more importantly, this apparent gap in the treatment is justified by my larger purpose in this book. The orthodox theory of exchange in private goods is not itself the source of major confusion about the role of the state. The same cannot be said of the complementary theory of public goods.

As an additional limitation, the emphasis will be on postconstitutional "social contracting" in its purest form. I shall not treat the interesting analytical and practical issues that arise when consumption jointness and/or nonexclusion efficiencies suggest many-party bargains over groups that are smaller than the membership of the total community, a membership which is assumed to be set exogenously.[1] That is to say, neither fiscal federalism nor the theory of clubs will be examined.[2] Discussion of these issues, intrinsically interesting as they are, would distract attention from those problems in many-person social contract which I want to discuss in this book.

In this chapter I shall continue to work within what is essentially a timeless model; contracts are assumed to be immediately carried out, and by the same persons who enter the agreement.

Market Failure and the Free-Rider Problem

If individual rights are well defined and mutually accepted by all parties, persons will be motivated voluntarily to initiate trades in partitionable goods and services, those that are characterized by full or quasi-full divisibility among separate persons or small groups. That is to say, markets will emerge more or less spontaneously out of the self-interested behavior of individuals, and the results will be beneficial to all members of the community. The potential gains-from-trade will be fully exploited, and all persons will be better off than they would have been by remaining in their initial postconstitutional positions, with well-defined endowments and capacities imbedded in a structure of legally binding human and property rights. The genius of the eighteenth-century moral philosophers (notably Mandeville, Hume, and

1. For a paper which discusses some of the problems which this neglect creates, see Dennis Mueller, "Achieving a Just Polity," *American Economic Review* 44 (May 1974): 147–52. Although Mueller develops his argument in the context of a critique of the work of John Rawls, much of his analysis is directly relevant to my argument in this book.

2. For two recent books which examine many of these issues in detail, see Wallace E. Oates, *Fiscal Federalism* (New York: Harcourt Brace Jovanovich, 1972), and Richard E. Wagner, *The Fiscal Organization of American Federalism* (Chicago: Markham Publishing Co., 1971).

Smith) lay in their discovery and application of this simple principle, which has been variously elaborated in modern economic theory, the principle which, directly or indirectly, served as the basis for organizing the institutions responsible for post-Enlightenment economic progress in the Western world.

A critical feature of the spontaneous and efficient order of markets is the two-party contractual setting which serves to reduce agreement or transactions costs to minimal levels. Trades are consummated when terms are established, and only two persons need agree explicitly. Furthermore, the fact that two-party exchanges are linked in a network of alternative options facilitates rather than retards agreement on terms. Increased numbers multiply the potential alternatives available to individual buyers and sellers and narrow the ranges of dispute inside particular exchanges and between specific trading partners.[3]

The thrust of the modern theory of public or collective-consumption goods is the demonstration that markets fail to emerge and to produce tolerably efficient results when potential contracts require the simultaneous agreement of many parties. Neither of the efficiency-generating elements of private-goods markets is present in the pure public-goods model. Agreement or transactions costs are much higher because of the large number of persons who must be brought into the same bargain or exchange. And this inclusiveness itself tends to eliminate potential alternatives for participants, alternatives which narrow the range over which terms of trade might settle. The basic behavioral contrast between private-goods exchange and public-goods exchange is often pointed up by reference to the "free-rider problem" in the latter, although this terminology is itself somewhat misleading.

In a simple two-party trade in divisible goods, each participant is aware that the behavior of his trading partner is directly dependent on his own action. If you have oranges and I have apples, and I want some of your oranges, I know that my desires can be met only by giving up apples, by paying some price. I can scarcely expect you to offer me oranges independent of my own behavior, nor could I expect to pick up the oranges without you invoking

---

3. For a discussion of the spontaneous order that emerges from market processes, see the excellent essay by Michael Polanyi, *The Logic of Liberty* (Chicago: University of Chicago Press, 1951).

rights of proprietorship. If I try this, or try to renege on a contract that I have made, I cannot expect to escape the costs that result from a breakdown in exchange. There is no way I can expect to get the oranges without cost. The behavioral setting for exchange or contract in indivisible or public goods is dramatically different. Suppose that many persons (1, 2, . . ., *n*) want something done, some "good" that is completely nonrival in usage. David Hume's example of the drainage of the village meadow is illustrative.[4] Suppose that each of the many villagers knows that the drainage would prove beneficial to him personally if the costs were shared equally among all members of the group. Even more desirable for an individual, however, would be the situation in which the meadow is drained by others, allowing the individual to escape without making any contribution. Each person will be motivated to refrain from voluntary initiation of action here to the extent that he expects his own behavior to be independent of that of other participants in the potential social interaction.

Each person has an incentive, therefore, to try to become a "free rider," one who secures the benefits of the jointly consumed good or service without participating fully in the sharing of its costs. As noted above, this "free-rider" terminology is somewhat misleading in that it suggests strategic behavior on the part of the individual participant. Strategic behavior designed to conceal from others the individual's true preferences for the public good will take place, however, only if the group is itself small and if the individual recognizes that his own behavior can affect others. With large numbers, the behavioral setting is quite different, although the results are similar. Here the individual participant does not behave strategically vis-à-vis his fellows; he treats their behavior as a part of his environment, and he does not consider that his own action can exert any influence on that of others in the sharing group. In this setting, the individual maximizes his utility by refraining from making an independent contribution toward the provision and the financing of the commonly shared good or service. In either case, some of the potential gains-from-trade that are available to all members of the group will not emerge spontaneously, even if individual initial rights are well defined and

---

4. David Hume, *A Treatise of Human Nature*, p. 538. The behavioral principle involved here has been recognized for centuries, or at least since Aristotle. See Aristotle, *Politics*, trans. H. Rackham (Cambridge: Harvard University Press, 1967), p. 77.

enforced. Exchanges in genuinely public goods will not be consummated voluntarily in the same institutional framework that facilitates exchanges in private goods.[5]

Exchange and Unanimity

Ordinary exchanges in private goods can be described as taking place under implicit unanimity. That is to say, if a buyer and a seller agree on terms, an exchange takes place and all members of the community outside this two-party relationship acquiesce in the outcome. Explicit agreement is not required on the part of these outsiders, and if any of this group should have desired to interfere with any observed exchange, he had the option of offering more favorable terms to either buyer or seller. So long as the spillover or external effects produced by the exchange are not significant, two-party trading under such implicit unanimity satisfies criteria for efficiency.[6] If, however, the characteristics of the goods are such that all members must participate explicitly in efficient sharing arrangements, the unanimity required becomes much more formidable. All persons must explicitly agree on the trading terms. Efficiency may require that the whole collectivity of persons be organized as an inclusive unit for implementing public-goods exchanges.

Knut Wicksell was the first scholar to recognize that a rule of unanimity for reaching collective decisions provides the institutional analogue to two-person trade in strictly private or partitionable goods.[7] The inclusive coalition of traders that is required to exploit fully all potential surplus will not, however, emerge naturally or spontaneously from the private, utility-maximizing behavior of persons who find themselves in a pure public-goods interaction. This remains true even if we ignore the agreement-transactions costs reflected

5. For a more detailed discussion of the basic analysis here, see my *Demand and Supply of Public Goods,* chap. 5.

6. For a summary discussion, see Ludwig von Mises, *Human Action: A Treatise on Economics* (New Haven: Yale University Press, 1949), p. 271.

7. See Knut Wicksell, *Finanztheoretische Untersuchungen* (Jena: Gustav Fischer, 1896). Major portions of this work are available in translation under the title "A New Principle of Just Taxation," in *Classics in the Theory of Public Finance,* ed. R. A. Musgrave and A. T. Peacock (London: Macmillan, 1958).

in higgling over terms of trade. A "natural equilibrium" in which some coalition of persons provides some of the public good and in which some other members of the community remain outside as free riders may emerge spontaneously in particular instances, but these results will tend to be inefficient. Careful analysis suggests that if efficiency criteria are to be met, some "social contract" among *all* persons must be made, a contract that requires all members of the community to participate in collective decisions which are, in turn, made under a unanimity rule. There is an apparent paradox here worth noting. A rule of unanimity will insure to each individual that he will not be harmed or damaged by collective action. But individuals, until and unless they are specifically organized under a "social contract" like that indicated, will not, privately and independently, attain efficient outcomes through voluntary trades or exchanges.

This poses a question of some importance for my discussion. Does a "social contract" in which all members of the community agree to make all collective choices relating to the provision and cost-sharing of a purely public good embody coercion as meaningfully defined? Ex ante, each participant knows that he will secure gains under such a contract, gains over and beyond those secured when none of the pure public good is provided. Recalcitrant members of the community may, however, expect to be able to secure differentially larger gains by remaining outside of the possible cost-sharing coalitions that would emerge to provide some of the jointly consumed good. Since, by our assumptions, Pareto optimality or efficiency is not attained until all persons are brought into the trading arrangements, there must exist mutual gains-from-trade as between potential cost-sharers and any potential free riders in this "social contract" sense. Hence, it would seem that an agreement to join a collectivity that would make its decisions only under a rule of unanimity could be reached noncoercively. Such an agreement might require, however, that certain members of the group be allowed differentially higher gains solely because of their unwillingness to cooperate. On the other hand, if this sort of differential treatment is granted, it might, in its turn, prove unacceptable to persons who would otherwise voluntarily agree to the contract. The basic principle of collective political order, that of equal treatment, would be violated at the outset. Paradoxical as it might seem, the conclusion must be that an all-inclusive collectivity could scarcely be organized voluntarily, even one that is severely limited to some required adherence to a rule of unanimity in making all collective choices.[8]

Unanimity, Voluntarism, and Exclusion

This result is modified if exclusion can be implemented. If those persons who do not choose to join in collective arrangements under which all cost-sharing decisions are to be made unanimously (surely a minimal set of requirements) can be excluded from any enjoyment of the subsequent benefits of public-goods provision, Pareto optimality or efficiency will tend to be attained voluntarily even in the pure public-goods case. Sharing arrangements will tend to emerge in which all persons will participate.[9] Potential free riders will not exist since each person will recognize that, should he refuse to participate, he will be wholly excluded from the enjoyment of public-goods benefits, benefits that he evaluates positively. Exclusion, as such, might never be observed in such a setting since the certainty of being excluded if they stayed outside would motivate all persons to join in the basic contract. Exclusion, if practiced, may in some cases be extremely costly to those in the sharing group, and in the case of a good that exhibits no rivalry in consumption or use, exclusion is always resource wasteful. Nonetheless, to the extent that the power to exclude and the willingness to exclude are known to exist, the sort of inefficiency generated by free-rider behavior will rarely, if ever, occur.[10]

More important for my discussion, however, is the problem of reconciling

8. For a discussion of the importance of others' behavior in influencing the willingness of individuals to participate in group decisions, see William J. Baumol, *Welfare Economics and the Theory of the State*, rev. ed. (Cambridge: Harvard University Press, 1965).

9. Note that I am defining a pure public good here in terms of the jointness rather than the nonexclusion property. That is to say, purity implies that additional consumers or users of any quantity may be added at zero marginal cost to those already in the group. It need not, in this context, be prohibitively expensive to exclude individuals from enjoying the benefits.

10. Exclusion from public-goods benefits is analytically equivalent to punishment for law violation, which will be discussed in detail in Chapter 8. The possible unwillingness of members of a cost-sharing group to exclude free riders because of the costs of the exclusion is conceptually equivalent to the possible unwillingness of law-abiding members of a polity to punish offenders because of the disutility involved in the act of punishment itself. In this, and other examples, an understanding of the central theory of public goods is helpful in understanding some of the issues involved in maintaining order under law.

a power of exclusion, regardless of cost, with the assumption that individuals' rights have been assigned, rights which are well defined and are mutually accepted by all parties. If we shift to the orthodox economist's model here and specify these in strict commodity dimensions, representing property rights as individualized claims to stocks of resources and final goods, complexities arise. Suppose that, in a community of n persons, $n - 1$ of them express a willingness to enter a binding contractual agreement to participate in sharing arrangements for the provision of a purely public good, with decisions as to quantity and cost shares to be made only under a rule of unanimity. When implemented, this would involve each of the $n - 1$ persons giving up some share of his initial endowment or stock in "exchange" for the expected return flow of public-goods benefits. But what about the nth person who refuses to enter the contract? We have implicitly presumed that, initially, he is a "member of the community," but we have not specified just what such membership means. Exclusion from enjoying the benefits of the public good must involve complete or partial expulsion from the community, as such. But this act seems inconsistent with the assignment of rights in basic constitutional contract, the assignment that defines an individual in terms of his initial endowments and entitlements which, presumably, incorporate physical location in a geographic community along with "social" location in a community which has adopted certain generalized rights of citizenship. Exclusion from the enjoyment of the public good may involve coercive intrusion into an individual's rights, defined independently of the public-goods decision.

There are two avenues of escape from this logical difficulty. We can either (1) reject the logical possibility of genuine social contract, even at the postconstitutional stage, while continuing to define individual rights in the manner suggested, or (2) redefine the assignment of rights in constitutional contract so as to embody exclusion. As the discussion indicates, the latter course offers a more explanatory model for exploring the complex issues of social order. Specifically, I propose that the initial assignment of individual rights emerging out of some prior constitutional contract embodies sets of personal claims to physically defined resource endowments (human and nonhuman) along with claims to share generalized rights of citizenship, limited or constrained by the minimal negation of such claims as may be required to implement exclusion from the benefits of public-goods provision upon the expressed unwillingness of claimants to participate in the postconstitutional contract under an effective rule of unanimity. Put somewhat more simply, this means that membership in a community is defined so as to compel participation in the genuine postconstitutional contracting for public goods, provided that an effective rule of unanimity is insured. Compulsion takes the form of exclusion from public-goods benefits, exclusion that may, if necessary, require the negation of specific "private ownership" claims.[11]

This setting allows us to analyze postconstitutional contract in a fully voluntaristic model. The individual, as such, is defined in terms of the rights assigned to him in constitutional contract. These include a specific imputation of initial endowments along with membership in a collective unit that makes decisions in accordance with a unanimity rule. The individual possesses no right to withdraw from the collectivity; to do so violates the constitutional contract just as clearly as the physical taking of endowments or goods that are assigned to other persons. Admittedly, this is a highly abstract and unrealistic construction, but it is necessary in order to develop the more realistic constructions to follow. The model suggests that, even when we restrict decision-making by a rule of unanimity, a collectivity, a state, must be an explicit element of and emerge out of constitutional contract. The inclusive exchanges in purely public goods that efficiency dictates will not necessarily emerge voluntarily from the behavior of individuals, each of whom is defined only in terms of initial endowments.

If, however, we make membership in an explicitly organized political entity an inherent component of each individual's rights, and if we restrict decision-making of this unit by a rule of unanimity, we can discuss all-inclusive, many-party exchange in public goods in voluntaristic terms, analogous to the two-party exchanges in private or partitionable goods implemented through market processes. As Wicksell recognized, the rule of unanimity offers the only ultimate test for efficiency in many-party exchanges, efficiency being measured by individualistic criteria. Or, to put this differently, any multiparty exchange that captures potentially realizable surplus can conceptually secure the unanimous approval of all participants. (In positive-sum

---

11. Mancur Olson has stressed the importance of by-product private goods as a means of enforcing exclusion in public-goods provision. See his *The Logic of Collective Action* (Cambridge: Harvard University Press, 1965).

games, all players can gain.) To get this result, however, individuals' incentives to invest in pure distributional gains must, somehow, be reduced or eliminated. A rule of unanimity provides each and every participant with a veto over final outcomes; it places each person in a position where he can bargain bilaterally with all others, treated as a unit. Because of this feature, the costs of agreement under a unanimity rule may be extremely high or even prohibitive. Recognizing this, Wicksell himself was willing to propose a qualified unanimity rule, by which he meant something like five-sixths of the total membership (or their representatives) for fiscal choice-making.

Individual Rights under Nonunanimity Rules

On grounds of institutional efficiency, departure from unanimity in the reaching of collective decisions seems necessary. Nonetheless, the importance of this change in any derivation of any postconstitutional "social contract" should be stressed. In *The Calculus of Consent,* Gordon Tullock and I analyzed the choice faced by an individual at the stage of constitutional contract on the presumption that his own cost-benefit position in subsequent decisions is unpredictable. We derived a logical basis for the adoption of less-than-unanimity rules, although we did not present arguments for any specific one among a large set of alternatives.[12] Indeed, one of our subsidiary purposes was to demonstrate that there is nothing unique about majority rule, the single alternative that is most often associated with nonunanimous collective action. But the problem of determining the rule to be chosen for postconstitutional collective choice is not my concern at this point. For present purposes, we may assume that any less-than-unanimity rule has been adopted, and we may use simple majority voting as illustrative. This rule is, presumably, chosen as one part of the more inclusive constitutional contract that defines the whole set of individuals' rights. My concern is the reconciliation of this majority rule with the multiparty exchange concept. What are individual "rights" in this setting? Can we discuss collective choice in terms analogous to voluntaristic exchanges

---

12. In the approach taken, there and here, unanimity offers the benchmark from which departures are dictated by reasons of efficiency in decision-making. Consent or agreement remains the conceptual ideal. For an argument which opposes this approach, see Douglas W. Rae, "The Limits of Consensual Decision" (Paper presented at the Public Choice Society Conference, College Park, Maryland, March 1973).

in private goods? Is it necessary to analyze collective decisions in a framework that is entirely different from that which is applicable for unanimity rule?

Under a unanimity rule, decisions if made at all are guaranteed to be efficient, at least in the anticipated sense. Individual agreement signals individual expectation that benefits exceed costs, evaluated in personal utility dimensions, which may or may not incorporate narrowly defined self-interest. With a purely public good, the individually secured benefits, as evaluated, must exceed the individually agreed-on share of costs, measured in foregone opportunities to secure private goods. From an initial imputation of endowments or goods, the multiparty exchange embodied in public-goods provision moves each individual to a final imputation, which includes public goods, that is evaluated more highly in utility terms. Each person in the collectivity moves to a higher position on his own utility surface, or thinks that he will do so, as a result of the public-goods decision reached by unanimous agreement.

No such results are guaranteed when collective decisions are made under less-than-unanimity rules. Under simple majority voting, for example, a person may find that a majority decision for public-goods provision shifts him to a lower rather than a higher position on his utility surface. What are his "rights" in such a postconstitutional change? It would seem that, for the person in question, this sort of change could hardly be called a "contract." Goods that he values are taken from him against his expressed desire. Coercion is apparently exercised upon him in the same way as that exerted by the thug who takes his wallet in Central Park. This manner of speaking is commonplace, but it tends to obscure much that requires careful analysis. The thief takes the victim's wallet. We should agree that genuine coercion is involved here because the victim, the thief, and external parties agree and accept the property rights. The wallet was the victim's by right of assigned and acknowledged ownership. Is this comparable to the situation of the citizen who finds that he must, on fear of punishment, pay taxes for public goods in excess of the amounts that he might voluntarily contribute? Is the collectivity, acting as directed by the effective decision-making coalition authorized in the conceptual constitutional contract, analogous to the thief? There is no question but that the collectivity is perceived in this image by many persons, and not only by those whose utilities may be directly reduced at a particular point in time.

This is one of the major sources of confusion in modern discussion of social policy, and it is related to a paradox of government that we shall examine in more detail in Chapter 6. If, as we have postulated, individual rights are defined as rights to do things with respect to some initial set of endowments or goods, *along with* membership in a collectivity that is empowered to act by less-than-unanimity rules, and, further, *if* these rights should be mutually accepted, it becomes inconsistent and self-contradictory for a person to claim that his "rights" are violated in the mere working out of the collective decision rules that are constitutionally authorized. At this point it is worth recalling once again that the analysis remains timeless. We are assuming that the *same* persons participate in the conceptual constitutional contract and in postconstitutional adjustments. From this it follows that, if a constitutional contract is made that defines separate persons in terms of property rights, and if these rights are widely understood to include membership in a polity that is authorized to make collective decisions by less-than-unanimity rules, each person must have, at this prior stage, accepted the limitations on his own rights that this decision process might produce. (Note that this statement need not imply that the prior constitutional contract was itself optimal or efficient. Note further that the justice or injustice of this contract is irrelevant here.)

To clarify the analysis, it will be helpful to distinguish two institutional structures of departure from a unanimity rule for collective action. In the first, collective decisions are made by less than full agreement of all members of the community, but these rules are externally constrained so as to guarantee outcomes that might, conceptually, have been attained under unanimity, without bargaining or agreement difficulties. That is to say, outcomes generated by collective choices must dominate the prechoice positions for all members of the community, evaluated in a utility dimension. In this restricted framework, it seems legitimate to refer to collective action as indirect *contract* or *exchange*. The decision rule embodying less than full agreement is necessary to avoid the behavioral effects of a unanimity rule, but the intent of the substitute rule is to accomplish essentially similar purposes. Even if an individual might have chosen differently from that outcome which the substitute rule produces, he has made a net improvement in his utility through participation in the collectivity. As later discussion will suggest, this restricted departure from unanimity is not without real-world application.

In the second set of institutions to be examined, collective decision rules are unconstrained, and when unanimity is dropped an individual may find himself actually suffering net utility losses from "participating." That is to say, he may end up at a lower utility level than he might have been able to sustain in the complete absence of collective action. (Recall that we are continuing to assume that there has been mutual acceptance of initially defined rights to endowments.) It would seem to be an improper use of language to call this process "contractual." In this case, collective action may seem to an individual to be equivalent to that taken by the thug in the park, or worse. Even here, however, care must be taken to specify just what protections the constitutional contract offers the individual against exploitative collective or government decisions. If the constitution embodies unconstrained collective action under less-than-unanimity rules, the individual does not really "own" the initial endowments or stocks in a manner at all analogous to "ownership" under the contrasting institutional structure. "Private ownership" takes on a wholly different meaning in this setting, a meaning that must be explored in considerable detail. Before such exploration, however, it will be useful to present the alternative structure somewhat more systematically.[13]

Indirect contract under less-than-unanimity decision rules

We may discuss the first of the two alternatives with the aid of a simple two-person model and a single diagram. In figure 3.1 we measure the utility of one person, A, on the ordinate, and the utility of the other person, B, on the abscissa. (The construction is similar to that of fig. 2.2, chap. 2 above.) The utility attained by each person from the establishment of constitutional contract is shown at C. Trade between the two persons in divisible or private goods shifts the position to E. There remain, however, further gains-from-

---

13. The whole discussion here is directly related to the issues involved in "just compensation." These are examined in the context of modern legal doctrine in an excellent long essay by Frank I. Michelman. See his "Property, Utility, and Fairness," pp. 1165–1258.

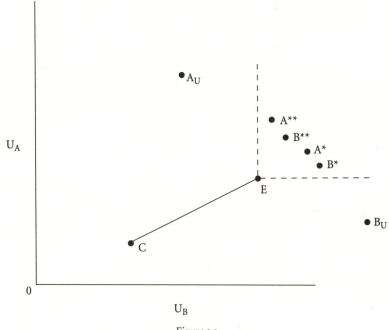

Figure 3.1

trade to be secured from the provision of a good that is consumed jointly. (The two-person model here is treated as being analogous to a many-person model; in an actual two-person interaction, few problems would arise in reaching agreement on joint or collective sharing.) If the group can attain agreement under a unanimity rule, this insures that a final outcome will be contained in the northeast quadrant from E, the area bounded by the dotted lines extending from E. In our extension to the many-person world, however, we have assumed that an effective unanimity rule is unworkable and that some less-than-unanimity variant is adopted constitutionally. In the two-person illustration, this means that decisions for the group will be made by either one or the other of the two persons, by either A or B, and independently of the preferences of the other.

We assume that collective decisions are limited to the purchase, provision, and financing of a single purely public good. Note that this assumption, in itself, severely constrains the set of outcomes that are possible. At best, the single ruler could impose all costs of the good on his cohort while providing the good out to his own satiety levels. This constraint alone would not, how-ever, normally be sufficient to insure that outcomes fall within the indirect exchange area bounded by the dotted lines of figure 3.1. As a further con-straint, let us assume that the basic constitutional contract also specifies a taxing institution. That is to say, there exist constitutional requirements that the single public good must be financed from a specific tax structure. We might select any one of the familiar patterns of taxation such as equal-per-head charges, proportional taxes on incomes, progressive taxes on incomes, or others. In this setting, if the tax institution is properly chosen, the results generated under one-man rule may be beneficial, in the net, to both persons. Ideally, choice of the tax structure could make the collective decision rule ir-relevant since all rules would produce the same outcome.[14] The ideal tax could not, of course, be selected at the constitutional level. But with some practicable choice of tax structure along with the limitation of collective ac-tion to the provision of genuine public goods, we might plausibly predict that outcomes would be bounded within the Pareto-superior area. Consider, as a supplement to figure 3.1, the demand patterns shown in figure 3.2, and suppose that equal-per-head taxes are required. If individual A is the ruler, he will choose a quantity Q_a; if individual B is the ruler, he will choose Q_b. Note that, in each case, the nonruler will still be enjoying a net fiscal surplus from participating in the public-goods arrangement. We might depict these separate outcomes in figure 3.1 as positions A* and B* respectively. Note that both fall well within the boundaries of the Pareto-superior set.

This means that either A* or B* could conceptually have been achieved from the working of a unanimity rule, given the chance pattern of bargaining toward solution that might have generated such outcomes. Given the tax in-stitution postulated, the nonruler, B, will not be satisfied at A*, or Q_a. He will not be in full marginal adjustment with respect to public-goods quantity and

14. Wicksell was the first to recognize the basic substitutability between tax institutions and collective-choice rules. By the introduction of more flexibility in tax institutions, more inclusive collective-decision rules can be accepted, with more guarantees against fiscal ex-ploitation. Wicksell did not, however, reverse the logical chain here. With effectively de-signed tax institutions, the potential exploitation that can be implemented through less-than-unanimity decision rules can be reduced, and, in the limit, wholly eliminated. For an elaboration of this relationship, see my *Demand and Supply of Public Goods*, and my *Public Finance in Democratic Process* (Chapel Hill: University of North Carolina Press, 1967).

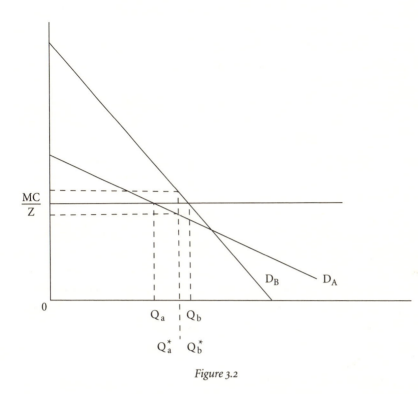

Figure 3.2

tax-price. If he should be made ruler, he would prefer to shift to B*, and Q_b. He will, therefore, be "unhappy" with the tax-budgetary decision imposed on him by A through the solution at A*. The same results would apply conversely to A if he should be the nonruler.

Differing constraints will, of course, generate different results, even under identical decision rules. Assume now that A remains the collective decision-maker, but that instead of head taxes, proportional income taxes are required. Furthermore, assume that B has a higher income than A, as indicated by the positions of D_A and D_B in figure 3.2. This tax will tend to reduce the quantity of good preferred by B and to increase that preferred by A. Under this scheme of taxation, individual A might optimally choose Q_a^* and individual B might choose Q_b^*. The utility positions attained under the alternative single-man rule are shown as A** and B** in figure 3.1. As depicted, both remain within the Pareto-superior region with relation to the initial position, E. This example suggests that there may exist a whole set of tax and budgetary institutions, or, more generally, constitutional constraints on fiscal process, which will insure that nonunanimity rules operate effectively as instruments to produce what we have called "indirect exchange" among individuals for purely public goods.

It is important to recognize both the purpose and the limits of the constitutional constraints that may be imposed on the operation of nonunanimity rules for collective decision-making at the postconstitutional stage of social interaction. To remain within what we may call broad contractual bounds, individuals must be assured that, in the net, operational politics will produce for them benefits rather than damages. There is nothing in the public-goods "exchange structure," however, that dictates uniqueness in the distribution of the gains-from-trade, nothing analogous to the unique distribution of the comparable net realizable surplus in private-goods trade, no unique price vector emergent from idealized recontracting. For this reason, there may be considerable variation in political-institutional structure, in rules, without forcing results out of the bounds of mutuality of benefits among all parties. In game-theoretic parlance, the core of the public-goods game is considerably more inclusive than that in the private-goods game.[15]

In a regime with perfect side payments and zero transactions costs, a unique allocative result for the provision of a purely public good will be generated only if income-effect feedbacks are neglected or absent. However, any allocative result achieved may, itself, be attained from any one of a whole set of distributive patterns. An allocative result requires that marginal prices confronted by separate participants stand in some specific relation one to another. There is no comparable relationship among average prices. The relatively loose restrictions imposed by the "indirect exchange" constraints require only that all persons secure net benefits. In the more general setting where

15. Formal proofs that the Lindahl "solution" to the public-goods game is in the core do nothing toward showing that there do not exist many other "solutions" that equally qualify for inclusion. In this sense, the Lindahl equilibrium in the public-goods game is not at all comparable to competitive equilibrium in the private-goods counterpart.

To make the geometrical illustration in figure 3.1 more relevant to the large-number setting, we could reinterpret position E as that which is attained from the completion of all interpersonal trades in private goods and in all trades in joint-consumption goods that involve coalitions of less than the full membership of the inclusive group. With this modification, the diagram and the discussion can depict the constraints imposed on political decision rules with respect to any one person vis-à-vis all others in the polity.

side payments are costly, the constraints also allow for considerable departures from the attainment of idealized allocative efficiency. The necessary condition is only that public-goods exchange, conceived as a game, be positive sum for all participants. There is no necessity that aggregate payoffs be maximized. To the extent that total payoffs may be influenced by the rules, one criterion of adjustment at the constitutional stage becomes that of predicted allocative efficiency. But, as we shall suggest, this criterion may well be dominated by distributive norms.

UNCONSTRAINED DEPARTURES FROM
UNANIMITY RULES

A categorically different model is introduced when collective decisions can be taken under nonunanimity rules with no constitutional limits or constraints. Recall that our basic schemata includes a conceptual separation between the stage of constitutional contract, at which individual rights are defined and collective decision rules are made, and postconstitutional contract, at which trades or exchanges take place among persons whose rights to carry out activities and to dispose of things are defined in the prior stage. This schemata allows us to discuss market process, private-goods trade, and those political processes that embody public-goods "exchanges" in the postconstitutional stage. We have incorporated the "indirect exchanges" that take place under constrained nonunanimity rules for collective choice. If, however, the delineation of rights in the constitutional stage allows the collectivity, the state, to make decisions on any less-than-unanimity rule without *constraint,* the proposed schemata appears to involve an internal contradiction. In the two-person example, we could scarcely argue that B's rights are defined in some prior stage if A's rights are all-inclusive and unrestricted. The model emphasizes the necessity of defining the "rights" or limits of the decision-maker for the collectivity as well as those of the separate persons within it. So long as the collectivity's actions are constrained as noted above, we are able to talk as if the contracting parties in postconstitutional negotiations are individual citizens. Although vastly more complex, political process becomes analogous to market process. But we are no longer able to think in such terms when all shackles are removed from collective action.

An attempt might be made to get out of the apparent contradiction here by resort to "probabilistic rights."[16] That is to say, we might consider that human and nonhuman rights are defined in the constitution subject to the actions to be taken by an unconstrained collectivity, operating under any of a large subset of specified nonunanimity rules for decision, ranging from the near-unanimity of a Wicksellian qualified majority, through simple majority voting, to one-man dictatorship. The value of any individual's actual claim over "goods," including over life itself, might then be represented by some "expected value," determined by the descriptive characteristics of the decision rule in being, by the social history of the collectivity, by the value of the nominal claim, and by the probability that this claim will be changed, upward or downward, by imposed action taken in the name of state or collective authority.

Consider, for example, the position of a person who, in nominal terms, has been assigned command over a relatively large share of "goods" in the community, but who holds membership in a collectivity that makes decisions on the basis of simple majority voting, without explicit or traditional constitutional constraints. In this setting, the probability of the person in question being able to retain the full nominal value of his "goods," as assigned, or to improve this by participating in public-goods trade, might be low. He should find it possible to compute some plausibly realistic "expected value" for his nominal claims. The question is whether this value might offer a basis for both private- and public-goods trades or exchanges. To the extent that trades can take place in terms of such expected values, it seems evident that risk elements will necessarily dampen pressures toward efficiency. A more fundamental problem arises, however, concerning the nominally assigned claims upon which such expected values might be computed. If the contractual setting is literally applied, why should a person have accepted the unconstrained collectivity in juxtaposition with his relatively favorable set of nominal rights? Even conceptually, why should he have ever acquiesced in the assignment of unlimited rights to the collectivity? These issues force us back into a discussion of constitutional contract itself which we have tried to relegate to a subsequent chapter. But a provisional answer may be advanced

---

16. For a related discussion in the context of theoretical welfare economics, see A. Mitchell Polinsky, "Probabilistic Compensation Criteria," *Quarterly Journal of Economics* 86 (August 1972): 407–25.

here. If an individual acknowledges the existence of an unconstrained collectivity that reduces the expected value of his net claims, he should rationally have preferred some initially defined constitutional reduction in his nominal claims along with an accompanying restriction on collective action. Similarly, if another person finds that the expected value of his net claims, under the operation of unconstrained collective action, exceeds that measured by the nominal value of his assignment, he should prefer a somewhat larger nominal assignment along with imposed limits on the collectivity. For both persons, uncertainty is reduced by restrictions on state action.

This would provide a logical basis for the imposition of constraints on the collectivity, as an acting unit, even if institutional necessity requires that this unit act independently from individual efforts. An additional basis for constitutional constraints on collective action is provided when it is recognized that, if there are no constraints, individuals have a stronger incentive to invest resources in attempts to secure control over collective decisions. Control over the collective decision-making apparatus becomes the instrument for securing the winnings of a zero-sum component of the game of politics. And, for the community in total, all resources invested in gaining this control are wasted. Incentives to gain control over the collective decision-making machinery are not, of course, wholly absent in the fully constrained model. As the simple diagram in figure 3.1 shows, it does make some difference in utility terms whether A or B is the effective decision-taker for the community. In the unconstrained model, however, individual A might look on the prospects of reaching some position like A_u that would result from his gaining control over the decision-making for the collectivity, while B might be similarly attracted by the prospects of moving to B_u if he successfully seizes the reins of government. It is clear that the incentives to invest resources in "politics" become dimensionally larger in the unconstrained than in the constrained model.

Corollary to this is the motivation for persons who control collective decision-making to use this means of generating directly enjoyable and divisible private and partitionable goods rather than producing genuine public goods which benefit all persons in the community. In a constitutionally unconstrained collectivity, it seems likely that net wealth and income transfers would bulk much larger in governmental action than they would in constrained constitutional regimes. The use of tax revenues collected from those

who are the "outs" to finance Swiss bank accounts for the "ins" is the familiar real-world example.

In a sense, the analysis of unconstrained collective action under nonunanimity decision-making brings us full circle. The very purpose, in the larger
"social" meaning, of defining rights in constitutional contract is to facilitate
orderly anarchy, to provide the basis upon which individuals can initiate and
implement trades and exchanges both of simple and complex forms. Having
defined and accepted a structure of rights, individuals can reduce their own
investment in defense and predation and go about their business of increasing utility levels through freely negotiated dealings with each other. To the
extent that collective action is allowed to break beyond the boundaries imposed by the mutuality of gains from exchange, both direct and indirect, the
community has taken a major step backward into the anarchistic jungle or
has failed to take the major step from this jungle in the first place.

The operation of an unconstrained collectivity could scarcely emerge from
rational constitutional contracting among persons. Historically, an explicit
stage of constitutional contracting may never have existed; the structure of
rights may have emerged in an evolutionary process characterized by an absence of conscious agreement. From this setting, the apparent contradiction
may be generated. More important for my purposes, even if something akin
to an initial contract may have settled the structure of individual and collective rights, this structure may be eroded over time. Although once constrained,
the powers of the collectivity may gradually be expanded so as to become,
for all practical purposes, unlimited. As we have noted earlier, the contractual models are not designed to be historically descriptive. They are, instead,
designed to assist in the development of criteria with which existing political-
legal systems may be evaluated. In this context, empirical evidence that the
collectivity as it exists is unconstrained suggests the hypothesis that general
agreement could be attained for genuine constitutional revision.

The analysis in this chapter, and elsewhere, is derived from the basic norms
of individualism discussed in Chapter 1. The position taken here stands in
apparent opposition to the allegedly "positivist" view that denies the possibility of constraining the collectivity in any ultimate sense. This was Hobbes's
position, and in his conceptual model the individual surrenders all rights to
the sovereign at the time of the initial contract. In the terminology employed
here, this amounts to saying that only the collectivity, the government, holds

anything that might be called "rights." Those claims to carry out specific activities, including disposition and usage of resources, that are expressed on the part of persons are subject at all times to arbitrary redefinition by government. And, indeed, the central role of government in this positivist model is the settlement of competing claims among individuals and groups, settlement which necessarily involves continual redefinition of limits.[17] I shall not defend the approach taken in this book against the positivist arguments. Whether it is possible to constrain the powers of government, to protect individual rights in a genuine usage of this term, can never be proven empirically. It is at this point, however, that individuals' attitudes toward reality seem more important than the reality itself. Governmental decisions are always made by men, and if these men act within a paradigm that embodies meaningful constitutional constraints, the "as if" analysis seems warranted, regardless of the ultimate power that may or may not remain unexercised.

Allocation and Distribution

The categorical distinction that I have made between constitutional contract and postconstitutional contract may seem familiar to economists. The distinction is related to the familiar neoclassical dichotomy between allocation and distribution, especially as the latter is treated in normative discourse in political economy. In the world restricted to private or partitionable goods and services, when property rights are defined, markets will emerge to allocate resources with tolerable efficiency and the gains-from-trade will be distributed among particular parties in a specific manner. Neoclassical, and mod-

---

17. Warren J. Samuels is an articulate modern spokesman for this positivist position. In an exchange devoted to a specific legal issue, the basic methodological differences between this position and my own are clarified. See Warren J. Samuels, "Interrelations between Legal and Economic Processes," *Journal of Law and Economics* 14 (October 1971): 435–50; James M. Buchanan, "Politics, Property and the Law: An Alternative Interpretation of Miller et al. v. Schoene," *Journal of Law and Economics* 15 (October 1972): 439–52; Warren J. Samuels, "In Defense of a Positive Approach to Government as an Economic Variable," *Journal of Law and Economics* 15 (October 1972): 453–60.

A more comprehensive statement of Samuels's position is contained in his "Welfare Economics, Power, and Property," in *Perspectives of Property*, ed. G. Wunderlich and W. L. Gibson, Jr. (State College: Institute for Land and Water Resources, Pennsylvania State University, 1972), pp. 61–146.

ern, economists have expressed little or no direct concern for the market's distribution of the *gains*-from-trade. They have been unwilling to accept the final distributional results largely because they remain unwilling to restrict their domain of evaluation to postconstitutional contract. The distinction developed here would have been helpful in clarifying much of the discussion in political economy because this would have indicated that the distributional problem arises, not with respect to the gross gains-from-trade, but with respect to the initial distribution of endowments or capacities—that distribution that provides the basis upon which individuals enter the trading process.

In this particular respect, discussion and analysis of public-goods exchange in postconstitutional contract have been considerably more sophisticated than the parallel analysis of the private market sector. Knut Wicksell recognized explicitly that the efficiency norms for the provision of jointly consumed goods and services which informed his search for the appropriate institutions for collective decision-making are applicable only in a setting where individual property rights are well defined and broadly acceptable. Wicksell recognized that the whole decision-making process must be modified when genuine constitutional contract is considered. In this respect, as in others, my own approach has been greatly influenced by Wicksell. In modern public-finance theory, R. A. Musgrave, in his basic treatise, makes a categorical distinction between the allocational branch of the budget and the distributional branch.[18] Especially in his response to attempts to extend allocational norms to distributional policy, Musgrave seems to make a categorical distinction between the fundamental decision processes that are involved.[19]

18. R. A. Musgrave, *The Theory of Public Finance* (New York: McGraw-Hill, 1959).

19. R. A. Musgrave, "Comment," *American Economic Review* 60 (December 1970): 991–93. The paper that prompted Musgrave's comments, along with those of several others, was Harold M. Hochman and James D. Rodgers, "Pareto Optimal Redistribution," *American Economic Review* 59 (September 1969): 542–57.

4. Constitutional Contract
The Theory of Law

As suggested above, postconstitutional contract has occupied the primary attention of economists for the whole period of their independent disciplinary existence. Despite the concentration of effort on the exchange processes, major analytical complexities remain unresolved. What then may we anticipate when we try to conceptualize constitutional contract, that human interaction in which individual rights may be initially defined, where the very rules for interpersonal behavior may be established, where "society," quite literally, replaces "anarchy"? Once we so much as open up this area for critical examination, is there much surprise in professional economists' proclivity to commence with the assertion that property rights are well defined? Is there any wonder that a genuine economic theory of law remains undeveloped?[1]

Strictures should not, however, single out economists. They can with some legitimacy claim exemption; their traditional domain is or should be limited to contract. Perhaps criticism is more appropriately directed at those whose professional emphases are on power relationships among individuals and groups. But political scientists have been reluctant to follow up the leads suggested by Thomas Hobbes. They have devoted much attention to the politi-

1. A development of significance in the 1960s and 1970s has been the emergence of the "economics of property" as a field of intense scholarly interest, along with the parallel introduction of more economic theory and more economists into the curricula of law schools. The primary emphasis of this movement has been, however, the influence on individual behavior exerted by the institutional or legal setting within which such behavior takes place. This emphasis is, in itself, praiseworthy, and it has yielded and will continue to yield useful scientific results. By contrast with this, however, relatively little emphasis has been placed on the possible explanations for the emergence of the observed institutions in the first place. See relevant footnotes to Chapter 2.

cal obligation of individuals, leaders and followers alike, but relatively little attention to the base positions from which behavioral obligations must be assessed. In its own defense, however, political science can claim to embody a more developed and sophisticated historical sense than economics. Once it is recognized that observed institutions of legal-political order exist only in a historical setting, the attraction of trying to analyze conceptual origins independent of historical process is severely weakened. The temptation becomes strong to assert what is essentially the positivist position that a structure of law, a legal system, a set of property rights, exists and that there is relatively little point in trying to understand or to develop a contractual metaphor for its emergence that would offer assistance in finding criteria for social change. There is merit in this approach, provided that it is not allowed to exclude complementary bodies of analysis. Some of the implications of accepting "law as fact" will be explored in Chapter 5.

In order to discuss or to analyze possible criteria for modifying the structure of rights, however, some understanding of conceptual origins may be helpful. As has been suggested, the problem is one of trying to explain and to understand the relationships among individuals, and between individuals and the government. And for this purpose, various "as if" models of conceptual origins may be necessary, regardless of the facts described in the historical records.[2] Stress should be placed on "explanation" and "understanding" since the temptation to introduce normative statement becomes extremely strong at this level of discourse. Precisely because the conceptual origins are discussed independent of observable historical data, the distinction between positive analysis and normative presupposition is difficult to detect.

Must we postulate a basic equality among men in some original setting in order to derive the structure of a free society from rational, self-interested

2. See S. I. Benn and R. S. Peters, *The Principles of Political Thought* (New York: The Free Press, 1959), p. 377.

Maine advanced the suggestion that the language and terminology appropriate to discuss the relationship between ruler and ruled in postfeudal society was found only in treatments of Roman law. Hence, "contract" theories of the state emerged, in part, because of linguistic history. In this connection, Maine's discussion of "quasi-contracts" is helpful, and this would perhaps be a more suitable term to apply to all discussion of "social contract." In "quasi-contract," there is no implication of explicit agreement, but the relationship is such as to make the contractarian framework for discourse helpful. See Henry Maine, *Ancient Law*, pp. 333–35.

behavior? We have often answered this question affirmatively, even if implicitly. In the process, we have made our whole "theory" of conceptual constitutional foundations highly vulnerable to positivist refutation. In this book, I am attempting to explain how "law," "the rights of property," "rules for behavior," might emerge from the nonidealistic, self-interested behavior of men, without any presumption of equality in some original position—equality either actually or expectationally.[3] In this effort, I make no claim to have escaped all normative influences. But I should argue that the approach taken is less normative than the familiar one which says, in effect, that any logical analysis of law *should* be based on the *as if* presumption of personal equality. We can substantially strengthen the foundations of freedom if we can succeed in demonstrating that, even among men who are unequal, a structure of legal rights can be predicted to emerge, a structure that retains characteristic elements that we associate with the precepts of individualism. Only after we have done this can we begin to offer constructive criticism of the veritable maze of confusion about constitutional order that abounds at the most basic levels of discussion.

Personal Inequality

In order to make an analysis of constitutional contract as general as is possible, allowance should be made for the existence of substantial differences among persons in the original conceptual setting. This is not the same as postulating inequality as fact. The analysis should be sufficiently general to be applicable if, in fact, persons should prove to be substantially equivalent. To be avoided is the dependence of the results on some unsupported presumption of natural equality. The degree or measure of inequality will, of course, affect the description of any initial position and the structure of rights that may contractually emerge.

Consider, then, some initial setting in which men are not equals. Following economists' practice, we can discuss inequality in two separate attributes:

---

3. It is in the expectational sense that the approach taken here differs sharply from that taken in *The Calculus of Consent*. In that book, individuals were assumed to be sufficiently uncertain about their positions under the operations of decision rules as to make them enter the negotiation stage as equals in at least this one respect.

(1) tastes or preferences, and (2) capacities.[4] It is necessary to avoid explicitly the tendency to slip exclusively into the familiar classification of persons by personal endowments of "goods," presumably measured in commodity dimensions. This procedure amounts to neglecting the very problems addressed in this chapter, to presuming that individual rights to commodities, to goods, have already been defined.

In the fundamental sense required for the analysis here, an individual possesses no "goods" or "resources." He can be defined initially by a preference or a utility function on the one hand and by a production function on the other.[5] The preference or utility function describes the rates at which the person is willing subjectively to trade off goods (and bads) one against the other. The individual's production function is less familiar. He will have, inherent in his physiological makeup, a set of capacities (skills, talents, abilities). These capacities, when exercised in a specified environmental setting, define for the individual a potential relationship between inputs (negative goods or bads) and product (positive goods). This relationship is his "production function."

As noted, persons may differ from each other either in tastes, in capacities, or in both. Or, persons identical in both tastes and capacities may find themselves in environmentally different situations relative to their capacities. A person with mediocre talents may be confronted with ample opportunities to secure positively valued goods while a person with superior talents may face less favorable opportunities. The position attained by a person is dependent on three basic elements: his preferences, his capacities, and his environmental setting. It would be wholly arbitrary to assume that all individuals face identical environmental settings; this would be as indefensible an assumption as that which postulates personal equality in preferences or in capacities.

Anarchistic Interaction

Consider two individuals who are wholly isolated from each other; each on his separate island with no social contact. Each man would attain a personal

4. For an analysis of the different implications of inequality in these separate attributes, see my paper, "Equality as Fact and Norm," *Ethics* 81 (April 1971): 228–40.

5. Note that we are removing the restrictions imposed by the no-production model analyzed briefly in Chapter 1.

behavior equilibrium, as determined by the interaction among his utility function, his basic or inherent capacities to convert input into output, and the natural environmental setting that he confronts. There would be no easy means of judging which of these two Robinson Crusoes is more favorably situated, or which one secures more "welfare." This two-Crusoe world is, of course, purely anarchistic. There is no law, and there is no need for a definition of individuals' rights, either property rights or human rights. There is no society as such. Nonetheless, this two-Crusoe world provides a useful starting point from which to begin consideration of the world where personal conflict may emerge. Suppose that the persons, whom we shall name A and B, no longer exist in complete isolation, but that, instead, they now find themselves in some spatially limited area, on the same island. This change, in itself, need not modify the preferences of either person, although such an effect should not be ruled out. The environmental setting of each person will, however, almost surely be modified. In the absence of law, each person will now consider the other as a part of the environment that he faces. The effects of this upon the rate at which bads may be transformed into goods may take on several patterns.

In a world of scarcity, mutual exploitation of the natural environment insures that, for each person, the terms-of-trade with his own environment are worsened relative to those confronted in the isolated setting where one person, alone, faces this environment. In effect, the natural environment becomes "common property," and the familiar reciprocal externality relationships emerge. Most economists would perhaps tend to stop the analysis at this point with little or no consideration of the remaining possibilities. But a second, and very different, sort of influence may operate. If production is not simultaneous with actual consumption of goods, individuals may store goods for future use. In this situation, the presence of B may prompt A to devote effort, a bad, to concealing hoards, and to defending and protecting these hoards from predation by B. Since this effort might otherwise have been used to produce goods directly, A's net rate of transformation is adversely affected by this necessity for defense.

An offsetting effect may, however, work in the other direction. Because of the presence of B, A now has available to himself a new opportunity. He may secure goods that were not available to him in the strict Crusoe setting. If B is known to be producing, and storing, goods, A may find that locating and taking these stocks from B is more productive than producing similar goods on his own. This effect, if it should predominate, tends to shift A's production function in a favorable manner. Once the prospects for defense and predation are recognized, it is clear that individuals may differ in their talents for these activities and that such differences need not be directly correspondent to their relative capacities as direct producers. Furthermore, individuals may differ in their tastes for defense-predation efforts relative to direct production efforts.

It is, of course, impossible to consider the effects of B's presence on A without, at the same time, considering the effects of A's presence on B. The two persons are necessarily in a reciprocal interaction; their behavior is interdependent even if there is no social structure within which interdependence takes place. As indicated in Chapter 2, this sort of interaction may be analyzed in externality terms, even if we are working with a model without law and rights of property. It is useful to think of the reciprocal external diseconomy model in which each person's behavior imposes harm on the other. Consider, first, the behavior of A in producing goods in the environment that is shared, but without overt dispute. That is to say, let us postulate initially that A and B allow each other to attain private adjustment independent of disturbance. Each man uses his talents as best he can to maximize utility on the assumption that the other will not take stocks from him and that he, in turn, will not take stocks from the other. This is strictly an arbitrary starting point, and it will not represent a final equilibrium in the interaction sequence. In figure 4.1, this no-conflict position is placed at the origin. Note that, at this position, A and B need not have equal quantities of the good, nor need they be accepting equal quantities of the bad to secure the position indicated. For purposes of illustration, let us assert that at the origin, A is exerting six units of effort (a bad) to get, in the net, ten units of bananas (a good), while B is exerting five units of effort in getting twelve units of good.

This arbitrary starting point does not qualify for a behavioral equilibrium because, in this position, each person has some incentive to initiate conflict, to engage in predatory activity vis-à-vis his cohort. Figure 4.1 shows that, if A thinks that B will remain in the position at the origin, he will initiate predatory action to shift toward position Y. Conversely, B will be motivated to try to reach position X. The reactions of A to every level of B's activity in defense-predation is shown by the ridge line, R_A. Similarly, B's reaction to every level

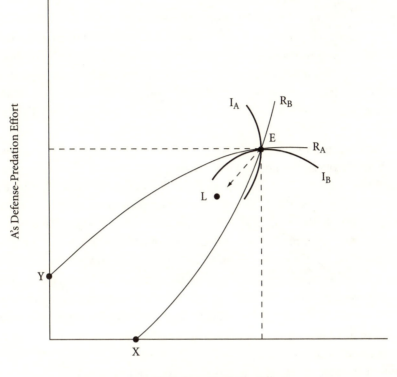

Figure 4.1

of defense-predation by A is shown by the ridge line, R_B. Equilibrium in this purely anarchistic setting is attained at E. At this point, neither person has an incentive to modify his behavior privately or independently. In this equilibrium, each person may be expending some share of his efforts in defending his stocks from the other, another part in taking stocks of the other, and another part in producing goods directly. The position of independent adjustment equilibrium describes the outcome or result that could be predicted in a genuinely anarchistic order. The distribution has been called the "natural distribution" by Winston Bush, and the two-person model may, of course, be extended to apply in a many-person setting.[6]

6. See Winston Bush, "Income Distribution in Anarchy." See also Winston Bush and Lawrence Mayer, "Some Implications of Anarchy for the Distribution of Property," mim-

I have emphasized in several places that there is no presumption of equality among persons in this independent adjustment or natural equilibrium. A second important principle is that this position cannot itself be attained contractually. Until this natural equilibrium is itself attained, there is no basis from which persons can negotiate contracts, one with another. The generation of this independent adjustment equilibrium is, therefore, the precontractual stage of social order, if indeed we can use the word "social" at all here.

There are no property rights in the strict sense of this term in the equilibrium so described. The position does, nonetheless, have certain stability characteristics, both for "society" and for the individual participant. There is no incentive for any person to modify his own behavior in the absence of exogenous shocks. In this equilibrium, therefore, each person knows with some degree of certainty what his own final command over ultimate consumable goods will be. Each person will, as noted, be expending resources in defending acquired stocks and in securing stocks initially acquired by others. But his net asset position, his final command over goods, will be predictable within relatively narrow limits. Chaos does not seem the appropriate descriptive word to apply to this genuinely anarchistic equilibrium if its meaning is taken to include unpredictability. Something akin to "property," therefore, emerges from the noncontractual struggle in anarchy. Individuals achieve identifiable bases from which it becomes possible to make contracts.

Disarmament and the Emergence of Property Rights

In natural equilibrium, each person uses resources to defend against and to attack other persons. Each person would be better off if some of these resources could somehow be turned to the direct production of goods. The most basic contractual agreement among persons should, therefore, be the mutual acceptance of some disarmament. The mutual gains should be apparent to all parties.[7]

---

eographed (Center for Study of Public Choice, Virginia Polytechnic Institute and State University, Blacksburg, Virginia, 1973).

7. This derivation of the conceptual origins of property has been advanced by several social philosophers. It was developed by Aegidius Romanus in the thirteenth century, and

This may be illustrated with reference to the interaction depicted in figure 4.1. By the definition of ridge lines, or lines of optima, we know that the indifference contours for A are vertical along R_A, while those for B are horizontal along R_B. Hence, at E, we know that the indifference contours intersect at right angles, in the manner shown by I_A and I_B. We know, further, that the indifference contours for A are concave to the left, while those for B are concave downward. This is because of the fact that the ideal position for A is at Y, where B makes no effort to defend stocks or to take stocks from A, and that the ideal position for B is the comparable one shown at X. In these configurations, the Pareto-superior region, that which includes positions reflecting mutual gains by comparison with E, lies to the southwest, indicated directionally by the arrow in figure 4.1. Positions that embody mutual gains must involve lower outlay on defense-predation for both parties. Suppose that an agreement is reached to move to position L. Note precisely what this agreement embodies. The contract is one of bilateral behavioral exchange. Individual A agrees to give up some share of his own defense-predation effort in exchange for a related behavioral change on the part of individual B. There is no incentive for either person to take this behavioral change unilaterally, and there is nothing in the initial agreement, as such, which requires or even induces any acceptance by the other of the legitimacy of either person's command over goods, either in the preagreement or postagreement stage. Mutual acceptance of "ownership rights" is not a part of this preliminary disarmament agreement. On the other hand, by negotiating such an initial agreement to limit defense and predation, "law" of a sort has now emerged. The two persons accept limits to their own freedom of action, to their own liberty. The first leap out of the anarchistic jungle has been taken.

Conquest, Slavery, and Contract

In the discussion of anarchistic interaction to this point, I have assumed implicitly that all persons will exist as independently acting defenders and pred-

---

was elaborated with surprising sophistication by Hugo Grotius in 1625. On these contributions, see Schlatter, *Private Property,* pp. 57f., 128–32.

The derivation is also closely similar to that presented by David Hume. See his *A Treatise of Human Nature,* vol. 3.

The contractual emergence of property rights from some anarchistic state of nature is opposed to the view taken by many scholars that "natural law" precepts are necessary.

ators both prior to and after a natural equilibrium is attained. If personal differences are sufficiently great, however, some persons may have the capacities to eliminate others of the species. In this instance, the natural equilibrium may be reached only when the survivors exercise exclusive environmental domain.

The complete elimination of other persons may not, however, be the most preferred course of action by those who possess superior capacities. Even more desired might be the state in which those who are "weak" are allowed to exert effort in producing goods, after which the "strong" seize all, or substantially all, of these for their own use. From this setting, the disarmament contract that may be negotiated may be something similar to the slave contract, in which the "weak" agree to produce goods for the "strong" in exchange for being allowed to retain something over and above bare subsistence, which they may be unable to secure in the anarchistic setting.[8] A contract of slavery would, as other contracts, define individual rights, and, to the extent that this assignment is mutually accepted, mutual gains may be secured from the consequent reduction in defense and predation effort. This may seem to represent a somewhat tortuous interpretation of slavery as an institution, but it is explicitly designed to allow the analytical framework developed here to be fully general.[9]

Trading Equilibrium and Direct Production

Economists who are familiar with the geometrical construction of figure 4.1, and the underlying postulates, will recognize that the minimal restrictions imposed on the locations and shapes of the indifference contours do nothing toward insuring that a final post-trade position where all gains are exhausted will be coincident with the origin, which describes the allocation or result that would obtain in the absence of all defense and predation effort. This direct-production position, in which each person retains for his own use

---

8. In terms of the model of figure 4.1, the natural equilibrium for one of the two persons would clearly be less desirable than the position at the origin, where, by assumption, he is allowed to retain what he produces.

9. For a different and more general discussion of the emergence of slavery, see Mancur Olson, "Some Historic Variations in Property Institutions," typescript (University of Maryland, 1967).

those goods that he himself produces, given his own capacities, his tastes, and his environmental situation, may or may not be Pareto-superior to the natural equilibrium at E; and even if the direct-production position should qualify as Pareto-superior it need not lie along the contract locus which would be generated by trading among the two parties.

The relationship between E, the position of equilibrium attained in the absence of law, and the origin, that position attained when each man keeps all that he produces, is important because of the dominant role that has been assigned to the latter in the historical discussions of property rights, notably those discussions in the natural-law tradition, and especially as represented in the theory of John Locke. In the conceptual origins of contract that have been developed here, there is no fundamental distinction between the position which allows persons to retain goods privately produced and any other position. The only distinguishable position, prior to contract, is that shown in the natural equilibrium at E.[10]

If the direct-production position is Pareto-superior to E, by which we mean only that both parties secure higher utility levels in the former position than in the latter, there may well be a strong attraction toward settling the negotiations at this point, even if the direct-production position does not qualify as falling along the strict contract locus. There are two related reasons for this. In the first place, initial agreements on limiting behavior would not be likely to take place in terms of finely tuned marginal adjustments. Instead, a once-and-for-all quantum leap might be suggested, without the tedious bargaining required for sophisticated adjustment. In this sense, any position within the lozenge confined by the indifference contours would qualify for a settlement prospect. Among this large set of Pareto-superior positions, those which seem the most likely candidates for agreement will possess Schelling-point characteristics. Positions which qualify here are those that are simple and known to all parties and which will tend to be selected in the absence of information and communication between the interacting parties.[11] An agreement to eliminate all predatory behavior might be a plausible outcome un-

10. If there is something inherent in the nature of man that inhibits theft, the natural equilibrium and the origin on figure 4.1 would coincide.

11. See Thomas C. Schelling, *The Strategy of Conflict* (Cambridge: Harvard University Press, 1960).

der this setting, in which case each person's production from the natural environment that he confronts becomes his "property" in some positive sense. The law might begin to take on positive features in a manner akin to that rationalized by John Locke.

The predominant role that has been assigned to the direct-production position may be based on the implicit assumption of natural equality among men. If we allow interpersonal differences to exist in the natural state, however, there is no assurance that the position attained in the anarchistic equilibrium, depicted at E in figure 4.1, is Pareto-inferior to the direct-production position at the origin. The latter position need not lie within the lozenge enclosed by the indifference contours drawn through E. At least one of the two persons may be better off, in utility terms, in anarchistic equilibrium than he would be if required to depend exclusively on his own production efforts (as in the slavery example noted). This outcome might emerge if the two persons were widely different in the ability to produce goods, either from a difference in natural capacities or from a difference in environmental situations. Also, such an outcome might arise if one person retains moral inhibitions against predation while the other does not, or even if one person values liberty of action so highly that he willingly sacrifices protection of goods produced.

When the direct-production position is not Pareto-superior to E, positive property rights to goods directly produced will not emerge from conceptual contractual agreement. Something other than an agreement on mutual limits to behavior is required to leap from the Hobbesian jungle in this case. Such an agreement on limits must be accompanied by a transfer of goods or endowments before a contractual settlement can be reached, and property rights positively established.

This may be illustrated with a different geometric construction, although still within the confines of a two-party model. In figure 4.2, effort is measured along the ordinate, and goods along the abscissa. Individual A is either favorably situated or is more capable of producing goods than individual B. The production function for A, if he is not interfered with by B, is shown by the curve P_a, which lies along the abscissa for an initial range, indicating that A can secure some goods without an outlay of effort. Individual B, by contrast, faces a much more unfavorable direct-production prospect. In the absence of all interference from A, he faces the production function shown by

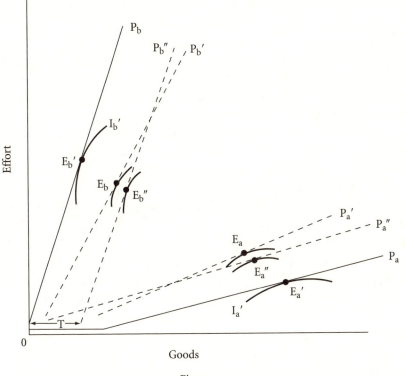

Figure 4.2

P_b. The direct-production position, that represented by the origin of the earlier figure 4.1, is attained when A attains point E_a' and when B attains point E_b'. In the situation where no rights of property are assigned, B may well find that his most productive expenditure of effort lies in predation, in stealing goods that are produced by A. If A undertakes no defense or protection effort, the anarchistic production function faced by B might be like that depicted by P_b', along which B would move to position E_b. This activity on the part of B would, of course, modify the situation faced by A. He would, privately, face the production function shown by P_a', if he undertakes no responsive action. In order to illustrate the relevant relationships in a diagram like figure 4.2, we shall assume that A does not find it advantageous to respond to B's predation. A's new equilibrium position would be that shown at E_a. Since we have assumed that A undertakes no defense or protection efforts, his actual production function is not modified, but he is producing a portion of his goods for B. The anarchistic equilibrium is that position indicated by the two points E_b and E_a in figure 4.2. It is clear that, for B, this is a more favorable situation than that which he attains when property rights are assigned in goods that are directly produced. Hence, B would never agree to the direct-production position. Contractual arrangements must include something over and beyond limits to behavior. In this setting, A might achieve B's agreement to respect an assignment of rights to goods that are produced privately or independently if he transfers to B some initial quantity of goods or endowments. One such transfer can be depicted on figure 4.2 by the amount T, as indicated. If this is transferred to B, his direct production function shifts to P_b'', and his attainable private production equilibrium to E_b'', which is on a higher utility level than E_b. The production function for A is shifted leftward by the initial transfer, to that shown by P_a'', but the attainable equilibrium along this function at E_a'' is superior in utility terms to E_a, the anarchistic result. Upon this transfer, B will agree to respect the assigned own-product of A and A will agree to similarly respect the assigned own-product of B. Positive rights may be established, once the initial transfer has taken place to bring the two parties into a setting where the direct-production assignment is, in fact, Pareto-superior to anarchistic equilibrium.

Despite the extremely simple and abstract nature of the geometrical models presented, the conclusions are significant for an understanding of the conceptual emergence of individual rights. The analysis demonstrates that there is no necessary basis for any initial agreement that will simply acknowledge the rights of persons to retain those stocks of goods that they can wrest from the natural environment by their own labor. Something other than the utility function employed in standard economic theory must be introduced in order to provide an explanatory foundation for a structure of property law that legitimizes individuals' (families') claims to stocks actually produced by their own efforts and independently from interference from others. Nowhere in the analysis am I denying the possible existence of internal behavioral constraints that may serve to inhibit man's seizing stocks of goods produced by others or invading physical domain initially inhabited by others. I remain agnostic on this as on many other aspects of human nature. My emphasis here is that such constraints, if they do exist, are over and beyond those normally introduced in economic behavioral models. With this proviso, the result stated becomes important. To secure an initial agreement on positive claims to goods or to resource endowments, some transfer of goods or endowments may be required. That is to say, some "redistribution" of goods or endowments may have to take place before a sufficiently acceptable base for property claims can be established. As the simple two-person model indicates, there may be many such redistributions that will meet the minimal requirements. Once any of these transfers takes place, if one is required, and/or behavioral limits are mutually accepted, positive rights of persons in stocks of goods or in resource endowments capable of producing goods may be settled. From this base, trades and exchanges in the postconstitutional stage already discussed can be implemented. These trades may, in utility terms, shift all persons to positions that overwhelmingly dominate either the natural equilibrium in anarchy or that distribution of goods and endowments that is settled on the initial establishment of positive individual rights.

Defection and Enforcement

To this point, attention has been concentrated on the conceptual bases for the formation of an initial social contract. The analysis has been aimed at isolating and identifying the mutuality of gain to be secured from a primal disarmament agreement accompanied, if necessary, by some unilateral transfers of goods or endowments. In this initial inclusive contract, all parties gain from the potential elimination of socially wasteful outlays on defense and predation. At the immediate postcontract stage, persons claim positive rights in stocks of goods, in resource endowments, and in specific spheres of activity. To this point, we have implicitly assumed that the set of rights agreed to will be respected by all participants.

This assumption cannot, of course, be justified. Even at this most elementary level of examination, the problem of enforcing contractual agreements must be introduced. Straightforward utility maximization will lead each person to defect on his contractual obligation if he expects to be able to accomplish this unilaterally. This may be illustrated in figure 4.3 (a duplicate of figure 2.1), which presents a two-by-two matrix for the two-person example. We are interested only in the net payoffs received by each of the two parties, A and B, in each of two possible positions. Each party has two behavioral options; he may keep his agreement, which amounts to respecting the de-

	B	
	Respects Rights 0	Respects No Rights V
Respects Rights 0	Cell I 19, 7	Cell II 3, 11
Respects No Rights V	Cell III 22, 1	Cell IV 9, 2

Figure 4.3

fined rights of the other person. This is the action indicated by the 0 row and column of the matrix. Or, alternatively, each person may abide by no agreement and act strictly in narrow self-interest. This option is defined by the V row and column. If both persons take the V option, and refuse to abide by contracts made, the result is equivalent to that which was described earlier as the natural anarchistic equilibrium. If both persons respect the terms of contract, both are better off, and the 00 result in figure 4.3 represents the contractually agreed-on set of rights discussed earlier.

The numbers in the cells are utility indicators for the two persons, with the left-hand numbers indicating utility levels attainable for A, the right-hand numbers those attainable by B. As the numbers indicate, each person has an incentive to defect on the agreement provided that he expects to be able to do so unilaterally. If A defects, while B respects A's rights, the result is in Cell III, which is the most preferred of all positions shown for A. Similarly, if B defects, while A respects B's rights, a Cell II result emerges, which is the most favorable of all positions for B. The situation is analogous to the classical prisoners' dilemma in game theory.[12] Any positive structure of rights is, therefore, extremely vulnerable to defection if continued adherence to the contractual basis depends on voluntary and independent "law-abiding." In our illustration, A can obtain three units of utility by defaulting unilaterally from the result in Cell I; individual B can gain four units by defaulting uni-

---

12. For a generalized discussion which extends the dilemma to many social interactions, see Gordon Tullock, *The Social Dilemma.*

laterally and securing a result in Cell II. And if both persons defect, the system lapses back into a Cell IV outcome, and ultimately to the anarchistic equilibrium discussed.

In the simplified two-person interaction illustrated, however, it is surely plausible to suggest that rationality precepts will direct each person to adhere to the initial contractual terms. Each person will recognize that unilateral defection cannot succeed and that any attempt to accomplish this would plunge the system back into a position that is less desirable for everyone than that which is attained upon adherence to contract. As the payoffs or utility indicators in figure 4.3 suggest, neither A nor B would allow the other person to defect and get away with it. Once a defection has occurred, the other party can improve his own position by bringing the system back to the Cell IV position.

It is important to recognize explicitly the behavioral motivation that lends stability to the contractual solution in the two-person setting. Each person may respect the agreed-on assignment because he predicts that defection on his part will generate parallel behavior by the other party. Each person realizes that his own behavior influences the subsequent behavior of the other person and does so directly.

It is precisely this aspect of the interaction that is modified, in kind, as we shift from a two-person to a many-person setting. As more parties are added to the initial contractual agreement, in which an assignment of rights is settled, the influence of any one person's behavior on that of others becomes less and less. As an element inhibiting individual defections on an initial contract, this influence tends to disappear completely after some critical group size is reached. In large-number groups, each individual rationally acts as if his own behavior does not influence the behavior of others. He treats others' behavior as a part of his natural environment, and he adjusts his behavior accordingly. In this large-number setting, man ceases to be a "social animal" at least in this explicit behavioral sense. This setting remains analogous to an n-person prisoners' dilemma, but it is one in which fully voluntary compliance with contract, or law in any form, cannot be predicted. Each person has a rational incentive to default; hence, many persons can be predicted to default and the whole agreement becomes void unless the conditions of individual choice are somehow modified.[13]

---

13. The divergence between individual utility-maximization and group interest is char-

This relationship between voluntary adherence to mutually accepted rules of social interaction, whether these be ethical standards or property-rights assignments, and the size of the interacting group is familiar, but it does have specific relevance to our analysis here.[14] The problem of enforcing any original contract becomes more difficult in large than in small groups. Any set of property rights, any legal structure, becomes more vulnerable to violation, and hence requires more than proportionate outlay on enforcement in large groups than in small. In respect to the conceptual origins of law and contract, this relationship alone suggests that contractual or quasi-contractual arrangements commence among individuals (families) that are involved in relatively small-number settings, with movement toward more inclusive contractual order taking the form of arrangements among smaller groups. These complexities are important, but they need not occupy our attention here.

If individual parties to an initial contract in which property assignments are established mutually acknowledge the presence of incentives for each participant to default and, hence, recognize the absence of viability in any scheme that requires dependence on voluntary compliance, they will, at the time of contract, enter into some sort of enforcement arrangement. Individuals' claims to stocks of goods and endowments will be accompanied by some enforcement institution that will be aimed to secure such claims.[15] The nature of this enforcement contract or institution must be carefully examined. Each person will receive some benefit from the assurance that his established claims will be honored by others in the community. And there are mutual gains to all parties from engaging in some joint or collectivized enforcement effort. Enforcement of property claims, of individuals' rights to carry out designated activities, qualifies as a "public good" in the modern sense of this term.

Enforcement is, however, different from the more familiar examples of

---

acteristic of many other situations in addition to that which involves adherence to law in the narrow sense of the term.

14. For a general discussion, see my "Ethical Rules, Expected Values, and Large Numbers," *Ethics* 76 (October 1965): 1–13.

15. The necessity for including enforcement provisions in the initial agreement distinguishes the social contract from other contracts which are made within the framework of a legal order. John C. Hall emphasizes that the recognition of this feature of social contract is central to the ideas of both Hobbes and Rousseau. See John C. Hall, *Rousseau: An Introduction to His Political Philosophy* (London: Macmillan, 1973), pp. 86–92.

public goods in several essential respects.[16] In order to be effective, enforcement must include the imposition of physical constraints on those who violate or attempt to violate the rights structure, on those who break the law. It is this characteristic that creates problems. There is no obvious and effective means through which the enforcing institution or agent can itself be constrained in its own behavior. Hence, as Hobbes so perceptively noted more than three centuries ago, individuals who contract for the services of enforcing institutions necessarily surrender their own independence.

Consider, say, a hundred-man community. In the absence of enforcement, let us say that B violates the contract that settles all property claims. He does so by stealing goods from or by interfering with the designated personal liberties of A. The latter will, of course, have some incentive to react privately by a counterattack on B. But if this becomes the general pattern of behavior, the system rapidly degenerates toward the precontractual position of anarchistic equilibrium.[17] Individuals C, D, E, . . ., however, have no direct interest in punishing B for stealing from or interfering with A. They have an indirect interest insofar as such punishment makes their own claims more secure, but unless they make such a connection in their own conception of enforcement, they may be reluctant to approve particularized punishment. This problem may be handled by an agreement by all persons on the purchase of the services of some external enforcing agent or institution that will, in all particular cases, take the enforcing-punishment action required. The "public good" is the generalized security of rights or claims, and not the particular enforcement action which produces this security.

In an idealized sense, the enforcing institution is necessarily external to the parties that reach agreement in the initial contract. The analogy to a simple game may be helpful. Two boys mutually acknowledge some division of marbles between them, and they seek to play a game. Each boy may know, however, that his opponent will have a strong incentive to cheat unless he is closely monitored. They agree and appoint a referee or umpire, inform him about the specific rules under which they choose to play, and ask that he en-

---

16. This point will become clear in the more general discussion of Chapters 7 and 8.

17. Historically, the state's more general role in criminal law emerged from its early role as enforcer of the process within which private quarrels were settled, by physical combat or otherwise. See Henry Maine, *Ancient Law.*

force adherence to these designated rules. This is precisely the functional role assigned to the state in its law-enforcement task. The state becomes the institutionalized embodiment of the referee or umpire, and its only role is that of insuring that contractual terms are honored.

This analogy exposes a recurrent fallacy in many discussions of property rights and of the role of the state in enforcing these rights. Enforcement of claims is categorically different from defining these claims in the first place. Claims are conceptually agreed upon by all parties in the constitutional stage of social contract. The state is then called upon to monitor these claims, to serve as an enforcing institution, to insure that contractual commitments are honored. To say that rights are defined by the state is equivalent to saying that the referee and not the players chooses both the initial division of the marbles and the rules of the game itself.

The Protective State and the Productive State

The distinction between the constitutional and the postconstitutional stages of social contract allows us to interpret the state, the collective agency of the community, in two separate roles. Failure to keep these roles distinct, in theory or in practice, has produced and continues to produce major confusion. At the constitutional stage, the state emerges as the enforcing agency or institution, conceptually external to the contracting parties and charged with the single responsibility of enforcing agreed-on rights and claims along with contracts which involve voluntarily negotiated exchanges of such claims. In this "protective" role, the state is not involved in producing "good" or "justice," as such, other than that which is embodied indirectly through a regime of contract enforcement. Explicitly, this state cannot be conceived as some community embodiment of abstract ideals, which take form over and beyond the attainment of individuals. This latter conception is and must be foreign to any contractarian or individualistic vision or model of social order. Nonetheless, because of each person's interest in the security of his agreed-on rights, the legal or protective state must be characterized by precepts of neutrality. Players would not consciously accept the appointment of a referee who was known to be unfair in his enforcement of the rules of the game, or at least they could not agree on the same referee in such cases.

"Fairness" or "justice" may emerge, therefore, in a limited sense from the self-interest of persons who enter the enforcement contract. It will not emerge from the acceptance of overriding ideals for society at large.

This legal or protective state, the institutions of "law" broadly interpreted, is *not* a decision-making body. It has no legislating function, and it is not properly represented by legislative institutions. This state does not incorporate the process through which persons in the community choose collectively rather than privately or independently. The latter characterizes the functioning of the conceptually separate productive state, that agency through which individuals provide themselves with "public goods" in postconstitutional contract. In this latter context, collective action is best viewed as a complex exchange process with participation among all members of the community. This process is appropriately represented by legislative bodies and the decision-making, choosing process is appropriately called "legislation." By sharp contrast, the protective state which carries out the enforcement task assigned to it in constitutional contract makes no "choices" in the strict meaning of this term. Ideally or conceptually, enforcement might be mechanically programmed in advance of law violation. The participants agree on a structure of individual rights or claims that is to be enforced, and violation requires only the findings of fact and the automatic administration of sanctions. A contract or a right is or is not violated; this is the determination to be made by "the law." Such a determination is not "choice" in the classic sense that the benefits of one alternative are weighed against opportunity costs (the benefits foregone). "The law," enforced by the state, is not necessarily that set of results which best represents some balance of opposing interests, some compromise, some median judgment. Properly interpreted, "the law" which is enforced is that which is specified to be enforced in the initial contract, whatever this might be.

I am not, of course, suggesting that ambiguities are wholly absent or that the actual enforcement task of the state is purely mechanistic. These aspects should not, however, distract attention from the characteristic and central feature of the enforcement contract, which is designed to implement the detection of violation and the punishment of violators of explicitly accepted and well-defined rights and claims. As noted, "the law" steps beyond the bounds of propriety when it seeks, and explicitly, to redefine individual rights.

If, indeed, the state is conceived in this sense, genuine choice is involved since the benefits and costs of various schemes for redefinition would have to become relevant.

From nothing more than this brief and introductory discussion, much of the modern confusion can be appreciated. Appropriately, the judiciary, as an element of the enforcement structure, is independent of the choice-making arm of the collectivity, the legislature. However, as the judiciary itself violates the terms of its own contract by explicitly engaging in legislation, in genuine "social choice," its independence from choice-making rules has been properly brought into question. The legal or protective state, as such, is not "democratic" in the sense that collective decisions are reached through some voting process, whether this be majority voting or otherwise. In determining the facts of contractual agreement, plural rather than individual or unitary judgments may be invoked, and these may be combined in many ways. In many jurisdictions, all members of a jury must be in agreement before a verdict can be established. Appellate courts may require only a simple majority. In all such instances, however, it should be clear that plurality rules are nothing other than devices aimed at producing somewhat more accuracy in a final finding of fact. With genuine choice-making, "accuracy" is not an appropriate descriptive word. Genuine collective choice may be rational or irrational; benefits and costs may or may not be properly weighed one against the other. But choices cannot, in themselves, be accurate or inaccurate, since it is values that are at issue, not facts.

Rules as Indirect Rights

To this point in the discussion of constitutional contract, we have assumed that agreement is reached on the limits to behavioral interaction and on the positive set of claims to endowments of goods, accompanied by some enforcement contract with the protective state. In an all-private-goods world, this would be the end of it. Trades and exchanges among persons in postconstitutional stages would more or less naturally emerge, as discussed in Chapter 3. However, when we allow for the presence of jointly shared collective or public goods and services, the collectivity as the productive state and its rules for operation must be taken into account. The political constitution, which in our context is only one aspect of the broader constitutional contract, becomes important here, and the rules for making collective decisions concerning the provision and the cost-sharing of public goods must, themselves, be settled at the ultimate constitutional stage of negotiation. It would, as noted in Chapter 3, be of relatively little moment to define an individual's nominal claims to goods only to leave these claims fully vulnerable to unconstrained political exploitation.

An earlier work, *The Calculus of Consent*, written jointly with Gordon Tullock, was devoted largely to an analysis of the constitutional choice among rules for making collective decisions. In that analysis, Tullock and I assumed implicitly that individual participants in constitutional deliberations over alternative rules faced uncertainty concerning their own interests in future collective decisions. Nonetheless, we did not question the independent establishment of their ultimate rights and claims to property, human and nonhuman, beyond the range of collective-decision rules. As I have suggested, this approach was an extension and application of orthodox economic methodology, which has tended to neglect the critical problems of establishing individual rights. This book differs from *The Calculus of Consent* in this fundamental respect; here I am trying to analyze the initial contract that assigns rights and claims among persons. This difference allows collective-decision rules to be interpreted in a somewhat modified setting, namely, as an integral part of a more inclusive contract rather than a strictly political constitution superimposed on some previously negotiated settlement. In the earlier book, we argued that the criterion of acceptability or efficiency lay in agreement, in unanimity. Further, we argued that insofar as participants remain uncertain as to their own specific roles in subsequent operation under the rules chosen, they would tend to reach agreement on reasonably "fair" and "efficient" working rules.[18] We did not postulate initial equality among individuals in property rights or in capacities, but our presumption of uncertainty served to generate a plausible basis for agreement on rules for collective action.

In the model incorporated here, by comparison, I allow quite explicitly

---

18. In this respect, as noted earlier, our approach had considerable affinity with that of John Rawls, who has attempted to derive general principles of justice in a similar manner. Rawls's earlier papers appeared in the 1950s, but his work is presented in detail in his book *A Theory of Justice*.

for personal inequality in the natural equilibrium, the anarchistic base from which primal disarmament contracts are conceptually negotiated. As the analysis in the earlier parts of this chapter indicated, however, the establishment of positive claims to stocks of goods or endowments may not be possible until and unless some unilateral transfers are made. This potential for transfer allows us to introduce an additional dimension of adjustment which may possibly facilitate the reaching of agreement among parties in contract. When we recognize that the rules for collective decision-making at the postconstitutional stage are also to be settled as a part of the initial contract, we have available yet another dimension for adjustment.

Consider the calculus of an individual whose position in anarchistic equilibrium is not significantly worse than that which he expects to secure under a simple disarmament agreement. When he also recognizes the problems of enforcement, including those which involve constraining the enforcing agent, this individual may be quite reluctant to enter into the basic social contract at all. Suppose, however, that one of the many clauses in a proffered contractual settlement states that "public goods" are to be financed by progressive income taxes, and that the person in question has either higher-than-average expected demands for public goods or lower-than-average income-wealth expectations. This proposed part of the larger social contract now represents, for this person, a positive supplement to the set of claims that he might otherwise secure from the unamended disarmament agreement. The collective decision rules present him with something akin to additional "rights" and upon which he may place a positive value. He may be motivated to enter into the constitutional contract under such conditions, even without a unilateral transfer of goods, although this would be an alternative means of making the proposal attractive to him.

The Constitutional Mix

The inclusive constitutional contract embodies elements that may appear in alternative combinations or mixes. The terms must include, first of all, some statement of limits on the behavior of any person with respect to the positions of other persons in the community. This element was referred to earlier in this chapter as the disarmament contract. As they enter genuine society from anarchy, persons lay down their arms; they accept rules governing their own behavior in exchange for the like acceptance of such rules on the part of others. Secondly, the basic contract must define the positive rights of possession or domain over stocks of goods, or more generally, over resource endowments capable of producing final goods. These endowments include human capacities (the rights to one's own person which have been widely discussed in the theory of property), as well as nonhuman factors, including domain over territory. These ownership rights or claims may simply reflect the pattern of possession established directly when interpersonal interferences are eliminated, which we have called the direct-production imputation, but, as the analysis disclosed, certain "exchanges" of resource endowments or goods and behavioral constraints may be necessary before clearly acknowledged ownership imputations are possible. Along with the limits on behavior and the rights of ownership, the inclusive constitutional contract must also make explicit the terms and conditions of enforcement. This set of terms will specify in detail the operation and limits of the protective state that is established as the enforcing agent. Finally, the basic contract must define the rules under which the collectivity must operate in making and in implementing decisions concerning the provision and financing of "public goods." This set of terms will specify in detail the operation and the limits of the productive state, the legislative aspect of collective organization. The rules and institutions of this productive state may, in themselves, incorporate several dimensions. The contract should indicate the allowable range over which collective action may take place. That is to say, some restrictions on the type of goods to be provided and financed collectively must be included. At least in some rough sense, the dividing line between the private and the public or governmental sector of the economy should be settled in the basic constitution. Within these defined limits, allowable departures from unanimity in reaching collective decision should be specified. Such departures need not, of course, be uniform over all decisions. Institutions for cost-sharing, that is, tax institutions, may also be imbedded in the inclusive constitutional structure.

It is not my purpose here to develop criteria for efficiency in constitutional contract in any specific setting. The mix among the various elements in this inclusive settlement will be functionally related to several identifiable characteristics of the community of individuals. This will include the size of the membership itself as well as the environmental setting. The features of the anarchistic natural equilibrium, whether or not this is ever actually realized, will influence the relative positions of individuals and groups in the final constitutional settlement. The degree as well as the distribution of the inequalities among persons will be important in this respect. Individuals may differ, and may be thought to differ, in relative capacities to produce goods and to secure gains by predation on their fellows. These differences, along with differences in individuals' tastes for productive and predatory activities, will have predictable effects on the initial settlement. Expectations about demands for publicly provided goods and services along with expectations about relative income and wealth levels will also affect individuals' willingness to accept rules for collective action.

The most significant point that emerges from this very general discussion is the interdependence among the several elements in the constitutional mix. Contrary to orthodox economic methodology, the rights of persons to property, the rights to do things privately and individually with physical resources, cannot be treated in isolation from those rights which are indirectly represented by membership in a collectivity that is constitutionally empowered to make decisions under predetermined rules. Consider, for example, the position of a person who holds nominal ownership rights to an income stream from a scarce and highly valued resource (human or nonhuman). This private ownership claim may be tempered by the membership rights in the collectivity, the governmental institutions of the community, that are held by other persons, membership rights that may offer other persons some indirect claims on the differentially higher income stream in question. This is not to suggest that the specific constitutional mix chosen need be the most efficient. As noted in Chapter 3, all parties might have gained by an initial transfer of claims with substantially greater stability of nominal ownership claims.

This approach allows us to look somewhat differently and in a positive manner at the perplexing issue of income-wealth redistribution. Under certain constitutional structures, those persons who are relatively "poor" do not properly claim, on the basis of overriding ethical norms, a share in the economic returns or assets of those who are relatively "rich." They *may* claim some such share indirectly on the basis of commonly held membership in collectively organized community under specified constitutional contract. The relatively "rich," in their turn, may legitimately expect their "private rights" to be respected and honored, and violations of these rights enforced, only as a component part of the more inclusive contractual arrangement which predictably requires that they pay differentially higher shares in those goods and services provided jointly for the whole community.[19] In this larger and more inclusive contract, all individuals and groups should find it advantageous to adhere to the rules established, to respect the claims as tempered, and to conduct themselves in such fashion as to attain maximum individual liberty within the constraints of acceptable order.

19. For a more detailed examination, see my paper "The Political Economy of the Welfare State," Research Paper No. 808231-1-8 (Center for Study of Public Choice, Virginia Polytechnic Institute and State University, June 1972).

See also Earl Thompson, "The Taxation of Wealth and the Wealthy" (UCLA Department of Economics Working Paper, February 1972).

5. Continuing Contract and the Status Quo

The Ethics and Economics of Contractual Obligation

Preceding chapters offer a conceptual explanation of how social order might emerge contractually from the rational utility-maximization of individuals, social order that would embody a definition of assignment of individual rights and the establishment of a political structure charged with enforcing rules of personal behavior with respect to these assigned rights. Even if the contractarian framework is fully accepted, the analysis is applicable only in a community where persons live forever. Time has not been introduced into the model, and even in a community with permanent membership, the influence of time itself on rational choice would introduce complications.

One of the continuing criticisms of any contract theory of social order is closely related to the timeless attribute of the model. As noted earlier, many critics have opposed the contractarian explanation on the grounds that, historically and empirically, no formal contracting among individuals was observed to take place. More important, they have suggested that, even if some such original compact might have taken place historically, there is nothing which binds men who did not themselves participate in the contractual settlement, nothing that binds them to honor commitments which they could not personally have made.

This is an important and relevant criticism of a contractarian argument that has essentially ethical foundations, and which seeks to locate the legitimacy of social order in implicit contract. Contractual obligation, expressed by the willingness of individuals to behave in accordance with specified terms, depends critically on explicit or imagined participation. Individuals, having "given their word," are "honor bound" to live up to the terms. This remains true even if, subsequent to agreement, these terms come to be viewed as "unfair" or "unjust." Defection or violation runs counter to widely accepted moral codes for personal behavior. When existing rules for social and political order, including the definition of individual rights, are simply inherited from the past, no such moral sanctions may be present. It may matter little whether or not ancestors participated in a contractual settlement; there may be no strong honor-bound commitment transmitted intergenerationally in an individualistic social structure.[1] Any ethical or moral basis for stability in rules and in institutions is severely weakened once participation is shown to be historically nonexistent and/or outside the memories of living members of the community.

This is the setting descriptive of the real world, and the question must be asked: Why will persons voluntarily comply with the rules and institutions of order that are in being? These institutions will, of course, include standards for enforcement along with punishment for violations. In the context of enforcement-punishment, however, genuinely voluntary compliance means little in itself. Almost any person will "voluntarily" comply with dictated patterns of behavior if he knows that departure from these patterns will be punished with sufficient certainty and severity. Of interest for our purpose is voluntary compliance independent of enforcement-punishment—behavior which can scarcely be observed. Nonetheless, it is clear that there is a relationship between potential voluntary compliance independent of enforcement-punishment and the resource investment that will be required to attain specified behavioral limits. It is through such a relationship that the structure of the existing "contract" becomes relevant, even to those who are recognized to be nonparticipants. Under what conditions are individuals most likely to adhere to the inherited rules of order, most likely to respect and to honor the assignment of individual rights in being?

This question can only be answered through an evaluation of the existing structure, *as if* it were the outcome of a current contract, or one that is continuously negotiated. Individuals must ask themselves how their own positions compare with those that they might have expected to secure in a re-

---

1. This conclusion would need to be modified for a social structure in which the continuing or permanent family rather than the individual is the dominant unit.

negotiated contractual settlement. If they accept that their defined positions fall within the limits, they are more likely to comply with existing rules, even in the acknowledged absence of any historical participation. This approach offers a means of evaluating social rules, legal structure, and property rights. But one point needs to be made in passing. That set of rights which might be widely accepted as being within the limits of what we may call here the "renegotiation expectations" of individuals will not be uniform over communities and over time. As the analysis in Chapter 4 demonstrated, the contractual terms, including the mix among the several elements in the constitution, will depend directly on the personal differences that exist in fact or that are thought to exist. The degree and distribution of these differences will not be uniform as among separate groups. This suggests that there can be no resort to idealized general standards through which a legal or constitutional structure in a particular community at a particular stage of historical development might be judged. At best, an observer can make some inferences about existing institutions from his assessment of the behavior of individuals living under them.

The approach to contract taken in this book is economic, and, as shown earlier, there is an economic basis for constitutional contract among persons. There is, similarly, an economic basis for adherence to any existing set of rules, to those that define the status quo. This economic basis is not nearly so dependent on the fact of participation or on the historical existence of settlement as its ethical counterpart. On the other hand, there are individually rational economic reasons for default from any contractual agreement. In large-number groups in particular, individual utility-maximization will dictate defection from agreed-on contractual terms in the absence of enforcement provisions or unless constrained by ethical precepts. It is important to recognize that the strictly economic motivation for defection is not influenced by the presence or the absence of individual participation in contract. The individual who has personally entered into an advance commitment has the same strictly economic motivation for default as the person who inherits the contract from his forebears, or who finds himself in a setting without contractual foundations at all. It is the ethical constraints that may be sharply different as between these cases, not the privately rational economic choice, with rationality here measured in quantifiable economic dimensions.

In recognition of individual motivation for defection, any legal structure will include rules for enforcement and for punishment of violators. On strictly economic grounds, there is no a priori reason why an individual would defect more quickly from rules and institutions that do not fall within his reasonable renegotiation expectations set than from those that do. Even for the person whose assigned rights in the status quo seem to be more favorable than he could reasonably expect to secure in a genuinely renegotiated settlement, the incentive to violate law is present, provided he expects to be able to accomplish this unilaterally and to escape punishment. Again, in a strictly economic calculus, whether a person will violate the terms of existing contract, whether he will abide by the set of legal rules, institutions, and rights in being, will depend on his assessment of the probability of and the severity of punishment rendered by the enforcing agent. This expected value is directly dependent on the willingness of the community, acting through the protective state, to make commitments to enforcement and punishment. These commitments, in their turn, are functionally related to the levels of voluntary compliance predicted. And, as noted, these levels will depend on the strength of ethical constraints on individual behavior. Through this sort of causal linkage, we can trace the relationship between enforcement and the "distance" of the status quo from the set of "renegotiation expectations."

Consider an example. Suppose that there is, in fact, an initial contractual settlement, and that only nominal violations are predicted to occur in early periods of the agreement. For a given resource outlay on enforcement, a specific degree of adherence to contractual terms is guaranteed. For purposes of illustration, say that only .001 percent of all behavior is explicitly violative of agreed-on rights. Time passes, and the structure of rights is not modified. But sons inherit fathers' positions in the community, and sons no longer feel themselves ethically committed to the initial contractual terms. More important, the existing rules may not be within the set of renegotiation expectations of at least some members of the second generation. For both of these reasons, more sons than fathers will respond to the strictly economic motivations for default. With the *same* enforcement, therefore, we should expect to find that the percentage of behavior that is violative of "social contract" rises to, say, .01 percent. That is to say, more persons will "break the law" unless it remains in their strictly economic interest not to do so.

There are two ways that the community might respond to an increasing "distance" between the status quo and the set of renegotiation expectations for a large number of its members. It may, first of all, increase resource commitments to enforcement, along with the accompanying moral commitments required, thereby making departures from the set of rights defined in the status quo more costly to potential violators. Second, the community may attempt to renegotiate the basic agreement, the constitutional contract itself, so as to bring this distance back to acceptable limits. As the analysis in subsequent chapters will show, the first alternative may be extremely difficult to implement, and, indeed, there may well be pressures for reducing rather than increasing enforcement-punishment commitments. In practice, the only alternative may be that of attempting to renegotiate the basic constitutional contract, at least along some of the margins of possible adjustment. Before such renegotiations can be discussed, however, we need to define the status quo more clearly.

Contractual Changes in the Status Quo

The whole set of rules and institutions existing as of any point in time defines the constitutional status quo. This set includes more than an imputation or assignment of private ownership claims, along with the rules under which these claims may be exchanged among persons and groups. The existing situation also embodies rights of membership in the polity, the collective organ of community, and this entity in its turn carries specified powers or rights to undertake the provision and financing of public goods and services. The constitutional status quo should not be interpreted to embody rigidity in social interaction. Shifts in individual claims may take place, provided that these are themselves processed through defined rules, which may also define the responses of the system to exogenous shocks. What is important is not stability but predictability; the constitutional status quo offers the basis upon which individuals may form expectations about the course of events, expectations which are necessary for rational planning.

The uniqueness of the status quo lies in the simple fact of its existence. The rules and institutions of sociolegal order that are in being have an existential reality. No alternative set exists. This elementary distinction between the status quo and its idealized alternatives is often overlooked. Independent of existence, there may be many institutional-legal structures that might be preferred, by some or many persons. But the choice is never carte blanche. The choice among alternative structures, insofar as one is presented at all, is between what is and what might be. Any proposal for change involves the status quo as the necessary starting point. "We start from here," and not from someplace else.

The necessary recognition of this does not amount to a defense of the status quo in any evaluative sense as is sometimes charged. Privately and personally, almost any one of us would prefer some alternative structure, at least in some of its particulars. There is nothing Panglossian implied when we insist that improvements must be worked out from the status quo as fact. How can we get "there" from "here"? This is the appropriate question to ask in any attempt to assess proposed sociopolitical change. What qualities of legitimacy does the set of rights existing at any point in time possess, qualities that are present due simply to the fact of existence? This can be turned into a further question. Should the enforcing agent, the protective state, punish those who violate the set of rights defined in the status quo? Put in this way, the question almost answers itself. These rights are the only ones that the agent could possibly enforce, since no others exist.

If a clearly defined set of rights exists (and I shall simply assume this here; at a later point I shall examine problems that arise when ambiguities are present), and if this set is effectively enforced, how can change in structure, basic constitutional change, take place at all? In order to answer this question, it is necessary again to avoid the confusion in thinking of rights in terms of imputations of goods or resources among persons. This static model would suggest erroneously that the assignment of rights remains always a zero-sum game; hence, there could be no agreed-on modifications in structure. Contractual or quasi-contractual readjustments in basic constitutional structure are, by definition, impossible in this limited model.

In a dynamic opportunity-cost framework, however, contractual or quasi-contractual agreements might be struck which would include reductions in nominally measured values of the rights of some members of the community. If the predicted course of events over time should be such that these nominally measured values are to be reduced, those holding such vulnerable claims may accept present reductions in exchange for greater security. If the individual holder of a right or claim, defined in the status quo, comes to predict that this claim will be eroded or undermined unless the structure is modified, he may willingly acquiesce in some current reduction in this claim's value as a means of forestalling the possibility of larger damage.

Such predictions may be based on imagined shifts in the natural distribution in anarchistic equilibrium which always exists "underneath" the observed social realities. This may be illustrated in a two-person numerical example. Suppose that A and B, in anarchistic natural equilibrium, secure final stocks of consumables measured at ten units and two units respectively. These stocks are net of the effort expended in defense and in predation. A disarmament contract is negotiated, and the postconstitutional imputation becomes fifteen units for A, seven units for B, with each person having secured the equivalent of an additional five units. This settlement continues to be in existence for some time, but let us assume that, after X periods, the relative strengths of the two parties are thought to change. Although the natural distribution, in anarchy, is no longer observable, let us suppose that A now thinks that the two parties would fare equally in genuine anarchy, that the distribution would, in fact, be closer to 6:6 than to the original 10:2. In such a situation, A may well recognize the extreme vulnerability of the 15:7 imputation in the status quo, its vulnerability to violation by B. In order to secure for himself some greater assurance that predictable order will continue, A may willingly accept a proffered change in nominal rights, a move to a new distribution, say that of 13:9.[2]

The two-person model is, of course, somewhat misleading in that it tends to obscure the enforcement problem that arises critically only in large-number settings. In strict two-person interaction, enforcement is implemented through the continued threat of having the whole system plunged back into anarchy by any one of the two participants. In the large-number community, the comparable model becomes more complex. Here the changes that may be contractually or quasi-contractually reached arise not directly out of in-

---

2. For a more extended discussion of this example and the general problem, see my paper "Before Public Choice," in *Explorations in the Theory of Anarchy,* ed. Gordon Tullock (Blacksburg, Virginia: Center for Study of Public Choice, 1972), pp. 27–38. For the development of a similar model which emphasizes the shift in the underlying structure of "fall-back" imputations consequent on changes in technology introduced because of association, see Donald McIntosh, *The Foundations of Human Society* (Chicago: University of Chicago Press, 1969), pp. 242–44.

creased danger of individual violation of rights, since this danger will always be present, but out of the danger that the enforcing agent will become increasingly unwilling to punish violators effectively. A simple three-person model, an extension of the same illustration, may be used, although this is taken to represent a large- rather than a small-number setting. Assume that the three-man community, A, B, and C, finds that the imputation in anarchistic equilibrium is 10:2:2, and that, on settlement of the initial disarmament contract, this becomes 15:7:7, and that all parties accept these terms. Accompanying the contract is the appointment of an enforcing agent, the protective state, which is assigned the duty of insuring respect for the 15:7:7 imputation. As before, assume that time passes during which, relatively, the strengths of the separate members of the group are thought to change. Suppose that we reach a period when A thinks that a true reversion to natural equilibrium would be described roughly by a 6:6:6 imputation rather than the one in being. So long as A retains faith in the enforcing agent's power and willingness to enforce the terms defined in the status quo, A has no worries and he will not voluntarily accept any change in his own nominal claims. He may come to recognize, however, that the enforcement contract also has a dynamic dimension. The agent may become increasingly reluctant to guarantee a set of individual rights as the relative positions of individuals diverge increasingly from what is seen to be the natural equilibrium in anarchy "underneath" the existing order. Hence, the linkage between shifts in the presumed or imagined natural distribution and the stability of rights represented by the status quo may be essentially identical in large-number and small-number communities.

In this discussion of the possible changes in the status quo distribution of rights, changes in the basic constitutional contract, I have emphasized the economic bases. I have not explicitly introduced the concept of justice, as this might or might not inform the attitudes of persons concerning the establishment of, or the changes in, structure. To the maximum extent that is possible I attempt to derive the logical structure of social interaction from the self-interested utility-maximization of individuals and without resort to external norms. Factually and historically, it may well be necessary that some notion of "social justice" or "social consciousness" characterizes the thinking of at least some part of the population if a society embodying reasonable personal freedom is to exist. I want neither to support nor to oppose this presupposition. My point is that I do not want to rely on the presence of such an attitude at this stage of the analysis.

It is useful to mention the concept of justice at this point, however, because in those situations where individuals may have rational economic reasons for accepting some reassignment of rights, where genuine constitutional change may be possible, the public discussion may be conducted in the rhetoric of "justice." Even the advocates of structural change may not be fully aware of the rational or utility-maximizing motivation that lies at the base of their proposals. This offers a partial explanation of the behavior that is often observed in the scions of wealthy families, behavior which makes them appear to be more interested in "justice" than other members of the community. If individuals find themselves in nominal possession of ownership rights that they know to be insupportable in anything that might resemble genuine anarchistic struggle, they will perhaps recognize that the means of protecting their position is through some surrender of claims in a genuine constitutional rearrangement of rights. Such persons are quite likely to support proposals for constitutional rearrangements and to argue in support of these proposals in terms of justice, which may or may not be hypocritical at base.[3] Arguments which may find their origins in rational economic calculation, which might otherwise be the basis for organizing genuine contractual or quasi-contractual modifications in the structure of legal order, when presented under the disguise of justice tend to attract support from those elements of the community whose primary motivation is to arrange preferred redistributions of rights among *others* than themselves, and who make no pretense or effort to undertake contractually approved or Pareto-superior changes. The behavior of individuals in this latter respect is important in shaping modern governmental policy toward redistributions of individual property claims, but this behavior is not directly germane to the analysis here.[4]

In considering individual behavior in support of basic constitutional

3. In his analysis of nonaltruistic motivations for transfers of income and wealth, Brennan mentions the self-protection motive and discusses the relevant literature. See Geoffrey Brennan, "Pareto Desirable Redistribution: The Non-Altruistic Dimension," *Public Choice* 14 (Spring 1973): 43–68.

4. For an extended treatment, see Gordon Tullock, "The Charity of the Uncharitable," *Western Economic Journal* 9 (December 1971): 379–92.

change, a distinction should be made between human and nonhuman capital. To the extent that individual claims in the status quo take the form of ownership rights to nonhuman resources, the relative value of these claims may be readily separated from the value which inheres in the person, and which could, presumably, be more invulnerable in anarchy. The separation here is accentuated when claims to nonhuman resources are transmitted intergenerationally, in which case there may remain little or no relationship between the relative value of such claims and the relative share that the holders think they can secure in either genuine anarchy or in a renegotiated constitutional contract. On the other hand, and by contrast, if an individual's claims to final goods are measured largely by his ownership of human capital, embodied in his relative skills, talents, or capacities, his relative standing in the natural distribution or in any renegotiated settlement might not diverge categorically from that which is observed in the status quo. There will not, of course, be any precise correspondence here. An individual's skill as a concertmaster may be worthless in the Hobbesian jungle, and almost worthless in any renegotiated settlement that reduces substantially the specialized demands for concerts that emerge from the status-quo distribution of wealth. Even here there is, however, a categorical difference between human and nonhuman capital. An effective transfer of the rights to the product of human capital may be impossible since explicit behavior by the owner may be required. No such behavioral link exists between nonhuman capital and the person who holds rights to its product. Insofar as human capital takes the generalized form of physical and/or intellectual capacity, the relative ability of a person to survive in anarchy itself or to secure terms in renegotiations is likely to be mirrored somewhat closely in the status quo. From this we should predict that support for major structural changes in rights, along the contractual lines suggested, is more likely to be located among those who hold relatively large claims to nonhuman resources than among those who hold comparable claims to human capital.

Imposed Changes in Constitutional Rights

I have discussed the possible bases for contractual or quasi-contractual changes in the status-quo distribution or imputation of constitutional rights—the rights of persons in the community to claim ownership over physical resources, to undertake specified courses of action with respect to such resources, to participate in collective choice and in the sharing of governmentally provided goods and services—under the unstated presumption that only such contractual changes in structure can take place. This is parallel to the initial derivation of contract, the first leap out of the anarchistic jungle. As our earlier treatment suggested, the initial distribution *from which* this initial step is taken could not itself emerge from contract; instead it must emerge in the opposing strength of persons in interaction, hence, the term "natural distribution." The question now at issue concerns change in the initially assigned structure of rights, without a lapse back into anarchy. A structure of legal order exists, the status quo, even if none of the persons in the community share any sense of participation, directly or remotely, in the constitutional settlement. It matters little whether a settlement, as such, was ever made.

Why need a presumptive rule of unanimity be adopted for genuine constitutional change, even if the contractual metaphor for the emergence of rights be accepted? Alternative structures of legal order are equally or perhaps more deserving of moral-intellectual support. What is then wrong with an imposed and arbitrary shift in the pattern of individual rights toward some alternative structure that may, by certain external criteria, be awarded comparable or even superior merit to that which is reflected in the status quo?

These questions deserve careful consideration since they get us directly to a source of major confusion. They point toward the further question that is so often left unasked (and unanswered). If imposed and nonvoluntary changes in the structure of legal rights are to be made, *who* is to do the imposing? What individual, what group of persons, what institution of collective decision-making, is to be granted the right (or power) to impose arbitrary and noncontractual changes in rights, to rearrange the distribution of property claims among persons away from that which exists? By what process can we derive such an ultimate right? In what primal contract?

It seems self-evident that if the status quo defines a structure of basic constitutional rights, these cannot be arbitrarily changed. To say this is possible would amount to semantic contradiction. If basic rights can be changed without agreement, they could scarcely be called either "basic" or "rights." Consider an example in which a person holds what he thinks to be an ownership claim to, say, ten units of productive resource or capacity. Suppose that some external force or entity simply "takes" one-half of this endowment, reducing the patrimony to five units. In ordinary language this seems straightforward, but if the external entity or force holds the power to decide and to implement the change indicated, did the individual in question really hold the claim in the first place? Some revision in the ordinary manner of discussion seems to be required here. If the person in the example holds ten units subject to the taking of the external entity, he does not "own" these units in any basic constitutional sense. At best we might say that he "owns" these claims subject to arbitrary external interference or that these claims are nominal rather than real.

This issue is brought into focus by the familiar assertion that property rights are defined by and subject to change by the "government" or the state. As noted in Chapter 3, this amounts to saying that only the government or the state has rights, and that individuals are essentially parties to a continuing slave contract. This is the Hobbesian vision or model of the true relationship between the sovereign and the individual members of the community. The only meaningful contract here is the initial surrender of power to the sovereign in exchange for the order that is imposed and maintained. But this vision is contrary to the whole notion of constitutional contract among persons, each of whom disarms himself in exchange for some guarantee that his assigned rights will be accepted and that violations will be punished by an enforcing agent appointed for this limited purpose, the state. In this alternative conception of constitutional contract, which in these respects is more Lockean than Hobbesian, the enforcing agent is restricted by terms of the initial agreement. Individuals hold rights or claims vis-à-vis the enforcing agent as much as against other persons. The government is, itself, held strictly within the law of the constitutional contract.[5]

I am not suggesting that individual rights cannot be modified coercively and without consent. Far from it. Simple evidence could not be thrown out in so cavalier a fashion. I am suggesting that rights which legitimately form a part of the expectations of a person or group can only be modified by agreement *if* the constitutional contract, implicit or explicit, is not itself to be violated. But this basic contract, as with all contracts, may be violated by

---

5. Cf. John Locke, *Second Treatise of Civil Government* (Chicago: Henry Regnery, Gateway Edition, 1955), pp. 116ff.

any of the parties. The analysis suggests only that such violations be recognized and discussed as such. There is no point in assuming the existence of something that simply does not exist. If "the government," represented through the decisions of persons who arbitrarily modify the assigned rights of individuals, violates the basic terms on which the social structure operates, there is no requirement that its actions be "honored" with ethical sanctions. If "the government," which is conceived as an enforcing agent for individual rights, itself captures powers to change the legal structure, individuals are deprived of rights and their existence becomes equivalent to that described in Hobbesian anarchy. Much of what we observe in the 1970s can pessimistically be described in precisely these terms. But because the basic set of rules has been eroded beyond recognition in many respects, there is no reason for us to refrain from discussing the elements of structure that might exist.

In this, as in other respects, my analysis lends potential support to modern-day anarchists, who deny the legitimacy of much of the action implemented by the governmental-bureaucratic apparatus. Legitimacy is "earned" by government's adherence to the terms of the legal structure that allows individuals' claims to remain within a set of reasonable renegotiation expectations, at least for most members of the community. If government oversteps these bounds, it is not "legitimate" in the strict definitional sense of the term, and its acts may be regarded as "criminal." This conclusion follows regardless of the manner in which decisions are made, so long as unanimity is violated. To say that any act of government is legitimate because that act is sanctioned by a majority or a plurality of the community's members, or by a majority or plurality of their elected representatives in a legislature, or by their elected, appointed, or anointed designates in executive or judicial roles, is to elevate collective or governmental institutions and process to a position superior to content. Unconstitutional behavior cloaked in the romantic mythology of majority will or judicial supremacy in some circumstances may proceed further than behavior which lays no claim to procedural rights.

Prior Violations and the Status Quo

The argument that I have presented above might seem persuasive in the context of a timeless model. If the structure of legal rights, described in the status quo, should have remained unchanged after an initial agreement, if there was, in fact, such an agreement made, and if participants remained as members of the community, there might be general acceptance of the principle that basic changes require the adherence of all parties. But our concern in this chapter is precisely with the problems that arise in the absence of some or all of these conditions. Specifically, we must ask (and answer) the question: What justifies the status quo when an original contract may never have been made, when current members of the community sense no moral or ethical obligation to adhere to the terms that are defined in the status quo, and, what is important, when such a contract, if it ever existed, may have been violated many times over, both by the government and by individuals and groups that may have succeeded in evading proper punishment? Does the presence of any one or all of these negations remove legitimacy from the status quo?

Again it is necessary to repeat the obvious. The status quo defines that which exists. Hence, regardless of its history, it must be evaluated as if it were legitimate contractually. Things "might have been" different in history, but things are now as they are. The fact that government may have violated implicit terms excessively and repeatedly does nothing toward modifying the uniqueness of the status quo. Prior violations may, however, make it more likely that the existing legal order diverges significantly from that set of orders which satisfy the renegotiation expectations of large numbers of persons in the community. Violations that remained unpunished in prior periods, whether by government or by persons and groups, make enforcement more difficult and provide an incentive for further violations.

Evaluation of the status quo as if it were legitimate may yield results in either direction. The set of rights in existence at any point in time may or may not deserve the putative legitimacy that it claims. If it does not, or more correctly, if there are aspects of this set that do not, there should exist means of adjustment which could be agreed on by all or substantially all of the members of the community. Adjustment that must be imposed coercively can scarcely represent in itself a restoration of "legitimacy" in any genuine meaning of the term. This sort of change would, instead, amount to still further violation of the implied contract.

Consider a situation where, due either to a change in the relative capacities of persons or to explicit past violations of an agreed-on set of terms, the status quo has come to define a set of individual rights that are clearly inconsistent with the renegotiation expectations of a large majority of the community's membership. That is to say, the relative positions of persons cannot, through any stretch of the imagination, be reflective of the relative positions that might be attainable after a detour into anarchy and out again into a new constitutional contract. In this case, it should be rational for those who seem differentially favored in the status quo to accept reductions in the measured value of their assigned rights. If they do so, constitutional change can emerge through agreement, as previously discussed.

Those who are or may be differentially favored in the status quo may not, however, accept this as the rational course of action. Especially if they can control the activities of the enforcing agent, the government, they may consider their relatively advantageous positions invulnerable. They may be unconcerned about the alleged illegitimacy of the structure of individual rights in existence. It is this sort of setting that invites breakdown into disordered anarchy or revolution with a potentially new natural equilibrium in the offing followed by some new constitutional order. This is not to suggest that a rights structure may not survive and be enforced unless it mirrors, more or less accurately, one of the structures that might conceptually emerge in a renegotiation settlement. If "the government" is willing to enforce the status quo with sufficient determination, almost any set of rights can be maintained. But, in such a case, the state or government essentially becomes the enforcing agent for the coalition of persons whose rights in the status quo are unsustainable in plausible renegotiation. If "the government" is, at base, democratic in any ultimate sense, its activity in enforcing existing rights becomes more and more difficult as these diverge from the renegotiation expectations of large numbers of persons. Long-continued enforcement of unadjusted rights may become impossible. Agreed-on and quasi-contractual readjustment offers the only effective alternative to progressive deterioration in legal order, to continued violations of the implied contract by government and by individuals alike, to accelerated decline in the legitimacy of the whole constitutional structure, to general reduction in the stability and predictability inherent in the ordinary operation of the legal-political environment.

Insofar as they have discussed changes in status-quo imputations of individual rights, political economists have probably confused the issues. With only a few exceptions, political economists, along with other social scientists and social philosophers, have been unwilling to search for and to analyze the potential opportunities for voluntary or contractual changes in the constitutional order. Instead they have felt themselves obligated to propose changes that are derived from external ethical criteria, changes that are presumably to be imposed on the existing structure. This sort of discussion has tended to distract effort and attention from the less romantic but more productive approach involved in working out possible compromise modifications that would be agreeable to large numbers of persons in the community.[6]

Specification of Rights in the Status Quo

I have referred variously to a "set of legal rights," to a "distribution of individual rights," to a set of "property assignments." If the analysis is to have more practical relevance, it is necessary to be more specific. What are the descriptive characteristics of the structure? I have repeatedly warned against thinking of the structure of individual rights in terms of an imputation of either final goods or units of productive capacity among persons. This is a pervasive error that has been one of the reasons why political economists have neglected the problems discussed in this book. There is no constant-sum endowment of potential capacity to be somehow parcelled out among persons in the initial constitutional contract or enforced by the existing legal order. To adopt this as the paradigmatic basis for the analysis of the emergence and maintenance of a structure of property rights generates confusion from the outset. Individuals do not attain definitional identity with specifically measured endowments; they attain this through conceptual agreement, explicit or implicit, on a set of limits to their own behavior vis-à-vis one another. Within these limits, within "the law," they are allowed to develop and to utilize their capacities, human and nonhuman, and to secure "goods" ei-

6. I have in several other works elaborated the basic methodological position suggested. My own ideas, here as elsewhere, owe much to Knut Wicksell. For an early statement of my position, see the essay "Positive Economics, Welfare Economics, and Political Economy," *Journal of Law and Economics* 2 (1959): 124–38. This is reprinted without change in my *Fiscal Theory and Political Economy* (Chapel Hill: University of North Carolina Press, 1960).

W. H. Hutt should be mentioned as an important exception to mainstream political economists here. In a book written during World War II that has been too little known, Hutt proposed basic structural changes along strictly contractual lines. See W. H. Hutt, *A Plan for Reconstruction* (London: Kegan Paul, 1943).

ther through their own direct production or through exchange with each other. Included within these legal limits is participation in postconstitutional contracts, both in private and in public goods and services. In the latter, individuals may find it necessary to organize themselves collectively through political units and to impose on themselves decision rules that depart from unanimity, but rules which are themselves specified in the constitutional contract.

This summary is far from offering specific definition of the rights of an individual in any status quo. These depend both on the community selected for examination and on the time period chosen. No general set of individual rights can be derived independently in the approach taken here. In this sense, the whole analysis is relativistic. To define an individual's rights in the status quo, the particular community would have to be examined closely to determine just what the ongoing "constitutional contract" actually is. This is not an easy task, but it must be basically empirical and not analytical. Again in somewhat general terms, an individual's rights might be defined as that set of expectations about the relevant behavior of others in the community that is also shared by others in the community. Consider, for example, a right of land ownership. What does this mean? To "own" a parcel of land means that the owner expects others to refrain from using the land in certain ways and that others share this expectation, at least to the extent that they respect the penalties for violation. These attributes of ownership are required for the exchange of titles or rights. The status quo may be interpreted as the whole set of mutually shared expectations concerning the behavioral domains of individual members of the community, of variously organized coalitions and groups of individuals, including the political entity, the state.

There may, of course, be many ambiguities, uncertainties, and conflicting sets of expectations about individual spheres of allowable actions in any legal structure. Indeed almost all of the discussion of individual rights, human and nonhuman, as well as most of the practical litigation is aimed at the resolution of such ambiguities and conflicts. I have to this point deliberately refrained from discussing these because my main purpose has been first to derive the conceptual origins of social order on the presumption that rights are defined. I cannot, however, go further in analyzing structure without introducing problems raised by conflicts in definition.

One criterion by which we might evaluate any status-quo structure, a criterion that is wholly independent of qualitative value judgment, is offered by the amount of ambiguity and/or conflict among individual expectations. At one extreme, there is the model that we have to this point assumed, the model in which all rights are clearly defined and are acknowledged by all parties, including the enforcing agent. Violations may, of course, occur even in this model, but these are recognized as such, even by the violators, who are subject to punishment. Some uncertainty may be present even in this regime with well-defined rights. Particularly with respect to collective or governmental decisions on public-goods financing and provision, the individual may not be able to predict accurately his own final position on any specific collective outcome. This uncertainty is, however, consistent with the overall statement that rights are well defined since the rules for decision-making for the community are themselves clear, as well as the range over which such rules are allowed to operate. At the other extreme, we might conceptualize a setting where everything is in chaos, in which individuals have little or no ability to predict the behavior of others, including the government. The behavior of others may be wholly capricious, and the enforcing agent may or may not support nominal claims of the individual. In a certain sense, this extreme model might be less desirable psychologically for the individual than genuine anarchy because, in the latter, there does exist some predictability about final positions.

Any status quo will, of course, fall somewhere along the spectrum between these two extremes. Some ambiguities and conflicts will exist and, with these, individuals will not mutually share expectations about allowable and predictable behavior, either of each other or of the government. The individual "owner" of land who does not know whether his title is valid cannot predict with assurance just what behavior other potential claimants will undertake with respect to the land, and just what action the state may take to enforce rival claims. In the presence of such ambiguity, the value of "ownership" is reduced, and the exchange of rights becomes more difficult to implement.

The presence of ambiguity and conflict among individual claims is the source of major confusion about the protective-state role of government. To the extent that conflict emerges, adjudication of claims is necessary. Some search for and location of "the law" is required. In the process, the state, through its judicial arms and agencies, must make what appears to be quite arbitrary decisions of the either/or variety, decisions that are then imposed unwillingly on the losing parties to the dispute, and decisions which are subsequently enforced by the state. It is from observation of this sort of activity that the state is often described as *defining* rights, as making basic law. But there is a vital difference between adjudicating emergent conflicts among parties when ambiguities arise and in defining rights ab initio or in initiating explicit changes in rights when there is no conflict to be observed.

There must be an adjudication role for the collectivity. The purpose is that of accomplishing peaceful and orderly settlement of disputes that appear around the various borders or edges of acknowledged agreement. Adjudication by the state is designed to prevent the introduction of physical force by the parties. The role of adjudication is related to, but distinct from, the role of the state as the enforcing agent. Well-defined rights require enforcement; violations must be policed and violators punished even when each person's rights are acknowledged by everyone. In this sort of world, however, no adjudication of conflicts is required. The burglar does not seek to validate his legal claim on your "goods" through state judicial channels (at least not yet). When individuals disagree on their rights, however, when expectations diverge, adjudication is indicated. Each person behaves, or may behave, in exercise of what he claims as "his rights," and, in doing so, he does not acknowledge that he is violating any status-quo assignment. He seeks adjudication because he feels that his own claims are legitimate in the status quo.

The status quo should never be interpreted as defining an equilibrium in the structure of individual rights and claims. As of any point in time, there will exist some mutually inconsistent expectations on the part of some parties to the "social contract," and these will be on the way toward some resolution through formalized adjustment channels or otherwise. The equilibrium position toward which the system moves but never attains is closely analogous to that which has been described exhaustively in economic theory. Any system of rights will tend to be modified in the direction of some equilibrium in which lines dividing spheres of allowable actions are sharply drawn and in which individuals' expectations become mutually consistent. This tendency remains even if the path toward such an equilibrium implies resort to physical force rather than formalized adjustment. Just as with the more familiar economic interaction, however, exogenous shocks will continuously shift the target toward which the adjustment process converges.

The theory of the stationary economy, that state characterized by full equilibrium, has been highly developed, so much so that economics as a discipline has often neglected the dynamic adjustment processes which represent the economy's groping in response to a continuous series of external shocks. The comparable theory of the stationary legal structure, which would also be characterized by an equilibrium in which all individual and group rights are well defined and in which, as in the economy, all expectations are mutually shared, has scarcely been developed at all, and relatively too much attention has here been devoted to the dynamic adjustments in rights made necessary by the external forces of growth and technological change. As I have suggested, one possible criterion for evaluating any status-quo distribution of rights is its "distance from equilibrium," its place along the spectrum between the extreme with well-defined rights and that of disorderly chaos when individuals' expectations are maximally inconsistent. As in the economic theory analogue, equilibrium carries with it efficiency attributes. Any internal barriers or distortions that prevent the movement of the system toward the shifting equilibria reduce the efficiency of social intercourse.

6. The Paradox of "Being Governed"

Americans are dissatisfied with the status quo. This is more than mere assertion and more than reference to the discontented of all ages. There is a difference between the attitude of citizens toward the institutions of their society in the 1970s and the attitude that existed before 1960. Faith in the "American dream" has largely disappeared, and restoration does not seem in the offing. Who could have predicted that major American cities would prove so reluctant to host a celebration of the bicentennial of nationhood?

Some of the slogans of the 1960s can be meaningfully interpreted. The "participatory democracy" of the New Left took form in 1972, both in George Wallace's "send them a message" and in George McGovern's reforms of Democratic party structure. But paradox appears when we look at the results. The Wallace message is interesting primarily because it did not get through. Citizens' clamor for tax relief was translated into tax reform which, again translated, turned into proposals for increasing tax revenues. The budding "taxpayer revolution" of the late 1960s and early 1970s all but disappeared. The McGovern "democratization" of party structure amounted to near-destruction and was shelved quickly after 1972.

Dissatisfaction with the institutional structure, and most notably with the observed performance of government at all levels, remains widespread, but there is no effective means through which this shared attitude can be translated into positive results. Reactions against the excesses of bureaucracy provide the source for bureaucratic expansion. Frustrations with the status quo are noted by politicians and by actual and would-be self-serving "public servants." Proposals come forward for resolving "social problems," almost on an assembly-line schedule, proposals that necessarily require expansion rather than contraction in elements of structure that generate the evils. The infinite regress involved in what has been called the "public utility attitude" goes on. If something is wrong, have government regulate it. If the regulators fail, regulate them, and so on down the line. In part this is the inevitable result of public failure to understand the simple principle of laissez-faire, the principle that results which emerge from the interactions of persons left alone may be, and often are, superior to those results that emerge from overt political interference.[1] There has been a loss of wisdom in this respect, a loss from eighteenth-century levels, and the message of Adam Smith requires reiteration with each generation. (Modern economics must stand condemned in its failure to accomplish this simple task, the performance of which is, at base, the discipline's primary reason for claiming public support.)

There is more to it than this, however, and some miraculous rediscovery of eighteenth-century political wisdom would scarcely get us out of the woods. The surface paradox between observed frustrations with governmental processes and the resulting expansion in these same processes is itself based on a deeper and more complex phenomenon, one that itself involves a more permanent paradox. Hence, this chapter's title.

As noted earlier, the ideal society is anarchy, in which no one man or group of men coerces another. This ideal has been expressed variously through the ages, and by philosophers of widely divergent ideological persuasions. "That government is best which governs least" says the same thing as the "withering away of the State." Man's universal thirst for freedom is a fact of history, and his ubiquitous reluctance to "be governed" insures that his putative masters, who are also men, face never-ending threats of rebellion against and disobedience to any rules that attempt to direct and to order individual behavior. In a strictly personalized sense, any person's ideal situation is one that allows him full freedom of action and inhibits the behavior of others so as to force adherence to his own desires. That is to say, each person seeks mastery over a world of slaves. In a generalized social setting, however, and one that man can recognize as being within the realm of plausibility, the anarchistic regime of free men, each of whom respects the rights of others, becomes the utopian dream. Observed social orders depart from this dream,

---

1. In earlier and forthcoming works, F. A. Hayek has elaborated this point in detail. See his *Studies in Philosophy, Politics, and Economics* (London: Routledge and Kegan Paul, 1967); also see his *Law, Legislation, and Liberty*, vol. 1, *Rules and Order*.

however, and men (and scholars) who think of themselves as potentially ideal citizens stand doomed to frustration with the practical. Perhaps some recognition of the equivalence between the hopeless and the ideal, repeatedly stressed by Frank Knight, would be helpful here. But there remains what should be legitimate faith in "improvement," in "progress," faith that should not be wholly deadened. Improvement within limits, faith in progress tempered by reason, not romance—these are the qualities of attitude that prompt men to live with the institutions that they have while seeking change in orderly and systematic fashion. The reasoning and philosophical anarchist, which involves no contradiction in terms, becomes the only person who might construct the constitutional basis for a free society, who might elaborate changes from an institutionalized status quo, changes away from rather than toward the threatening Leviathan.

Why should the potentially ideal citizen adopt the conservative stance suggested? If all men are viewed as moral equals, why not institute the anarchist utopia in the here and now? Must the utopia remain unattained because some men cannot qualify as brothers? Is the problem centrally one of broadening the anarchist elite until all men become capable of the challenge? This line of thought may characterize the anarchist-cum-elitist, but it offers neither the direct nor the detour route to the construction of a free social order.

Man as Rule-Maker

Man looks at himself before he looks at others. The individual recognizes, and acknowledges, that he is neither saint nor sinner, either in existing or in extrapolated society. Man adopts rules. The rule-maker explicitly and deliberately imposes constraints upon himself in order to channel his own expedient behavior toward rationally selected norms. No one could claim that Robinson Crusoe is not "free"; yet a rational Crusoe might build and set an alarm clock, a device designed deliberately to intervene in his behavioral adjustment to changing environment.[2] It is rational to adopt rules that will ef-

2. After writing this chapter, I discovered that the alarm-clock example was used by John C. Hall to illustrate roughly the same point. More generally, Hall's careful and persuasive interpretation of Rousseau's work suggests that many of the elements of the contractual analysis developed here can be found in Rousseau. Those points where Rousseau

fectively "govern" individual behavior, and in this sense we say that Crusoe, even before Friday's arrival, is "governed." The concept of rationally chosen "self-government" is a necessary starting point for any analysis of "governing" in a many-person setting.[3]

Crusoe imposes rules on his own behavior because he recognizes his own imperfection in the face of possible temptation. This is not an acknowledgment of original sin but a simple recognition that behavioral responses are to some extent predictable by the person who chooses, and that some behavior patterns are better than others when a long-term planning horizon is taken. The rational Crusoe accepts the necessity of planning; his necessarily anarchistic existence may be carefully and systematically "planned" to make for a fuller and better life.[4] Before shifting from Crusoe to the individual in society, however, we should note that the alarm-clock example was not randomly chosen. Crusoe constructs his alarm clock, an impersonal and external device designed to impose constraints on his own choice behavior. He may, of course, also select internal rules or precepts which, once adopted, will be rigorously followed. But there remains an important difference between the two cases, one that has significance for the broader problems to be examined later in this chapter. With the alarm clock, Crusoe disturbs his dozing in advance. He closes off one behavioral option that would continue to remain open under voluntaristic rule. In a literal sense, Crusoe is "governed" by his clock with respect to his time of starting to work, even in his isolated one-man world.

A somewhat different way of putting this is to say that Crusoe "makes contracts with himself" when he works out his planning program. He recognizes that the pleasant life requires work while the sun is young in the tropical morn and agrees with himself during his contemplative moments that such work is a part of an optimal behavior pattern. But, knowing him-

---

departs from Hobbes, in Hall's interpretation, mark comparable limits of Hobbes for my own analysis. See Hall, *Rousseau;* the alarm-clock example is found on page 95.

3. Complex psychological issues are raised even in this simple model of self-government. As McIntosh says: "The idea of self-control is paradoxical unless it is assumed that the psyche contains more than one energy system, and that these energy systems have some degree of independence from each other" (*The Foundations of Human Society,* pp. 122f.). See also Gordon Rattray Taylor, "A New View of the Brain," *Encounter* (February 1971): pp. 25–37.

4. Cf. Rousseau, *The Social Contract,* p. 393.

self and his predispositions, he fears that he will not expediently and voluntarily live up to his own terms. The alarm clock becomes, for Crusoe, the enforcing agent, the "governor" whose sole task is that of insuring that the contracts once made are honored. For effective enforcement, the "governor" must be external to the person who recognizes his own weaknesses.

As the alarm bell arouses him from his nap, Crusoe faces one paradox of "being governed." He finds himself frustrated by an external constraint on his choice set, and he feels "less free" at that moment than he might have felt in the wholly voluntary act of rising from his bed. This sense of frustration may be repeated each and every morning, but Crusoe may continue to set the governing clock each evening. The rational rule-maker makes the trade-off between liberty and planned efficiency and includes an enforcement instrument in the contract.

I have discussed this choice calculus in some detail because the analysis is helpful in introducing problems raised by the enforcement of social contracts. Just as our Crusoe may choose to govern himself by the alarm clock, two or more persons may rationally choose to be governed by prior selection and implementation of enforcement institutions. Consider an elementary, two-person example. Once two men recognize each other's existence, potential conflict becomes possible, and some mutually acceptable disarmament agreement may be worked out, either before or after conflict takes place. This contract will embody agreed-on limitations on behavior which will, in turn, imply agreement on something that may be called a structure of rights. Each party will realize, however, that the agreement will have little effective value until and unless there is some security against violation by the other. Some enforcement mechanism, some device or institution, may accompany the initial contractual agreement, and each party will place a positive value on having such an instrument included.

At this point the two-person example distorts analysis by making enforcement seem less essential to contract than it is in the more general multiperson interaction. But the two-person example carries offsetting benefits in that it focuses attention on one feature of enforcement that may be overlooked. As noted, both men in the example will place value on the enforcement institution. The design and location of this institution becomes all important, however; neither party will entrust enforcement to the other, and, indeed, the delegation of such authority to one party in contract violates the meaning of enforcement. Both persons will seek something analogous to Crusoe's alarm clock, some instrument that is *external* to the participants (potential violators all) and which may be programmed in advance, which may be counted on to detect and to punish violations of the agreement, and to do so impersonally and impartially. Both parties will place a higher value on external institutions of enforcement than on adversely chosen internal ones.[5] (It is bad baseball when the catcher is required to umpire.) Both parties will prefer that the rules which they mutually choose be enforced by a third party, a stranger, by forces outside and beyond the participating group. Ideally, some wholly impersonal mechanism, a robot that could do nothing but follow automatized instructions, might be selected. Failing this, resort to third-party adjudication produces "government" of the ideal type in practicality.

The Protective State as Outside Referee

When the relative desirability of an external "governor" for enforcing contracts is understood, much of the continuing confusion and ambiguity in democratic theory may be clarified. The "government" or state that is conceptually derivative from this individualistic calculus is categorically different from that other "government" or state that emerges as an instrument of contract itself, as the means of facilitating and implementing the complex exchanges required for the provision of jointly consumed goods and services. This dual role for the state was discussed in earlier chapters. But it is sufficiently important to warrant elaboration and reemphasis here in a somewhat different setting. Failure to recognize this basic distinction provides a major source of the paradox of being governed.

For purposes of emphasizing the distinction, I have called that part of government which acts as the enforcing institution of society, the "protective state," and that part of government which facilitates public-goods exchanges, the "productive state." The task or role of the protective state is to insure that the terms of the conceptual contractual agreement are honored, that rights are "protected." As noted, in this role the state ideally must be external to and

5. Locke, *Second Treatise of Civil Government*, pp. 11ff.

divorced from the individuals or groups whose rights are involved.[6] Conceptually, the participants in social contract "purchase" the services of the external or outside enforcing agency, much as Crusoe builds and sets his alarm clock. Once selected and informed as to the agreed-on terms or rules, the participants have no voice, and could have none, in the "decisions" of the enforcing agent. Ideally, there are no "decisions" to be made, in the sense of a value-weighing of alternatives. The enforcing agent's task, conceptually, is purely scientific. The determinations to be made concern possible violations of agreed-on terms. These are almost archetype "truth judgments." While margins for discretion will almost always be present, the answer must be in the form of either/or. The terms or rules, "the law," were or were not violated, and there is no subjective moral evaluation in the agent's or referee's "choice." The terms will include specification of punishment or penalty to accompany violation. And, again it is inappropriate for the external agent to introduce its own evaluation into "decisions." (The basketball referee does not arbitrarily assign free throws to the shorter players.)

Precisely because "the government" (or the institutions of "the law," the protective state as enforcing agent) is and must be external to the parties in contract, unhappiness and frustration appear when sanctions for violations occur. Crusoe experiences displeasure when his clock arouses him; the person who violates social contract, who "breaks the law," and suffers punishment for it experiences comparable displeasure. This remains true despite the fact that, in both instances, the enforcing agent may have been rationally selected by the very person who is displeased. This suggests that, at the time of acknowledged or proven contract violation, with reference both to the policing and the imposition of punishment, "participatory democracy" that includes participation by those who violate the rules becomes an absurdity.

Even in the most idealized conditions of genuine social contract, the enforcement of terms that reflect agreement made in some prior stage will invoke displeasure of potential violators. To the latter, the protective state, as the enforcer of contract, becomes the enemy to be countered and outwitted if at all possible. This alienation from the enforcer state becomes much more severe, however, in the descriptive setting of the real world. The existing and

6. This principle was fully recognized at certain stages of English constitutional history.

ongoing implicit social contract, embodied and described in the institutions of the status quo, is exogenous to the participants, who have no sense of previous sharing in the making of the rules. To the extent that they divorce themselves from existing contractual order, their respect for "law" and for the agent assigned the enforcement task is diminished. Individuals come to feel that they are "governed" by institutions, by a system, that is external in any current participatory sense, which, as suggested, is a necessary condition, while, at the same time, they consider these institutions to be wholly exogenous in any contractual sense. That is to say, persons may feel themselves being forced to abide by terms of a "social contract" never made and subjected to potential punishment by an enforcing agent over whom they exert no control, either directly or indirectly.

This alienation of modern man from the protective state is exacerbated when he observes those persons who hold assigned roles in the functioning of this agency themselves to be departing from the rules defined in the status quo, either to aggrandize personal power or to promote subjectively chosen moral and ethical objectives. In this context it may become literally impossible for the individual to look on the state as anything other than arbitrarily repressive. Once this stage is reached, the individual abides by existing law only because he is personally deterred by the probability of detection and subsequent punishment. Indirectly, he may seek relief from arbitrary and capricious interference with his own freedom of behavior. All semblance of "self-government" may have disappeared, at least as this might exist at the margins or limits of actual governmental functioning.

The Productive State as Embodied in Postconstitutional Contract

As noted in earlier chapters, government, as observed, operates in a dual capacity. There is a part of government whose action is different, in principle, from that of rule-keeping or enforcement. In its postconstitutional role, what we may call the "productive state" is the constitutional process through which citizens accomplish jointly desired objectives, a means of facilitating complex exchanges *among* separate citizens, each of whom enters the contractual or exchange process with rights assigned in the more fundamental legal structure. In this role, government is *internal* to the community, and meaningful political decisions can only be derived from individual values as expressed at the time of decision or choice. Lincoln's "by the people" becomes appropriately descriptive of current choice-making procedures. In such a context, current participation in collective choice becomes a desirable attribute. And, as noted, Wicksellian unanimity offers the idealized rule for the reaching of decisions. Departures from this benchmark are justifiable only because of the excessive costs of attaining genuine consensus. Even when the practicably acceptable departures from unanimity are acknowledged, however, the decision-making process is properly conceived as a surrogate for a full consensus model.

In this role or capacity, the state is not "protecting" defined individual rights. Government is a *productive process,* one that ideally enables the community of persons to increase their overall levels of economic well-being, to shift toward the efficiency frontier. Only through governmental-collective processes can individuals secure the net benefits of goods and services that are characterized by extreme jointness efficiencies and by extreme nonexcludability, goods and services that would tend to be provided suboptimally or not at all in the absence of collective-governmental action.[7] In this capacity, government decision-making involves agreements on quantities and cost-sharing. Outcomes are reached by compromising among conflicting desires, by making full use of various devices for compensation, by facilitating and promoting indirect trade-offs among persons and groups. The "truth-judgment" characterization of outcomes or decisions applicable in the enforcer or protective state is wholly foreign in this second governmental role. In providing and financing national defense, for example, the governmental process represents an adjustment among conflicting demands and generates some median level of budgeted outlay. This is not an either/or choice, and the level of outlay finally selected is not properly to be described as "true" or "false." The outcomes of the institutional processes of the productive state are not "scientific." These outcomes are derived from individual behavior, not from some objectifiable empirical reality. The results reflect the distribution of the value

7. The relationship between the set of goods and services which might have these characteristics and the particular assignment of rights in basic constitutional contract should be emphasized. The dividing line between private and public goods depends, in part, on how the property rights of persons are defined.

weights among persons that are inherent in the constitutionally determined rules for choice-making, and participation by affected parties is a necessary component of such rules because only through such participation can evaluations be revealed.

The outcomes that define the amount of publicly provided goods and services and the means of sharing their costs are themselves contracts, and, as such, these, too, require enforcement. This creates a necessary interface between the productive and the protective state. What we descriptively observe in government is an amalgamation of both of these, along with other components yet to be examined.

Experts and Democracy

The preceding summary of the dual capacity of government may be followed by a brief discussion of some of the implications. Consider, first, a setting in which no need for a productive state exists. There are no goods and services that may be consumed or used more efficiently through collective than through market auspices. In this setting, individuals have been assigned rights to resource endowments in a basic if implicit constitutional contract, enforceable by an external agent, the protective state. From this base, individuals are free to negotiate any and all mutually beneficial exchanges among themselves, and agreed-on terms will be effectively enforced by the agency. In such a world as this, there should be little or no concern expressed about the "form" of government. So long as the enforcing agency does not overstep its own constitutionally delegated bounds, the citizenry should not bother itself with the detailed means through which the agency operates. There is, in conception, no more need for concern here than Crusoe might feel as between alarm clocks made of hickory or of coconut wood. So long as the device works well, the details of construction and operation are not relevant.

There may, of course, be a relationship between the efficiency of the enforcing institution and its organizational form. And, more important, the probability of departure from its delegated role may be affected by organization. But concern for either of these matters is different in principle from that which is appropriately expressed for governmental "form" in the productive state. The jury may offer a familiar example. Operating as an inherent part of the enforcing agency, the jury's verdict is a "truth judgment," and the efficiency in attaining correct or accurate decisions may vary somewhat as the organization is modified. A jury of twelve men may be more efficient than one of ten men or one of six men, or vice versa, but there is no inherent reason for selecting one form rather than another. Much of the same applies for the inclusiveness of rules for verdict; whether unanimity is or is not required may affect the accuracy of decision as well as the direction of bias, but there is no single best rule for all circumstances. Or, consider a different example, that of the judge in an isolated community. The selection of a person to fill this role by voting processes may be preferable to random assignment or to any of several other methods. But there is no logical reason why democratic process should be preferable here since the function to be performed is not one that derives ideally from individual valuations at all, but is, instead, ideally one of determining objective fact and initiating well-defined action. Some notion of the extent of modern ambiguity is suggested by familiar proposals for "representation" of interests on multijudge appellate courts, and even more dramatically by the observed action of modern appellate courts in requiring appropriate interest "representation" on juries.[8] This attitude appears to reflect simple blindness to the distinction between the protective and the productive state, between the external enforcement of contract and contract itself.

It may be argued that, in carrying out its enforcement role, the state should employ "experts," "scientists," "truth seekers," "fact finders"—persons who are particularly trained in the law. If confined to its appropriate limits there seems to exist a logical and rational basis for delegation of enforcing power to a judicial elite. The problem is, of course, that of keeping any such elite confined within any limits that might be specified, and it is in recognition of this problem that much of the modern ambiguity arises. Democratic procedures, including representation of interests, may be explicitly incorporated into the structure of the enforcer state because these seem to offer the only means of exercising ultimate control over the experts to whom enforcing tasks are delegated. If they cannot voluntarily withdraw from the game, players on all sides may insist on retaining some power of removing the referee,

---

8. Although it does not recognize the distinction made here, a recent paper applies a helpful economic approach to the institution of the jury. See Donald L. Martin, "The Economics of Jury Conscription," *Journal of Political Economy* 80 (July/August 1972): 680–702.

even when they recognize that this intrusion of player control will, ceteris paribus, introduce inefficiencies.

By a converse chain of reasoning, expert or scientific judgments become wholly inappropriate in generating outcomes in the productive state, and democratic procedures become necessary. The question of "form" becomes all important here, and, of course, the productive state is that aspect of government that spends billions, allegedly in promoting the "general welfare." The ambiguity in attempts to incorporate democracy directly into government's enforcer role is matched by that which holds that government should provide goods and services for citizens in accordance with "social goals" or "national priorities" rather than in accordance with citizens' own expressed desires. This latter view is, in part, fostered by the practical necessity of bureaucratic discretion and by the intellectual failure to distinguish procedural and substantive norms.

The costs of decision-making guarantee that wide discretionary powers rest with bureaucratic personnel. Representative assemblies, themselves already one stage removed from constituency demands, can scarcely vote separately on detailed items in a multipurpose budget. Allocative decisions are necessarily shifted to the executive branch, to the bureaucracy, and without criteria for determining citizenry evaluation, the temptation to introduce "experts" is strong. For those allocative decisions within his power, how is the bureaucrat to choose? On his private, personal preferences? Or, on the introduction of some presumed judgment of "general welfare" or "public interest"? Some choices are surely "better" than others, or so it would seem. To accept this implies, however, that substantive criteria have been subtly introduced over and beyond the procedural criteria that are embodied in the decision-making itself. To the external observer, *any* result reached by the procedure of voluntary contract among persons is equally desirable, provided only that the procedural norms are followed, that the process itself is efficient, and that the interests of the parties in contract are the only ones to be counted. This is clear enough when we discuss ordinary market exchanges among persons. But the issue necessarily becomes cloudy when we shift discussion to the actions of the government in supplying goods and services. As noted, governmental process here must be interpreted as a surrogate for a complex exchange among all citizens in the community. To the extent that this interpretation mirrors reality, all outcomes that are reached through agreed-on and efficient procedures for decision-making become equally acceptable. When it is recognized, however, that governmental process must include departures from any rules that would be fully analogous to voluntary exchanges, it is difficult to maintain a stance of full neutrality as among possible alternatives. Some of these do seem better than others.

Personal Loss Functions and Procedural Norms

Governmental decision-making in its operative form departs from voluntaristic contracting, despite the contractarian basis for the state's productive role. Indeed the relative efficacy of governmental institutions in providing genuinely public goods and services is presumed to stem from the cost-reducing impact of allowable departures from strictly voluntaristic negotiations. But, in their turn, these departures guarantee that some participants in almost every decision will be coerced into abiding with undesirable terms. Budgetary and taxing decisions are not reached through Wicksellian unanimity, and to the extent that they are not, some participants suffer losses in an opportunity-cost sense. The existence of these opportunity losses becomes an additional source for the basic governmental paradox.

Consider a politically organized municipality that has long operated under a constitution that specifies simple majority voting as the rule for making budgetary choices. Spending and taxing decisions are made in town meetings. (This simplest of models is used here to avoid unnecessary complexities that are introduced by representation.) Assume that a proposal is made to finance a new auditorium through an increase in the general property-tax rate. The proposal secures a majority in the assembly, and it is adopted. Each person who opposed the measure will, however, experience an opportunity loss consequent on the political action taken, a loss by comparison with his own individually preferred outcome. To these disappointed members of the losing minority coalition, the budget is too large, but observed voting behavior suggests that a proposal for reversal cannot carry the day. Members of this losing coalition, singly and in groups, will be motivated to search out and to propose other spending schemes which are personally preferred and which promise to yield benefits in excess of the allocable tax costs. Such persons, or a political entrepreneur who senses their interest, will try to locate new budgetary propositions that may succeed in generating majority support. But as a second such proposal, say, a new swimming pool, is added to the municipal budget, a new and different disappointed minority emerges. Even to some of those who approved the initial proposal for spending on the auditorium, the budget may now have become too large; they, too, will experience opportunity losses. To persons outside either of these two majorities, the opportunity loss increases as the budget grows, and they are now more strongly motivated to secure "budgetary justice" by getting the enactment of at least some projects that they value differentially.

In a continuing process of this sort, and so long as the tax institution remains more general in incidence than the particular benefit projects, each member of the community may experience opportunity loss from governmental action. The total outlay may seem too large to each and every citizen; the budget will contain items of spending that are valued less than the corresponding tax obligation. This conclusion holds even if each budgetary project, considered independently, is "efficient" in the strictly allocative sense. There is, of course, no assurance that all majority-approved projects will be allocatively efficient, especially in the absence of smoothly working monetary side payments. The introduction of logrolling possibilities allows for the enactment of projects that benefit specific minorities, but this does not modify the general conclusion about budgetary frustration.[9] The budget is, of course, symmetrical; outlays must be financed. And essentially the same process as that sketched above would apply to majority-approved departures from strict generality in tax distribution. Suppose that an initial proposal is made to reduce the tax shares of a majority of citizens, while increasing the shares of the minority. Anyone in the latter group senses the loss, and he seeks relief by organizing a somewhat different majority, insuring his own membership, that will support additional departures from tax generality. As the process continues, each person may be placed in the position where he feels that the whole tax structure is "unfair" and "inequitable," which translates into the notion that the "loopholes" available to others than himself are unwarranted.

The direction of overall budgetary bias which majority-voting decision processes may generate is wholly irrelevant to my argument at this point. It does not matter whether the results are budgets which are "too large" or "too

9. For elaboration of this analysis, see Buchanan and Tullock, *The Calculus of Consent.*

small" by normal efficiency criteria, or that offsetting biases produce overall budget sizes that are "just right." If the productive state operates strictly within the procedural norms laid down for it in the constitutional stages of decision, and even if its provision and financing of genuinely public goods and services represents the most efficient institutional arrangements possible, the individuals who are the final recipients of benefits and the final bearers of costs may feel that they are being coerced. And coerced here in a somewhat different sense than that which must be felt by any person who is required to live up to contractual terms that he has himself agreed to at one time. Even if the contractarian basis for governmental action is acknowledged in the abstract, so long as departures from unanimity are descriptive of the collective decision rules, the individual's sense of being compelled to abide by unacceptable terms must be treated as fact. This sense of coercion is enhanced precisely because of the internal nature of the productive state, precisely because the basis is seen to be contractarian. The individual may accept "rules" enforced by the protective state as being exogenous to his own influence. He abides by law because it is there, and he may see no way that his own behavior can modify this. He may not be so willing to abide by democratically evolved budgets, on either the spending or taxing side, because he is encouraged to consider his own influence on budgetary outcomes, his own participation in democracy at work.

This fiscal frustration with government that is experienced by the citizen necessarily increases as the size of the governmental sector grows, relative to that of the private or market sector of the economy. As government, and notably the central government, commands a larger share of the economy's total resources, as more specific functions are taken over collectively, the citizen's personal benefit-cost criteria are increasingly violated. Consider an example. If government limits itself to an enforcer role, all exchange is private and voluntary. The individual's ability to opt out of any particular agreement guarantees that enforced acceptance of unfavorable terms is minimal. (This principle holds true even if all markets are not fully competitive; the degree of monopolization will, of course, affect the comparability as well as the number of alternatives that each market participant faces.) If the government takes on a productive role, and if it assumes responsibility for the complex exchange process embodied in the provision of public goods, the average or representative citizen must anticipate that he will rarely, if ever, optimally prefer the particular budgetary package that he will be required to enjoy and to pay for. Given almost any budgetary package, the citizen must expect that he would prefer expansion in some items, contractions in others, even within the same revenue constraint. And, overall, he may prefer that the total outlay be larger or smaller than that to which he is subjected. On the taxing side, the citizen will, quite straightforwardly, prefer that his own cost-shares be reduced relative to those of others in the community. As the total size and complexity of the budget increases, the individual may become increasingly disappointed with governmental performance, even if all functions are carried out efficiently in the small.

Individual opportunity losses increase with increasing centralization in the public sector in much the same way as with increasing budget size and complexity. It has long been recognized that the individual's sense of participation in collective choice is relatively greater in localized jurisdictions, rationally so because the influence of a single person on group outcomes is inversely related to group size. A less familiar but still elementary fact is that governmental process is necessarily closer to genuine voluntary exchange at the local level because of the relatively greater freedom of migration. The limits to tax-budgetary exploitation of the individual are reached more quickly in local governmental units than in central governments. Migration thresholds need not be high in a multicommunity national economy that is characterized by high resource mobility, a description that has fitted the United States in the twentieth century.

Enforcement of Putative Contract

In the productive state that provides and finances public goods and services, costs of agreement dictate that decisions binding on all members of the community be made by some subset of the putative parties in contract. Once made, however, these decisions must be enforced just as those reached by negotiations among persons in genuinely voluntary interactions. To enforce its decisions, the productive state must call on its complement, the protective state.

To the individual citizen who may oppose a particular outcome, enforcement here is not one whit different from exogenous destruction in his rights. He is forced to abide by choices made for him by others, which may involve a net reduction in his own command over material goods. Taxes are levied on him, without his consent, to finance goods and services that he may value less highly than the foregone private-goods alternatives. The activity of the enforcing agent becomes quite different here than it is with reference to ordinary contractual agreements among separate parties. In the latter, rights are presumably well defined in advance, and the contractual terms are explicitly known and acknowledged. The task of enforcer is "scientific"; it must determine whether an explicit contractual agreement has been violated. This setting may now be compared with that involved in the enforcement of the putative fiscal contract that is reflected in a decision on providing and financing a public good. Suppose that a spending-taxing decision has been made by an appropriately required majority in a legislative assembly. The outcome is opposed strongly by a significant minority of citizens. Here the enforcing agent must assume a wholly different role. Problems arise in determining just what rights individuals possess prior to contract, and in determining the limits to which these rights, if they existed, may be coercively destroyed without consent in the putative fiscal contract that the decision reflects.

The enforcement agency's task may remain "scientific" at the purely conceptual level, but the discretionary limits are significantly wider here. The range over which the agent may make his determination is not narrowly confined, and, within this range, his own judgments may enter, judgments of "value," not of "truth." Consider a simple comparison with ordinary two-person contract. If A tells B that he will repay a loan of $10, the enforcer must decide only whether A has carried out the terms. But what if A and B join forces in a three-person collective group and, by majority vote, impose a tax of $10 on C to finance a joint-consumption project? Suppose that C objects and refuses to pay the $10. He has violated no agreement, no explicit contractual arrangement made with his peers. The enforcing agent or adjudicator here must do more than determine whether C fails to comply. The agent must also decide whether the putative contract is, in itself, "constitutional." As noted, this, too, is a factual or scientific question at the conceptual level of inquiry. But constitutions are unlikely to be at all specific with respect to the rights of collectively controlling coalitions to impose binding decisions on all members of the community. Historically, the United States courts have held only that overtly discriminatory treatment is prohibited. If taxes are plausibly "general," there is normally no "constitutional" basis for minority objection, regardless of the distribution of benefits or of the nonvoluntariness of the decision.[10]

The point of emphasis here is that the necessary intrusion of the external enforcing arm of the state into the putative social contract reflected in collective decisions concerning the financing and provision of collective-consumption goods places this arm or agency in a conceptually superior position. By necessity, the protective state must ride herd on the possible excesses of the productive state that is its complement. Majorities might, if left unchecked, impose discriminatory costs on minorities. Gross departures from anything that could plausibly be legitimate social contracting might be observed under majority rule without constitutional constraints. Nonetheless, the granting of review authority to the enforcing arm of the state carries with it a fundamental contradiction. Under the majoritarian governmental process that finances and provides public goods, the individual citizen who holds the franchise retains some indirect controls through the possible formation of rotating majority coalitions. Even if he remains dissatisfied and disappointed with particular results, there is a participatory element that is present which has some value save in those cases where the constituency is permanently divided. With respect to the enforcing agent, however, the individual does not have even this recourse open to him. The transfer of final authority to this part of the state must, therefore, reduce rather than enhance the individual's influence.

Enforcer's Encroachment on the Contractual Domain

The alienation of the individual citizen from government in the large is further increased when the enforcing agent expands its authority and encroaches on

---

10. For a detailed discussion of the uniformity requirement for taxation under the United States Constitution, as interpreted historically by the courts, and with especial emphasis on the asymmetry between the taxing and spending sides of the budget in this respect, see David Tuerck, "Constitutional Asymmetry," *Papers on Non-Market Decision Making* 2 (1967). (This journal is now *Public Choice*.) Or, more comprehensively, see Tuerck, "Uniformity in Taxation, Discrimination in Benefits: An Essay in Law and Economics" (Ph.D. diss., University of Virginia, 1966).

the domain that is or should be appropriately reserved for the putatively contractual state operating postconstitutionally. The temptation for such encroachment that is placed on the men who fill assigned enforcement roles is directly related to the authority granted and to the respect for this authority held by both private citizens and by those who hold positions in the contractual branch of government. If it comes to be widely acknowledged, and accepted, that only the enforcer (the judiciary) can determine whether or not a particular putative contractual proposal (for example, a budgetary scheme) is "constitutional," and, further, that there is no appeal from the enforcer's final pronouncement, there should be little surprise at the enforcer's failure to distinguish carefully between "constitutionality" and "public good," with the latter defined personally and privately. (If others treat him as God, man will come to think that he is God.) This is especially the case when legal and political philosophers themselves fail to sense the critical differences between these two categorically different sets of criteria.

In practice, some institutional ambiguity must always be present, and the conceptual boundaries between enforcement and contract itself can rarely be maintained inviolate. It remains nonetheless extremely important that these ambiguities be minimized, and that encroachments in either direction be called into account and corrected if possible. One of the primary reasons for the discontent with government that we observe in the 1970s is traceable to the failure of the separate agencies to respect the distinction between their separate roles. The federal courts in the United States, which must be a vital part of the enforcing agency but whose task extends neither to a rewriting of the basic constitutional contract nor to the providing of public goods and services, have sought, and gained, widely respected authority to define "public good," and their criteria for decision have come increasingly to be those of "social interest" rather than those of embodied contract, whether this be explicit or putative. Whether the values reflected by the thrust of particular judicial decisions are deemed desirable or undesirable to the observer, the role that has been assumed by the federal judiciary must be recognized to be grossly violative of the conceptual separation between constitutional contract and its enforcement on the one hand and between the enforcing agent and the productive state on the other. It is little wonder that the individual citizen stands bewildered. By this reference to the American setting in the 1970s, I am not suggesting that the political structure was conceived initially and has been operated along precisely the model developed in my analysis and that departures have taken place only in recent decades. The analysis will, I hope, provide a way of looking at the operating political structure at any point in time, a structure that is always, to an extent, "imperfect." I am suggesting that by applying critically the model for democratic political order to the modern American setting, the anomalies seem gross indeed. Furthermore, and in part because of the quantum increase in governmental size, these anomalies do much to explain the intensity of the basic paradox sensed by the ordinary citizen.

7. Law as Public Capital

Man makes laws; in this respect he differs from other animals. He chooses deliberately to impose constraints on his own behavior; he distinguishes between rational planning and response to stimuli. Self-imposed law in an isolated individual setting is wholly distinct, however, from agreed-on law in a social setting, in an interaction with other persons. In the latter, the individual accepts defined constraints on his own behavior, not because his own well-being would be privately enhanced by such constraints but in exchange for favors that take the form of acceptance of like behavioral constraints by other parties in contract. That is to say, the individual does not enter into social contract for the purpose of imposing constraints on himself; he could always accomplish this by more effective means. He enters into agreements with others to secure the benefits of behavioral limitation on their part. The individual will find his own adherence to law unprofitable except insofar as this is directly related to others' behavior. This constraint on his own liberty is the cost side of the contract. Rationality precepts, strictly interpreted, suggest efforts toward maximizing "law-abiding" by others and toward minimizing "law-abiding" by the party in question. Law is simply a reciprocal relationship among parties, an embodiment of contract. It is voluntaristic in a sense analogous to any contractual relationship; parties agree on the whole set of terms. This does not imply that unilateral adherence to these terms in the absence of effective enforcement is utility-maximizing. Each party has an incentive to violate the contract, to violate law, if he can predict that his own behavior will exert no influence on the behavior of others. A person has little private-personal incentive to adhere to the terms of a pure "external" contract, except insofar as this represents required "payment" for reciprocal action offered by contractual partners. Law-abiding by a single party, treated independently, exerts a pure external economy on other parties.

In the discussion contained in Chapters 2 through 4, the constraints on individual behavior embodied in law were conceived to emerge from basic constitutional contract. Until and unless some such constraints are in existence, individuals are not themselves "defined" with sufficient precision to allow postconstitutional trades or contracts to be implemented. As there noted, both the theory of private goods and the theory of public goods are normally based on the presumption that a well-defined set of individual rights and claims exists, as imbedded in a functioning legal structure. Although not often made explicit, there is also a presumption that there exists a clear demarcation between those interactions in which behavior is limited by formal law and those which continue to utilize anarchy as the organizing principle. It is this latter presumption which must be relaxed at this point. The formation of constitutional contract is continuous. "Law" is in a continual process of change and modification; communities are observed to be adopting new constraints on individual behavior, to be shifting additional areas of human activity from anarchy to law. At the same time, communities are observed, or should be observed, to be shifting yet other activities from law to anarchy. The effective constitutional status quo is dynamic. The trade-off between the individual's liberty of person that is present only in the complete absence of law and the order that is present only with formalized legal constraints on behavior is subject to change as tastes, technology, and resources change.

The purpose of this chapter is first to discuss this trade-off with the concepts of public-goods theory, although the differences as well as the similarities between the two applications of analysis will become apparent. As a second cross-classification, the capital-goods characteristic of legal structure is examined.

Law and Public Goods

To the extent that law embodies the contractual origins discussed above, or that law may be conceptually explained on the "as if" presumption of such origins, law-abiding exerts a *pure* external economy. This feature distinguishes law from the more orthodox public-goods interactions among persons. For comparison here, we may look at one of the classic examples, the provision of lighthouse services for a community of fishermen. In the absence of collective action, a single person may provide at least some of these services; if he does so, he exerts significant external economies on others in the group. But in the process he will also be securing some share of the total benefits. The external economy is not pure; others than the acting person receive less than the totality of benefits that the action produces. In this lighthouse-type case, the presence of significant external benefits allows us to predict that in-dependent, individualistic behavior will result in suboptimal levels of service; too few resources will be invested in the activity under normal conditions. We cannot, however, predict that there will be no services made available in the absence of collective contract. Individuals may well invest some resources under certain cost configurations and certain community sizes.

With "law," however, no such results emerge, regardless of group size. Pre-cisely because law-abiding is a pure external economy, and as such involves behavior from which the actor secures no private, personal reward, an eco-nomic model would predict an absence of all such behavior in the strictly individualistic setting. (I am abstracting here from any moral or ethical pre-cepts that may lead persons to act as if some contractual basis for reciprocally advantageous behavior exists. Abstraction from such considerations for the purpose of analysis is not, of course, equivalent to asserting that such pre-cepts are nonexistent, or, if existent, that they are empirically unimportant.) In somewhat more technical language, "law" of the sort analyzed here qual-ifies as a pure collective-consumption or public good,[1] and one for which in-dependent adjustment yields corner solutions for each person. No person will provide, by his own restricted behavior, the benefits of law-abiding to others. I define "law-abiding" here to mean a generalized respect to the de-fined rights of all others in the community, as opposed to a particularized or directed result. Probabilistically, if a single person, A, chooses to respect the rights of *all* others in the group of size n, each person in the $n - 1$ set be-comes more secure in the possession of his rights.

A second possible difference between "law" and the more familiar light-house example of public good may be mentioned. In the latter, even if cost configurations suggest that no person independently invests resources in gen-erating the external economy, cooperative, club-like arrangements may be

---

1. For a general paper which covers material similar in many respects to that treated here, see W. H. Riker, "Public Safety as a Public Good," in *Is Law Dead?* ed. E. V. Rostow (New York: Simon and Schuster, 1971), pp. 379–85.

made among two or more persons but substantially fewer than the whole community membership. Two or more fishermen may find joint provision of lighthouse services advantageous, and they may carry out such a venture even when they recognize that they will confer significant external benefits on remaining members of the community, benefits for which no payment can be exacted. Again "law" may be quite different. Privately arranged contracts that take the form of cooperative, club-like arrangements among relatively small numbers of persons may emerge, but those who remain outside the contract but within the larger community need not secure spillover benefits comparable to those received in the familiar public-goods examples. Indeed, the result may be just the opposite. Small groups may be motivated to form coalitions, but the law-abiding that is embodied in agreement may be strictly *internal* to members of the coalition. The law that emerges may well be selective and discriminatory, with a sharp difference between the specified behavior of a person toward members of the coalition and that toward outsiders. The primal disarmament contract may be limited; predatory behavior vis-à-vis persons and groups that remain outside the boundaries of agreement may continue and perhaps accelerate. (This setting is, of course, descriptive of the world when we look on nation-states as the effective coalitions of persons.) Those persons who do not form a part of the internal agreement may secure no spillover benefits from the behavioral constraints that are accepted by members. For the ideal-type public good, exemplified by the lighthouse, technological attributes of the good itself make it impossible or inefficient to exclude noncontracting persons from benefits. The good, as produced, is necessarily nonexcludable. With law, conceived in this publicness context, that which is produced tends by its nature to be selective. Exclusion tends to be efficient in this case, and self-interest will insure its presence.

If, from an initial anarchistic equilibrium, a preliminary coalition forms, members of this coalition secure differential advantages over persons who remain outside the subgroup. The latter persons suffer costs because of the increased productivity of predatory efforts that may be directed against them by members of the coalition, who have by agreement ceased internal predation. This effect will be present even if there are no scale advantages in either defense or predation; if scale economies exist, the differentials will be larger. This situation becomes almost the converse of the more familiar free-rider problem when nonexcludability of public-goods benefits is present. Unorganized persons are confronted with a choice set that places greater incentives for (1) joining the initial coalition, or (2) forming another coalition. As some of the persons unorganized take either of these steps, those left still unorganized find their own situations further worsened. Their incentives to join existing coalitions or to form new ones increase further.

If several independently organized coalitions emerge, each of which embodies internal agreements on law, movement toward an all-inclusive legal contract for the whole community may take the form of bargaining among the separate coalitions. In either case, there should be potential gains to all parties from contractual arrangements that extend the legal structure to the appropriate limits of community membership. The existence of major discontinuities in the interaction sequence, such as those produced by defined spatial boundaries, may reduce the potential gains. The many complexities introduced in attempting to construct a plausible conjectural history for the emergence of a general legal system, with law being made coextensive with membership in the community, need not occupy too much discussion. The point of emphasis is the "publicness" of law itself, the attribute which allows us to use the tools of modern public-finance theory to shed some light on pressing social issues of our time.[2]

The Benefits and Costs of Law

Law-abiding on the part of an individual is the cost that he pays as a part of the overall legal-social contract between himself and others in the community, treated as a unit. In a private, personal utility sense, any limits on indi-

---

2. The analysis applies only to "law" which does, in fact, lend itself to the "publicness" description. In technical terms, "law" which involves the elimination of general external diseconomies or the creation of general external economies is the subject of analysis, not "law" which attempts to regulate individual behavior that may be unrelated to the extent of external effects. For example, a law that requires me to vaccinate my dog against rabies clearly qualifies because, in so doing, I am exerting external economies on all others in the community. By contrast, a law that might prevent me from purchasing the services of a prostitute could hardly be brought within the "publicness" description.

My use of "law" in this respect is similar to that employed by Rousseau. See Rousseau, *The Social Contract*, p. 399.

vidual behavior are "bads." But rational persons accept such limits in exchange or trade for the "goods" which law-abiding on the part of others
represents. This behavior on the part of others creates "goods" because of
the predictable order, security, or stability that it generates in the individual's
choice set. To the extent that other persons respect the limits laid down in
law or rules, and to the extent that these are known by everyone, the individual can make his own private decisions in a reasonably predictable and stable
social environment. This feature is applicable for many rules that might be
called "laws," whether these be simple rules of the road, such as right-hand
driving, or complex arrangements, such as those required among different
owners of condominium units. For purposes of illustrating the analysis, we
may think of law as embodying general agreement to respect a set of rights
or disposition over physical property. Individuals in the community, having
agreed on or having accepted this assignment of rights, are said to abide by
law if they do not attempt to secure others' assigned rights without consent.
It is not difficult to see that a legal structure confers benefits on all members
of the community in most cases, benefits that stem from the order that is
introduced. The appropriate comparison is with the anarchistic alternative
which is, in the limit, characterized by a total absence of behavioral constraints.

These benefits are achievable only at the cost of limiting individual freedom, only at the sacrifice of personal utility which the spontaneous adjustment to changing circumstances would offer. To an economist, this benefit-
cost framework suggests that there is some optimal or efficient amount of
law for any person, some level of generalized behavioral restriction that is
preferred to alternative levels.[3] Each of us would probably agree that some
traffic laws are beneficial, whether these specify right-hand driving, as in the
United States, or left-hand driving, as in Britain. There is probably not a single person who values his own freedom of choice so highly that he would
prefer a nation without traffic rules. On the other hand, for each of us there
are probably some laws or rules in existence that yield benefits insufficient to

3. For a general discussion, see Paul Craig Roberts, *Alienation and the Soviet Economy*
(Albuquerque: University of New Mexico Press, 1973), Chapter 3; idem, "An Organizational Model of the Market," *Public Choice* 10 (Spring 1971): 81–92.

offset the sacrifice of personal freedom involved. The Virginia Pollution Control Board, acting as empowered by the legislature, prohibits open brush- and leaf-burning, clearly a restriction on my own freedom of action, and one that is not offset in value to me by the prediction that other persons will also follow the regulation.

These examples point up a third difference between law and the standard public good, a difference that is of major importance. The achievement of "efficiency" in the overall quantity of law becomes extremely difficult, and, furthermore, the normative properties of any "efficiency" criterion become much less persuasive. This difference involves the adjustment in relative cost- shares among persons. In the standard public-goods model, all persons in the community share in the benefits of a uniform quantity of the nonexclud- able good or service, despite their possibly differing marginal evaluations of this quantity. Separate persons may, however, be brought into agreement, or closer to agreement, on this common quantity by appropriately made ad- justments in marginal cost-shares or tax-prices. (These tax or cost-share ad- justments among individuals substitute for the more familiar adjustments in individually demanded quantities in markets for private or partitionable goods and services, where prices are uniform over separate buyers.) The ag- gregate cost of a public good or service, that which must be shared among beneficiaries in some fashion, is determined exogenously, and this cost is based, ultimately, on the alternative product values that might be produced by the resources used. This may be contrasted with the adoption of a general law or rule that does qualify under the "publicness" rubric and that con- strains the behavior of all members of the community. As noted, the exis- tence of and adherence to this law introduces greater stability into the be- havioral environment for all persons and in this way qualifies as a purely public good. The costs of this rule or law are measured in the losses of utility suffered by each person due to the restrictions imposed on his range of choice options. These utility losses may indirectly reflect subjective estimates for ob- jectively measurable opportunity losses. But the relevant consideration here is that these costs are not exogenous to the choice of the "good" itself. That is to say, the mere adoption of a law or rule carries with it a specific cost- sharing scheme; the law or rule must be generally applied to all citizens. Each person is subjected to a "liberty tax," to use an appropriate term coined by

Thomas Ireland,[4] a tax that need not be, and normally will not be, valued uniformly by all persons, even if values should be reduced to commodity or money dimensions. It is as if, in the standard public-goods paradigm, some arbitrarily determined tax-sharing scheme should exist which is independent of the relative evaluations of individuals, a scheme that must remain inviolate.

Under these conditions, one dimension of adjustment, one degree of freedom is lost. In the provision of orthodox public goods, this dimension is used to produce more widespread agreement among persons on quantity and/or to accomplish specific by-product distributional objectives. Each of these uses of the flexible tax system in financing orthodox public goods may be briefly discussed for purposes of comparison here. If the utility losses inherent in the adoption of a law or rule, applied uniformly to all persons in the community, vary among individuals, and/or if the evaluations placed on the benefits vary, the preferred quantity of law will be different for different persons. (For analytical clarity we assume that the restrictiveness of law or rules is continuously variable rather than discrete. This allows us to treat the collective decision calculus in the familiar economic model. All-or-none choices can be introduced, but the analysis becomes more complex.) There is no way that the structure of cost-shares can be modified so as to produce more agreement among separate persons. From this it follows directly that, unless side payments or compensations separate from the liberty tax are somehow introduced, *any* collectively chosen quantity of law will leave large numbers of persons in nonpreferred positions, either with overly restrictive law or with law that allows for too much liberty. Without compensations, there is no way that political entrepreneurs, even in some proximate sense, can move toward consensus, toward something that might approach Wicksellian unanimity. "Tax reform" is simply unavailable as an instrument of adjustment or compromise. To the extent that "tax adjustment" in real-world political structures is or may be successfully used to attain greater consensus on the level and mix of public spending on orthodox public goods, we must

4. See Thomas R. Ireland, "Public Order as a Public Good," typescript (Chicago: Loyola University, 1968). Ireland's discussion is one of the few that seems to be based on a recognition of the central points made here.

conclude that, by comparison, individuals will be somewhat less frustrated with budgetary outcomes than they will be with laws, rules, and regulations that directly affect their behavior.[5] The individual loss-function aspects of the paradox discussed in Chapter 6 are necessarily present. Groups may divide sharply between those persons who consider existing law to be overly repressive and those persons who would sacrifice further behavioral options for greater social order and stability.

A variation on this sort of adjustment that may often be available in the provision and financing of standard public goods, represented by components in a governmental budget, involves logrolling among intense supporters of separate items. But this avenue of adjustment may also be closed with respect to collective decisions on laws or regulations of behavior. The direct or indirect exchange of votes on separate budgetary items allows individuals and groups to express intensity as well as the direction of preference. For example, even under a predetermined tax-sharing scheme, those groups that intensely desire some expansion on outlay in, say, space exploration may secure this objective, at least to some partial extent, by agreeing to support expanded outlay, on, say, higher education, which may be intensely desired by a different pressure group, one that is not particularly interested in space. Such logrolling is possible, however, only to the extent that the relative intensities of different groups are differently directed.[6] With the imposition of laws or rules that restrict individual behavior directly, the scope for logrolling or vote trading may be very limited. Those persons who place relatively higher value on the maintenance and expansion of their own choice options are likely to be in agreement over most, if not all, of the proposed limits. The same

5. This argument may appear to be related to the analysis of direct regulation and effluent charges as policy alternatives in dealing with pollution, but on closer examination the two arguments are quite distinct. The pollution analogue concerns collective decisions on the quantity of clean-up (the public good) and the means of sharing the costs. Direct regulation does embody a determinate cost-sharing scheme, imposing differentially higher costs on those whose liberty of action is more highly valued. This is the equivalent of the adoption of any quantity of behavioral restrictiveness or law, as discussed in the text. The levy of effluent charges provides an alternative means of attaining chosen targets, along with alternative means of sharing costs. But effluent charges are not analogous to modifications or adjustments in the distribution of tax-prices so as to produce more widespread agreement on preferred quantities in the orthodox public-goods model.

6. For extended discussion, see Buchanan and Tullock, *The Calculus of Consent*, especially Chapter 10.

applies to those who place relatively little value on freedom of choice. "Law and order" advocates are likely to desire more restrictive regulations on pornography *and* on drugs.

We may now discuss the second use of the adjustment in tax-shares in the financing of orthodox public goods and demonstrate that this use, like the one of attaining agreement, is not available with respect to public restrictions on behavior. Even if no attempt is made to adjust taxes so as to secure more agreement on budgetary outlays, the possibility of manipulating relative tax-share offers a means of accomplishing by-product objectives through the fiscal structure. This adjustment is best discussed with the aid of a political model which assumes that a benevolent and omniscient despot makes decisions for the whole community. He can determine the quantity and mix of public goods to be provided, and we may assume that he chooses in accordance with efficiency criteria, derived from the individual evaluations of citizens, evaluations which the despot is assumed to be able to determine. This allows the financing or cost-sharing side of any fiscal decision to be divorced from the expenditure side of the budget. Through changes in relative cost-shares, a certain amount of income-wealth redistribution may be achieved, while maintaining overall efficiency in provision. In the real world, some elements of this political-decision model are always mixed with the alternative democratic-decision model which implicitly informs most of the analysis in this book.

Any observed public-goods provision and financing can be interpreted as embodying some mixture of efficiency and equity results.[7] If, for example, some redistribution of real income and wealth from the relatively rich to the relatively poor is the acknowledged distributional objective, the variability in tax-shares, in total and at the margin, allows this to be achieved while retaining tolerable efficiency in the levels and mix of provision. But no such by-product redistribution can be accomplished by the enactment of laws or rules that are generally applied to all persons, even though these behavioral

7. For a development of this approach, see H. Aaron and M. McGuire, "Public Goods and Income Distribution," *Econometrica* 38 (November 1970): 907–20; M. McGuire and H. Aaron, "Efficiency and Equity in the Optimal Supply of a Public Good," *Review of Economics and Statistics* 51 (February 1969): 31–39. See also William H. Breit, "Income Redistribution and Efficiency Norms" (Paper presented at Urban Institute Conference on Income Redistribution, 1972, forthcoming in conference proceedings volume).

restrictions fully qualify as "public goods" under the standard definitions. The "liberty tax" structure is endogenous to the efficiency calculation, and it is not possible to vary the cost or tax-shares among persons. If the benevolent despot is fully informed about individual utility functions, he can determine the "efficient" level of behavioral restriction or regulation. He cannot, however, vary the relative cost-shares which this efficient level of regulation involves so as to promote a secondary purpose. Under normal configurations of preference functions, the efficient level of law may be unique, and this will, at the same time, require a unique distribution of costs among persons. There is a specific distributional result, but this result need not be, and normally will not be, related to plausibly acceptable equity criteria. Those persons who must, willy-nilly, bear the lion's share of the costs generally are those who place the highest value on freedom and liberty, relative to order and stability in the sociobehavioral environment, particularly those who place the highest value on the actions that law inhibits. Those who bear relatively little costs are those who do not generally value freedom of choice and action highly, particularly those who place little value on the freedom to carry out the activities that the law prevents.

Both sides of the individual's benefit-cost calculus must be included, and no generalized conclusions about distributional or efficiency results can be reached from cost-side or benefit-side comparisons in isolation. From benefit-side comparisons alone, it seems reasonable to suggest that persons in possession or command of relatively large quantities of private assets, the relatively rich, would place relatively higher values on the general application of behavioral restrictions. Those persons need not, however, optimally prefer more behavioral restrictiveness than those who command smaller asset endowments, provided that the restrictions are constitutionally required to be generally applicable to all members of the community. The utility losses suffered by the relatively rich in having their own choice options closed by law may also be highly valued in terms of a numeraire or common denominator. The relatively poor man may have relatively little to be protected by the behavioral limits to be placed on others, but neither does he need to place great value on his own freedom of choice and action. It is quite possible that the persons who command relatively little in private assets will optimally prefer more restrictive general laws than their more fortunately endowed compatriots. Consider auto theft as an example. A more restrictive law may take the form of intensified vehicle checks for registration and title. The poor central-city resident may consider the interferences with his personal freedom which such procedures involve to be a relatively small price to pay for the greater stability in possession that is promised.[8] The rich suburbanite, by contrast, may think that the constraints on his own freedom which general application of the proposed law requires are not worth the increased order that is anticipated to be produced. This possible difference in attitude toward law may become even more pronounced when collective decisions concerning severity of punishments are considered, the general subject to be examined in Chapter 8.

Agreement on Constitutional Change

The earlier analysis (in Chapter 4) of the conceptual origins of the constitutional order demonstrated the general advantages of defined behavioral limits, and, through this, the possibility of securing unanimous agreement on rules or law. No attention was given to nonunanimous and imposed changes in constitutional structure, although departures from unanimity were discussed in connection with postconstitutional collective decisions on the provision and financing of public goods. These operational departures from unanimity were, however, themselves conceptually derived from general, and presumably, unanimous agreement in constitutional contract, which specifies rules for reaching operational collective decisions in addition to defining individual behavioral limits. In this chapter, we have introduced the public-goods framework to discuss behavioral limits, or laws, which emerge as part of the basic constitutional contract, and the analysis has indicated that individuals are quite likely to disagree on the extent of restrictiveness preferred and that means of compromising individual differences available in standard public-goods decisions are likely to be of little assistance.

The undiscussed question remains that of how changes in the set of rules defining behavioral limits, the changes in law, are themselves to be made, and on what criteria. Note that this is not the same question analyzed in Chapter 5, which involved agreement on changes in the distribution of individual rights, best conceived in property terms. For those aspects of the basic constitutional contract, the analysis suggested that agreed-on changes from the

---

8. For an application with disturbing racial overtones, see Andrew Hacker, "Getting Used to Mugging," *New York Review of Books,* 19 April 1973.

status-quo distribution of rights were possible, provided that the status quo is conceived in a dynamic rather than a static setting. The question that arises from the analysis in this chapter is quite different, since we are now concerned with a different aspect of basic constitutional contract, a different aspect of general legal structure, that which draws the line between those activities which are to be subjected to behavioral restrictions and those which are not. Changes here are not strictly distributional; they are organizational. The issue concerns individual comparison between anarchy and law; and, as suggested, individuals may differ. The problem of securing general agreement on behavioral limits in this setting was discussed in Chapter 4 in the particular geometrical variation of figure 4.1 where the origin lay outside the lozenge enclosed by the indifference contours through the position of anarchistic equilibrium. As suggested at that point, agreement on rights, or limits, in this case requires something beyond disarmament, something beyond mutual agreement to respect limits to behavior. Compensatory payments in commodities or in a numeraire good may be required to secure general willingness to accept new laws, new rules or restrictions on behavior, or to relax or repeal existing laws.

The analysis suggests that there will be major difficulties in securing agreement, but, conceptually, unanimous agreement on basic structural or constitutional changes remains possible, even when individual preferences for behavioral restrictions differ. And there is no other criterion than agreement with which we might evaluate the overall efficiency of such rules, in the absence of the omniscient despot who is so often conveniently invoked. As noted in Chapter 5, however, constitutional changes can be imposed without agreement. Political constitutions which are at all explicit normally require more inclusive rules for changes in the constitution than for ordinary collective decisions. In practical fact, basic legal rules are modified through long-observed but condoned departures from explicit rules, through judicial fiat, through legal precedent, through encroachment by the legislature on what should be the separate function of constitution-making, and through numerous other instruments. As stated earlier, there is no suggestion that imposed nonagreed changes in legal structure do not occur. The suggestion or implication to be drawn is only that such nonagreed changes as do occur cannot be logically derived from individual evaluations, and hence at this level they have little claim to be called "legitimate."

Formal and Informal Law: The Role of Ethics

To this point the analysis has been based in the implicit assumption that formal, codified rules and regulations, requiring explicit collective implementation, make up the primary if not the sole content of "law." Before we consider further causes of observed breakdown in law-abiding, it is essential to incorporate some treatment of the role that ethical precepts play in maintaining social stability. First of all, as noted in earlier chapters, if there is no conflict among separate persons, there is no basis for social contract; there is no need for law, as such. By the same token, however, there is no need for ethics; there is no function of a moral code. In the strict no-conflict setting, pure anarchy remains ideal without tempering. When conflict does emerge, however, anarchy in its pure form fails, and the value of order suggests either some social contract, some system of formal law, *or* some generally accepted set of ethical-moral precepts. It is important to recognize that these are alternative means of securing order. To the extent that ethical precepts are widely shared, and influence individual behavior, there is less need for the more formal restrictiveness of legally imposed standards. And vice versa, although the superiority of securing tolerable behavioral order and predictability through ethical standards should be apparent. To the extent that the trade-off between narrowly defined self-interest and the putative general interest is internalized, and made to take place among the arguments within the individual's own preference or utility function, the resort to external coercive force is minimized. Ordered anarchy, organized voluntarily through privately imposed constraints on behavior, through adherence to basic norms of mutual tolerance and mutual respect for acknowledged rights, is surely preferable even to an idealized formal constitutional structure that might generate a like degree of order, along with a comparable degree of efficiency. And, of course, such a relative valuation would be enhanced when it is recognized that any practicable legal structure must diverge sharply from an idealized one. Significant differentials in levels of predictable behavior may be required before formalized law would be chosen over anarchy, although individuals may vary in their trade-off positions just as in their evaluations of the degree of restrictiveness of law, once chosen. Both anarchy and formalized constitutional structure must be distinguished from a setting in which individuals behave strictly in accordance with customary or traditional modes of conduct, with little or no connection with rationally selected norms. This alternative is likely to be grossly inefficient, and it must be placed beyond the extreme limits of formalized legal structure in its coerciveness. Under such a regime, order is present in the predictability sense, but this order need bear no relationship to the "publicness" of the rules or customs that are being followed.

Fortunately, perhaps, communities do not face either-or questions with respect to basic organizing principles. The status quo rarely presents the stark alternatives: (1) anarchy with full dependence on internal ethical constraints as the only means of resolving conflicts outside war itself, or (2) inclusive and rigid formal laws with a complete absence of internal ethical constraints. At any point in time, behavior that may be observed in a community reflects individual utility maximization, and the pattern of behavior is influenced by the arguments in the preference functions of participants, along with the internal and subjective trade-offs among these arguments, *and* by the formally imposed legal constraints on behavior that participants confront, constraints that are nominally embodied in formal rules accompanied by enforcement instruments, *and* by constraints imposed by custom and tradition which, although nonformalized, remain external to the individual and carry their own enforcement processes.

As mentioned in Chapter 1, many aspects of social intercourse are organized anarchistically, which means that the observed orderly behavior depends critically on mutual acceptance of certain informal precepts by all parties. Life in society, as we know it, would probably be intolerable if formal rules should be required for each and every area where interpersonal conflict might arise. An indirect test of the cohesiveness of a society may be offered in the range of activities that are left open to informal rather than formal control.

The individual who restricts his own behavior voluntarily, who limits his own freedom of choice because of built-in ethical standards, who acts in accordance with something like a Kantian generalization principle, is continually confronted with a dilemma of sorts. His narrowly defined self-interest may dictate departures from that pattern of behavior required by adherence to his ethical-moral standards. He is in a position analogous to that faced by the potential free rider in public-goods theory, as discussed earlier in this chapter. So long as a significantly large proportion of the community's total membership abides by the same standards, the temptation placed on any individual, although always present, may not be sufficiently great to cause him to modify his cooperative behavior. However, if and when some persons, or a critically large minority of persons, are observed to violate ethical precepts that previously have been accepted by almost everyone, and to act on self-interest grounds, those who might continue to adhere to the precepts find themselves subjected to what may seem to be exploitation. Once a critical limit is passed here, the standards may erode rapidly as more and more individuals revert to narrowly defined self-interest. The situation is in most respects similar to that in which individual behavior is restricted out of some precept of obedience to formal laws which carry with them no enforcement procedures.

This suggests that one of the most important ethical precepts may well be that of obedience to and respect for formalized law, as such. If individuals place a high value on obedience to law, as laid down through observed political-decision processes, utility-maximizing norms may produce surprising adherence even in the total absence of enforcement and punishment instruments. If individual preference functions embody this principle, it is the announcement and enactment of the rule or regulation that imposes limits to behavior that matters; enforcement and punishment institutions assume secondary importance. Casual empiricism suggests that this attitude may, in fact, explain much of the order that we observe, an order that exists even in those aspects of behavior when most persons recognize that enforcement of formal rules is nonexistent or woefully inadequate.[9] As with the more general ethical precepts, however, this principle of respect for law, as such, may be subject to rapid erosion once a critical minority is observed to violate the principle. In such instance, unless effective enforcement and punishment are

---

9. An alternative, but related, explanation of observed order is based on the hypothesis that individuals follow rules not because these are formally enacted as law or because of the acceptance of ethical precepts but simply because they are rules which exist. The origin of rules, in this view, is essentially evolutionary in an unpredictable sense. This hypothesis is supported by F. A. Hayek. See his *Law, Legislation, and Liberty,* vol. 1, *Rules and Order.* Hayek cites, in elaboration of the specific hypothesis of "man as rule follower," a book by R. S. Peters, *The Concept of Motivation* (London, 1959).

forthcoming, formal rules or laws may become inoperative as means of producing social stability.[10]

The Generation of "Public Bad"

The position of the individual under law, whether this be formal or informal, is comparable to that present in any "publicness" interaction so long as law itself qualifies under this rubric. In the absence of effective enforcement, external or internal, persons are always motivated to violate the standards laid down. This is true quite independently of a person's preferences with respect to the appropriateness or the inappropriateness of the standards themselves, considered as rational collective institutions generally applied or as viable and widely shared ethical norms. Even the person who places the highest benefit-cost ratio, in total or at the margin, on the extension of behavioral constraints through law may be motivated, in his private, personal capacity, to violate these constraints. He is, as noted several times, in a position akin to that of the potential free rider with ordinary public goods. Economists have adduced the free-rider dilemma to explain the failure of voluntaristic, market-like institutions to supply jointly consumed goods efficiently. A more directly relevant application explains the necessity of coercion in the instruments of taxation. Individuals may not voluntarily pay taxes even if their private-personal benefits from public spending exceed their nominal tax liabilities. Consider the person who has explicitly been party to the putative public-goods contract in which his assigned share of tax is matched against expected public-goods benefits. Suppose that he succeeds in evading his assigned tax obligation; this has the effect of reducing the total revenues available for providing-purchasing the jointly consumed good, the benefits from which are shared by other members of the collectivity.[11] In evading his tax obliga-

10. An excellent example of this interrelationship is provided in the testimony of Jeb Magruder before the Senate Watergate Committee in June 1973. Magruder justified the departures from formal legal requirements by the Nixon supporters on the grounds that the antiwar militants of the late 1960s and early 1970s had been repeatedly observed to violate formal laws without being subjected to the penalties which were presumably attached to such violations.

11. For a specific discussion of this effect in an externality setting, see my "Externality in Tax Response," *Southern Economic Journal* 32 (July 1966): 35–42.

tion, which is economically rational for the individual, he creates a "public bad." The person in question imposes an external diseconomy on all others in the sharing group, all potential beneficiaries of the jointly consumed good or service financed from tax revenues.

This is, of course, nothing more than the converse of the "public good" that is created by law-abiding. Failure to produce "public bad" is equivalent to the creation of "public good." And the failure to provide "public good" is equivalent to the production of "public bad." The choice between constructions here depends largely on the purpose to be served by analysis and on the relevance to real-world problems. If, as in traditional public-goods theory, the purpose is to explain why market institutions fail and why governmental action may be necessary, attention should be paid to the "public good" that collective action might generate. Much the same applies to explaining the requirement that law be established collectively. If, by contrast, the purpose is one of trying to explain why long-established institutions of "law and order" break down without effective enforcement, it is best to change the focus of analysis and to concentrate on individual behavior in generating "public bads," despite the basic equivalence in the underlying models.

There are, of course, many important modern applications of the theory of public bads, notably those which are introduced in analyses of environmental quality. The treatment of law violation in this section is, in almost all respects, identical to that which could be, and has been, applied to explain pollution in basic behavioral terms. To pollute the air or the water or to despoil the natural environment is to create "public bad." To violate established law, whether this be codified or present in prevailing ethical norms, is formally the same. The whole discussion might be subsumed under the general rubric of environmental quality if we are willing to recognize that the sociobehavioral environment is as important for the quality of personal life as the natural environment. The analysis becomes a theory of behavioral pollution.[12]

Why does an individual pollute? Why does the Los Angeles motorist add

---

12. For related discussion, see my "A Behavioral Theory of Pollution," *Western Economic Journal* 6 (December 1968): 347–58; and my "Public Goods and Public Bads," in *Financing the Metropolis*, ed. John P. Crecine, vol. 4, Urban Affairs Annual Review (Beverly Hills: Sage Publications, 1970), pp. 51–72. Also see James M. Buchanan and Marilyn Flowers, "An Analytical Setting for a Taxpayers' Revolution," *Western Economic Journal* 7 (December 1969): 349–59.

his bit to the already smog-laden atmosphere? Why does the family on a picnic dump its litter in the park? If the behavioral bases for pollution in such familiar cases are well understood, the extension to the less familiar terrain of law and order becomes straightforward. The individual pollutes, he creates public bad, because it is in his private, personal interest to do so. In creating public bad, the individual is creating or producing private good. It is through no malevolence or evil intent that the Los Angeles motorist adds to smog. He is not deliberately imposing external harm on others; his behavior produces this harm only as a by-product of his straightforward utility maximization, given the choices that confront him. The individual may recognize full well that there is a conflict between his behavior as a private decision-maker and that behavior which, if generalized to all persons, would produce results more desirable to him. But, in his private capacity through which he must act, there may be no means for the individual to influence the behavior of others, at least directly. Hence, it remains rational for the individual to do the best that he can under the circumstances. And since this is simultaneously true for all persons in the interaction, the aggregate result is pollution, deterioration in environmental quality, a result that may be desired by no one.[13]

The interaction need not reach what we might call full pollution equilibrium, in which each and every participant behaves strictly as directed by narrowly defined self-interest. Saints may continue to exist in every social group. And if ethical standards influence the behavior of some individuals and groups in the community, these may limit their own actions while others are allowed to create the public bads of pollution. If the two sets of actors are heterogeneous, and if the polluting groups remain within certain critical size limits, an equilibrium of sorts may be reached with widely divergent behavior patterns. Even here, however, the situation may be far from optimal, even to those who are the polluters. Despite the possibilities for such a quasi-equilibrium, once pollution on the part of some members of the social group becomes the observable and predictable response pattern, the forces at work tend to

13. For a general discussion that introduces several helpful examples, see Thomas C. Schelling, "The Ecology of Micromotives," *Public Interest* 25 (Fall 1971): 59–98. Also see his "Hockey Helmets, Concealed Weapons, and Daylight Saving," Discussion Paper No. 9, Public Policy Program (John F. Kennedy School of Government, Harvard University, July 1972). For a discussion applied to ethical standards, see my "Ethical Rules, Expected Values, and Large Numbers."

shift the system toward some full pollution equilibrium. This conclusion holds even if all parties recognize that they would have been better off had the erosion process never commenced. In the sequence of events, however, each party may have acted rationally, given the choice situations that were presented to him.

As of any moment in time, at any status quo, the sociobehavioral environment embodies some explicit adherence to ethical standards, some implicit obedience to informal rules stemming from custom and tradition, some obedience to formal law simply because it is law, some obedience to law that is due to effective enforcement and punishment expectations. These motivations may be mixed within the behavior pattern of a single person, and they may vary over persons in their relative weighting. From such a status quo, suppose that one person shifts his behavior pattern, and specifically that he departs from that behavior which would reflect acceptance of something like a Kantian generalization principle. He pollutes; he imposes an external diseconomy on all others in the community. By changing his behavior, the single person has modified the environment, he has changed the conditions of choice for others.

Consider a single example, that of auto theft. Suppose that one person who previously refrained from theft changes his behavior and becomes a thief. The precise object of his theft is, of course, under the ownership of a single party, and in this sense the external diseconomy is not general. But in making the behavioral change, which is presumably in his own private interest, the thief imposes diseconomy on all persons in society, over and above the directed harm to the owner of the automobile. Policing services must be increased if the same degree of order is to be maintained; these must be financed from general taxes. Private protection against theft must be increased, and this involves investment by all persons, and not only by those who have their property stolen. Insurance rates go up for everyone who owns an automobile. The predictability under which a person may own and operate an automobile is reduced. The quality of the sociobehavioral environment is reduced by the behavioral pollution that theft represents.

Although it is familiar in a sense, this example may be partially misleading because theft is normally forbidden explicitly in formal law, and enforcement and punishment institutions do exist. The behavioral pollution instanced here can occur only because of some failure of these institutions to accomplish their objectives. That things are not nearly so simple, even here, will become apparent in the discussion of Chapter 8. The pollution of the sociobehavioral environment may, however, be illustrated readily with other examples.

Consider the situation in the orderly anarchy that was the university community in the late 1950s. Although there may have been a few notable exceptions, most university communities were then characterized by relatively pure standards of free expression. Almost any student or faculty group could invite almost any speaker on almost any subject in the assurance that the event would be allowed to take place without disruption. The intellectual environment of the university embodied free expression, and expectations were made on the basis of this fact. In the 1960s, much was changed, and much more than has yet been realized. Certain individuals and groups, acting in accordance with their own privately dictated norms which may or may not have been based on some ultimate ethical values, chose deliberately to preselect speakers and topics of discussion, and to disrupt meetings by speakers and on topics that were beyond the limits. This sort of behavior cannot be generalized to all members of the university community without rapid degeneration into something akin to the pollution equilibrium previously noted. In the 1970s, the student or faculty group that considers extending an invitation to a visiting speaker must make some predictions about potential acceptability to dissident elements. Can anyone seriously dispute the statement that the quality of the intellectual environment was lower in 1970 than it was in 1960? And, once commenced, how can erosion be stopped? How can behavioral standards which allowed the university community to remain an ordered anarchy for so long be recovered once they are lost?

Legal Structure as Public Capital

The question directly suggests a critically important feature of law and lawabiding that has been left aside to this point. The structure of law, whether this be described empirically in formal or informal terms, represents social or public capital stock, the yield from which accrues through a sequence of time periods. The "public good" that law provides is analogous to the lighthouse as initially constructed; it is not analogous to the "public good" that is offered in the municipal fireworks display on July 4, something to be enjoyed jointly but only in the instantaneous time frame. This capital-goods feature is emphasized in the isolated Crusoe example. The very purpose of adopting laws or rules is to restrict behavior in future periods, restrictions that will, in turn, allow planning to incorporate more accurate predictions. The isolated person secures greater efficiency, he accomplishes more good for less bad, if he lays down rules for his own behavior in advance.

This element or feature does not change when the analysis is shifted to the many-person social setting, where laws and rules are designed to restrict behavior in the interest of mutual but not unilateral gains. It would, of course, be possible to analyze the possible emergence of behavioral rules or laws that apply only to a single time-period. Robin Hood and Little John may agree on a "law," with no implications that this would apply on other subsequent crossings of the footbridge. It seems apparent, however, that the capital-stock characteristic of law has been implicit in almost all discussion and, indeed, the word "law" would scarcely be appropriate in a strict consumption-services setting.

This capital-goods characteristic is important both in the initial formation of law, in constitutional contract, and in the maintenance of existing law. To the extent that an initial agreement on law, or on changes in law, involves major bargaining and transactions costs, the benefits of agreement may be insufficient to warrant enactment of formalized rules at all if the applicability of these is anticipated to extend only over a short time-period. Many rules that might be acknowledged to be mutually beneficial over time might remain nonexistent if negotiation and agreement should be required anew at the onset of each specified point in time. This point is indirectly supported by widespread practice of resorting to generalized rules for interactions that are known to be short-lived but which require some means of ordering the proceedings. Robert's Rules of Order for single meetings is perhaps the most familiar example. Groups acquiesce in these rules, not because they are necessarily the most efficient for the circumstances of the moment, transactions costs neglected, but because they are in existence and the inefficiencies may be less than the costs of negotiating a particular set of rules for the short-lived interaction.

The limited time-span of decision-makers is important in relation to the capital-goods feature of law. An individual, as he participates in the formation of or change in basic law which restricts his own behavior along with the behavior of others will make his own benefit-cost calculation for an expected life-cycle planning period. From this it follows that the individual's own expected benefits from the establishment and maintenance of law may be significantly lower than the measure of present-value benefits to an idealized person who expects to live forever. From this it follows that the legal structure which might emerge from the choice behavior of mortal men might be somewhat less restrictive on behavior, somewhat less inclusive, than the structure which might be judged to be ideal by some omniscient being external to the community. The divergence will depend on the subjective discount rate in the utility functions of members of the community, and if these rates are sufficiently low the divergence may be insignificant. An important positive hypothesis can be deduced here; a shift in the subjective discount rate held by members of the community will modify the optimal or efficient levels of behavioral restrictions that they mutually impose on themselves and which are embodied in law.

The most important consequence of the capital-goods feature, however, involves maintenance of the capital stock through time. As we have discussed in earlier chapters, the political-legal structure, the existing "social contract," need not be based on explicit choices made by those whose behavior it restricts. There need be present no consciousness of individuals having been party to the initial "investment" decisions that the existing constitutional structure describes. In this particular respect, there seems to be no basic difference between public and private capital. The person who inherits an embodied capital stock, measured in claims to private assets, need not feel himself to have been party to the investment decision, need not recall the sacrifice of consumption potential necessary for the initial capital formation. With a private capital stock, however, the legatee acquires full rights of disposition over both the capital asset and the income flow from the asset. He has a private incentive to maintain the source of the income flow that the capital asset represents. With a public capital, by contrast, the individual beneficiary has no such incentive, precisely because of the public-goods feature already discussed. By acting so as to maintain the public capital asset that the existing legal structure describes, the individual confers pure external economy on others in the current time-period as well as on those who live in subsequent time-periods. It may be privately rational for the individual to create "public bad," to destroy the existing public capital, to convert this asset into privately enjoyed "income." It is in this context that the term "erosion" properly applies. An individual's decision may erode the basic structure, reducing the stability of social interaction not only for his fellows but for those who come later.

We may pursue the application of simple investment theory further. By converting capital into income, future incomes are reduced. To restore these to earlier levels, abstention from consumption is required. Consider a simplified numerical example. An existing private capital stock has a present value of one hundred units; it yields an annual income of ten units over and above full maintenance. Let us suppose that, during some period, the owner "eats up" or consumes ten units of stock, along with the yield, generating for himself a consumption flow of twenty units during that period. This action reduces the capital stock to ninety units, and the subsequent yield to nine units per period. For *all* periods after this disinvestment, income must remain lower than before. If the owner decides to rebuild his stock, he must abstain from consumption by the full ten units, a feat that may prove difficult since his maximum consumption has already been cut back to nine units per period.

The numerical example is helpful, but it does not fully indicate the results of behavioral changes that might be interpreted as amounting to erosion in the capital value of an existing legal order. In the numerical example, capital yields income immediately on its investment, and at the same rate as that yielded on capital that has been invested for many periods. In application to law, however, it seems clear that benefits are yielded, in enhanced stability of interpersonal relationships, at an increasing rate over many periods of time. That is to say, the benefits from law increase in rate as the investment matures. It is as if, in the numerical example, investment would yield the full 10 percent return only if the asset is maintained for, say, ten years, and that this rate might, say, increase to 20 percent if the asset should be maintained for twenty years.

If the relationship between the yield on the public capital embodied in the legal-constitutional structure and time is such that a constant perpetual stream may be restored, once it has been destroyed, only over a period that exceeds personal planning horizons, the model moves close to one that involves "mining" rather than merely disinvestment. For all practical purposes, public or social capital may be permanently lost once it is destroyed. It may be impossible to secure its replacement, at least on the basis of rational decisions made by individuals.

If a diagnosis of society suggests that individuals, organized groups, and governments are creating "public bads" by departing increasingly from traditionally honored limits for behavior, by increasingly violating both formal and informal law, then a recognition of the capital or investment aspects of the genuine "public goods" that are being destroyed makes corrective action much more urgent than any application of a consumption-goods paradigm might suggest. (Perhaps it really does not matter too much if vandals disrupt the fireworks display; but if they bomb the lighthouse the crisis takes on more serious overtones.)

Law Reform and the Status Quo

Somewhat contradictory implications for reform or change in constitutional contract, for modification in law, emerge from the public-goods and the capital-goods paradigms. It will be useful to discuss these separately. When we examine legal structure in the publicness framework, with no reference to the capital investment feature, the relationship between efficiency and the underlying system parameters becomes apparent. The level of behavioral restrictiveness embodied in formal laws or rules that is optimally preferred by any individual, the level that might be deemed efficient by the omniscient and benevolent despot, the level that might emerge from a plausibly effective collective decision process—any of these will depend on the preferences of persons in the community, on the existing technology, and on the resources available to the community. An exogenous shift in any of these basic parameters will modify the behavioral restrictiveness described by the legal structure considered in its totality. We can best discuss this set of relationships in terms of the choice calculus of a single person as he tries to decide on his own most preferred quantity of general law, applied equally to himself and to others, and treated as a continuous variable. If we interpret ethical norms as affecting behavior through changes in the weighting of arguments in individual preference functions, the interdependence between formal law and preferences is obvious. Consider one individual, and we shall assume that his own preferences do not change. However, for other members of the community, treated as a unit, suppose that ethical norms lose some of their previously effective influence in constraining behavior in potential conflict situations. To the individual in question, the direction of effect on his most preferred quantity of formal law is readily predictable. He will optimally prefer a somewhat more restrictive legal system after the change than he did before the change in the preferences of his fellows. Similar relationships may be traced between technology and the optimally preferred level of law for the individual. These are familiar in modern discussions of the pollution of the physical environment. Until the advent of the internal combustion engine, no person may have rationally desired general laws restricting individual freedom to dispose materials in the air. In the 1970s, by contrast, he may find such generally applied restrictions desirable. The areas for potential conflict among persons, and hence those areas over which some trade-off must be made between unrestricted individual freedom of action and the behavioral limits of laws or rules, critically depend on the technology that is available and in use.

The effects of exogenous changes in the resource base are equally clear. In the most elementary economic sense, an increase in the resources available to the community reduces the potential for conflict. As resources become less scarce, as the economic problem becomes less acute, there should be less need for behavioral restrictions, for laws defining limits on individual rights. The primitive society cannot nearly so well afford the resource wastage involved in pure conflict as the modern, rich society, especially when engaging in certain sophisticated forms of conflict may itself provide utility. This elementary economic principle applies more or less directly to nonhuman resources. But what if the increase in resources takes the form of more human beings, relative to the nonhuman resources available? In this setting, the measure of nonhuman resources per person may well have declined while, overall, the community has become richer. The range of potential interpersonal conflict may have increased substantially with population increase, especially if space itself is treated as a nonaugmentable resource in the strict Ricardian sense. Increasing population concentration will tend to have the effect of increasing the optimally preferred level of formal restrictions on individual behavior. These parametric shifts may themselves be interdependent. An increase in numbers may, in turn, affect the influence of ethical norms on individual behavior. This generates a reinforced relationship between community size and optimally preferred restrictiveness.

If we can make the assumption that, for the individual whose calculus we are examining, the basic trade-off between freedom of choice and behavioral restrictiveness remains unchanged, a diagnosis of modern developments suggests that more rather than less formal law should be preferred in late twentieth century than in the late eighteenth or nineteenth century. Technological developments, increased mobility, and the increased density of population in space—these combine to suggest increasing interdependence and, what is the same thing, increasing areas of potential conflict. But, of course, we need not assume that the fundamental preferences of individuals for freedom and for order have themselves remained stable. Any diagnosis of modern society, especially since the 1960s, must also incorporate the observation that a fundamental shift in preferences has occurred at least for some individuals and groups, a shift toward individual freedom and away from constraints. Although its advocates may have exaggerated its extensiveness or its long-run importance, "the greening of America" is fact, at least for some members of society. The representative young person in the early 1970s does not value order so much as his counterpart in the early 1950s. The legal structure, along with still-influential ethical precepts, may seem repressive, which translates as embodying an excess of order relative to liberty of person. This person may stand willing to change the system in this direction even when he recognizes the opportunity costs as measured in disorder and behavioral unpredictability.

One of the most disturbing characteristics of modern society is the nongenerality of preference changes. If only a subset of the community's total membership undergoes the preference shift described above, while others undergo no such change, the disappointment or frustration with legal-constitutional structure increases, regardless of which set of preferences dominates the policy choice. If the new-found or rediscovered preferences for individual liberty characterize the politically dominant majority, or the institutions which assume the role of changing basic law, those who suffer from increased disorder will be harmed. On the other hand, if those groups that seek to maintain traditional standards of conduct, expressed in formal and informal laws, exercise sociopolitical dominance, those whose preferences have undergone the libertarian shift will suffer increasing utility loss through time. And, as noted earlier in this chapter, means of compromising divergent interests may be ineffective or nonexistent.

More generally, however, there is nothing in the public-goods paradigm which implies that the legal-constitutional structure should be stable through time. Quite the opposite. The analysis suggests that this structure is a function of the parameters of the society and that changes in these parameters will, and should, change the basic compact. There is nothing which appears to be particularly advantageous about stability in legal order except insofar as individual preferences include some positive evaluation on stability, as such.

This conclusion is, however, contradicted or opposed by an implication that emerges from the complementary capital-goods paradigm applied to law. Here the advantages of maintaining existing legal-constitutional rules, along with ethical-moral rules, because they are existing, because they define the status quo, appear. Law is not only public; law is public *capital*. Once this characteristic informs the analysis, proposals for reducing or for increasing the level of restrictiveness in society must surmount barriers that are not suggested in the complementary public-goods paradigm. This point may be demonstrated in an analogy to ordinary physical capital. Consider a person who inherits a capital asset, in some specific physical form, say, a building constructed in 1900. This asset yields an income stream of ten units per year, which, if capitalized, indicates the capital value of the asset to be one hundred. Let us make the further assumption that the owner cannot sell this asset in its current use. The scrap value of the building, which can be sold, is, say, twenty units. Aesthetically, the new owner may not like the architecture, and, economically, there may exist alternative opportunities for investment where one hundred units investment would yield 15 percent rather than 10. The building cannot, however, be converted into this most attractive alternative because of our assumption about its nonmarketability in its current form. Hence, despite the new owner's dissatisfaction with the asset, both aesthetically and economically, it remains rational for him to keep it rather than scrap it. Destruction would remove the income stream of ten units per year, with only twenty units of present value recovered. Rationality dictates holding on to the physical form of the capital until such time as the return on the scrap value equals or exceeds the return on the old asset.

This analogy is quite helpful when we consider law and the calculus of an individual concerning his optimally preferred level of legal restrictiveness. An individual might prefer that the legal structure, along with the prevailing ethical standards in society, take somewhat different form from that which he observes in the status quo. But he inherits the legal order as it is, not something else. And he cannot "sell" this order to third parties. His choice set reduces to the alternatives that the analogy suggests. He can scrap the structure and start anew, but, in so doing, he must realize that a large share of the income flow from the asset will be destroyed, a flow that may not be fully restored until new investments mature over time. Or, he can hold on to the structure as it now exists, despite his recognition that alternative structures would be more desirable over the long term and that higher yields might have been forthcoming under different historical circumstances. Straightforward economic analysis suggests that large thresholds may exist as between these choice alternatives. This is, of course, recognized in the traditional legal doctrine of stare decisis, and more generally in the basic mystique of orthodox conservatism. The analysis supports these in a framework of rational economic decision-making. The erosion of constitutional-legal order should be recognized for what it is—the destruction of social capital, with all of the consequences therefrom.

This does not, of course, suggest that changes in constitutional order should never take place. The public capital paradigm suggests only that the shifts in basic system parameters must be sufficiently large to surmount the threshold that necessarily exists between "eating up" capital and consuming an income flow.

8. The Punishment Dilemma

If man could but design a God who would punish for violations of man-determined rules, and would, at the same time, constrain his own impulse to power, stability and progress in social order might be insured. Only under some such scheme of things could the enforcer of basic constitutional contract be made genuinely external to the parties whose separate interests are to be protected without, at the same time, being granted power for potential exploitation on his own behalf. Only then could we think of social order as a game in which the umpire is neither himself among the players nor a potential seeker in the winnings. If all men should accept such a God on faith, on the "as if" assumption that such a God exists, and if all men behave accordingly, formal law embodied in the agencies of what we have called the protective state need not be observed. Abiding by the rules in existence, and secure in the prediction that others would follow the same rules, an individual could survive and prosper in an orderly regime of social intercourse provided that the rules themselves were tolerably efficient. But faith cannot follow design; the man who might imagine such a God could not himself faithfully abide by the precepts. Shivering man must rely on his own resources to pull himself from and stay out of the Hobbesian "warre."

As Hobbes perceptively noted three centuries ago, individuals at war with one another will join in contracting with an external peacemaker, and because they value peace so highly, they will surrender to him their own powers of resistance. In the Hobbesian model, the sovereign remains external to the parties who remain in potential conflict. For better or worse, Hobbes predicted the subjugation of individual men to a sovereign master, with the latter empowered to enforce "law" as he sees fit. But what if men acknowledge no sovereign to exist?

What if they recognize the necessity of selecting an enforcer from among their own ranks, one who has interests comparable to their own? How can the function of the protective state, the enforcer of the implicit contractual agreement embodied in law, be organized by those who are themselves to be protected? And, once organized, how can this state, this enforcer, be controlled? How is it possible to delegate enforcement power to an internal agent, and, once the power is delegated, to treat this agent as if it were external?

In this chapter, discussion will be confined to the issues raised by the necessity that the enforcement of law remain internal to the set of contracting parties. As the chapter's title indicates, these issues center around the dilemma of punishment, the treatment of those who violate law. In Chapter 9 the issues involved in controlling the enforcing agent will be examined.

Man cannot design a God, and man will not universally abide by the promises that he makes. The world is neither Christian nor Kantian, although Christians and Kantians inhabit it alongside their heathen and amoral brethren. The necessity for law enforcement must be squarely faced, regardless of our romantic yearnings for an imaginary paradise. Can man turn his scientific-technical talents toward the invention of some nonhuman agents, some robot-like entities, that will be internally constructed but which will function without moral impulse, without independent interest, without consciousness? Can an internal policing equivalent of the Doomsday Machine be invented and developed into a practicable institution? Are the constraints technical or are they based on Frankenstein uncertainties?

Questions such as these should not be dismissed out of hand. We need not reach into the extremities of science fiction to think of devices that could serve as automatically programmed enforcers. To an extent, such devices exist and are in operation, for example, electric fences and gun traps. But suppose that modern science, if applied with intent, could produce mechanical agents that would detect violations of law readily and, in the same process, impose severe penalties on violators in the form of physical pain. For example, suppose that it should prove possible inexpensively to install devices on TV sets that would cause them to explode violently if moved some specified distance from a preprogrammed location. The owner would, of course, have access to a code that would deactivate the device, allowing him to move the set about at will. A potential thief would not, however, have access to this code, and the device would be relatively invulnerable to deactivation in any other manner. This automatic enforcer would seem to meet formal requirements. It would protect individual ownership rights; those who were informed about the device would be effectively deterred from law violation. Those who were not informed would have nothing to fear unless they explicitly violated the law. There would be no danger that the device would do more than it was programmed for; it would not rise up and become the master.

Nonetheless, it is clear that modern value attitudes would probably not allow such a device or devices to be installed nor, indirectly, would they allow investment for research and development of such instruments. In fact, should a person install such a device and have his TV set stolen and should the thief be physically harmed, modern courts would probably force the owner to compensate the thief.[1] The basic punishment dilemma appears even in this quasi-fictional account of robot enforcement. Why are men apparently unwilling to punish those among themselves who violate the terms of the implicit existing contract, the law that defines individual rights?

The Cost of Punishment

From his professional base, the economist's primary contribution to discourse is his emphasis on the trade-off among conflicting objectives. His principle is that of opportunity cost; more of one thing can be secured only at the sacrifice of another. In Chapter 7 we discussed law, legal structure, as a public capital good, along with some of the implications that may be derived from this conception. As noted, there is for each person some efficient or optimal quantity of general law, defined in terms of a marginal equality between the costs of further restraints on liberty and the benefits of further order in society, with the increased stability that this embodies. Although it is less meaningful, and less operational, we might also define an efficient or optimal quality of law for the community by some aggregation over persons.

This derivation of the efficient or optimal quantity of law as discussed to this point is based on the implicit presumption that once some agreement is reached, once mutually acceptable limits are defined, each party abides by contract. As the analysis has indicated, however, each person retains a private

---

1. As witness the infamous gun-trap judgment in Iowa. For a general discussion of state laws, see Richard A. Posner, "Killing or Wounding to Protect a Property Interest," *Journal of Law and Economics* 14 (April 1971): 201–32.

incentive to default, and some behavior toward default can be predicted to occur in the absence of effective enforcement. Any enforcement is costly, however, and a more general model must allow for the simultaneous determination of the preferred or optimal quantities of law and the quantities of enforcement. Laws that might well be efficient in the presence of costless enforcement may be inefficient when the presence of potential violations and the costs of punishing violators are taken into account. The delineation of rights in constitutional contract, the definition of legal structure, is therefore related to the costs of enforcing rights, and exogenous changes in these costs will affect the system of rights that seem socially viable. When this is recognized, we must modify somewhat our earlier discussion of the protective state. Having once defined rights, individuals may be willing to turn over the enforcement task to an external agent, but with the proviso that this agent will carry out the enforcement task only to the limits preferred by the participants. The orders to the external agent cannot be, "Enforce these rights, regardless of cost," because the cost must be borne by those who assign the enforcement to the agent, and not by the agent itself. "Law-abiding," that which is achieved by enforcement, is a public good, but it is one that is not produced without cost.

Enforcement has two components. First, violations must be discovered and violators identified. Second, punishment must be imposed on violators. Both components involve costs. Resource outlays are required to search out violations and to identify those who are responsible; these outlays increase as the desired amount or quantity of law-abiding increases, given an unchanging set of individual preference functions. Once discovered and identified, however, violators must be punished or penalized for their failure to live up to the terms of the implicit contract under which law is established. Resource outlays are also required in punishment (prisons, guards, security systems, and so on). But the primary cost of punishment cannot be represented directly in a resource dimension. The basic costs of punishment are subjective, and these can best be conceived in a utility dimension. The imposition of penalties on living beings, whether or not these beings have violated law, causes pain, utility loss, to the normal person who must, directly or indirectly, choose these penalties. "Punishing others" is a "bad" in economic terms, an activity that is, in itself, undesirable, an activity that normal persons will escape if possible or, failing this, will pay to reduce.

This "badness" aspect of punishment is accentuated when the individual recognizes that he may himself fall victim to the very standards that he lays down. He may himself be among the "others" for whom the punishment is chosen. For some laws or behavioral rules, the individual's self-interest may override adherence, at least in certain circumstances. Traffic violations offer a good example here. Recognizing that he may himself violate traffic regulations on occasion, the individual may be reluctant to accept institutions that impose severe penalties, despite his preferences that all "others" than himself should be led to obey the general rules by sufficiently severe sanctions. Just as the individual prefers that all others abide voluntarily by law while he remains free to violate it, so, too, he prefers that differentially severe punishment for law violation be meted out to others than himself. Similar effects on a choice among institutions arise from the recognition that errors may occur in the enforcement-punishment process. Even if he knows in advance that he will violate no laws or rules generally laid down for the community, the individual must consider the prospects of becoming an innocent victim. In fact, "protection for the innocent" has been a central if not dominant objective in English and American jurisprudence.

Care must be taken to distinguish between the pain costs, the utility losses, that are involved in making a choice among institutions that impose pain or suffering on individuals for law violation, and the pain costs, or utility losses, involved in the actual imposition of the prechosen punishment. The former is under discussion and analysis; the latter may, in most cases, be delegated to an agent or agency. The "punishment dilemma" arises from the elementary fact that to secure the public good of law-abiding the public bad of punishment must be accepted.[2] We do not live in a world where men abide by law without threat of punishment; if we did, there would be no need for law, as such. We could achieve ordered anarchy.

The Time Dimension of Punishment

The benefit-cost calculus involved in determining a preferred level of punishment is more complex than a simple public-good, public-bad trade-off

2. For a discussion of the punishment dilemma in a different setting, see my "The Samaritan's Dilemma," in *Altruism, Morality, and Economic Theory.*

might suggest. Punishment, as carried out, is necessarily ex post; a person who violates law is punished after the fact. The objective of punishment, on the other hand, is ex ante; punishment institutions are chosen only for the purpose of preventing or deterring violations. Consider a person who is conceptually participating in a decision on the establishment of collectively determined rules for punishment of a particular crime. The benefits from punishment are measured in the anticipated deterrent effects; the costs of punishment are measured in the pain, or utility loss, suffered by the knowledge that overt damage must be imposed on those who are not deterred. This seems straightforward enough, until we recognize that, once a punishment rule is established and violation of law then occurs, the individual must suffer a quite different "cost of punishment" as he observed the rules in operation.[3] He observes persons being coerced and harmed by the rules, after violations have occurred. The damage that the violation itself represents has been done; no punishment will restore the status quo ante. At this stage, the individual member of the inclusive community, which includes the person who has violated law as well as those who are damaged by the law violation, may be strongly tempted to modify or to change the rules that he may have indicated to be preferred in his planning or constitutional frame of reference. The presence of uncertainty concerning the actual identification of the violator will serve to accentuate this mood. The normal person may suffer utility losses on punishing known criminals; he suffers even more from the prospect that some persons apprehended will, in fact, be falsely charged. In this context, the planning frame of reference may be jettisoned altogether; and persons may begin to juxtapose the observed costs of punishment measured in the suffering of offenders against the future benefits of having punishment carried out; the rationally chosen rules may well be abandoned or relaxed.[4]

3. For a generalized discussion of the different conceptions of "cost" that has relevance here, see my *Cost and Choice: An Inquiry in Economic Theory* (Chicago: Markham Publishing Co., 1969).

4. My discussion suggests that the observed punishment of offenders, ceteris paribus, imposes a utility loss on representative members of society. This may not be true, especially with respect to major crimes. In observing retribution or "justice done," individuals may actually secure benefits or utility gains. This will not modify the analysis, as such, although it will make the problem under discussion less serious than otherwise. In the

Insofar as currently observed infliction of punishment is allowed to inform decisions or choices about preferred levels of punishment generally, the subjective trade-off or discount rate between present and future will influence the outcome. As this rate rises, the preferred level of punishment will fall, providing that observed punishment inflicts utility loss on the observer. There are unstable elements introduced into the behavioral system once the effects of the subjective discount rate are recognized. Those persons who violate law also make their decisions in a time dimension. As noted in an earlier chapter, law violation amounts to a destruction of social capital. Those who violate law seek immediate gain; they try to compare the expected value of this gain against the expected and future costs that punishment involves. A decision to break law represents a trade-off between anticipated future loss and present gain. From this calculus, an increase in the subjective discount rate will lead to increased law violation. But, as noted, for those who are influenced by current infliction of punishment in their choice of optimal levels, an increase in the subjective discount rate will, ceteris paribus, lead to a decrease in punishment imposed. The analysis suggests that an exogenous upward shift in the subjective discount rate will simultaneously increase law violation and decrease punishment. This may, in turn, promote further violation on straightforward benefit-cost adjustments. As the observed breakdown in standards of order proceeds, the subjective discount rate may increase further. The system of order may be degenerative until and unless exogenous forces intervene to restore stability.

Exogenous changes in "tastes" may also set off unstable reactions under the conditions of the model implied here. A modern example is provided in marijuana consumption. The law, as it existed before the 1960s, nominally imposed severe penalties on those who consumed and traded marijuana. Presumably, during the 1960s, an exogenous change in taste occurred, increasing dramatically the number of marijuana users, and, predictably, the number of those who are subjected to punishment as established in law. The non-

---

extreme, if the average or representative person in the community should actually enjoy seeing others punished, the direction of the bias introduced by taking this into account would be the opposite from that which I have suggested. My own view is that modern social attitudes are much more accurately described by the model which my discussion implies than by its opposite.

using members of the public observed this punishment and, finding it unpleasant, began to clamor for a reduction or relaxation of legal standards. The effect is, of course, to increase demands for marijuana usage, with subsequent further demands for reduction in punishment, or "decriminalization." The sequence may be stopped only after the legal restrictions on behavior are abandoned and marijuana usage shifted to that set of social interactions that is organized anarchistically. The implication that may be drawn from the analysis, and the example, is that the basic social decision on whether such restrictions should be imposed should be made in an ex ante planning or constitutional stage and that this decision should not be influenced unduly by observed impositions of penalties.

The Strategic or Constitutional Dimension of Punishment

There is no escape from a punishment dilemma until and unless the relevant choices of institutions imposing punishment are made strategically, at the stage of constitutional choice-making, rather than expediently. The community will remain frustrated by its own complex institutional processes if it does nothing other than respond to violations of law, once committed. A response strategy can be, and will be, exploited profitably by potential law violators, and the community will be forced to remain in undesired positions, imposing less than efficient levels of punishment and accomplishing less than preferred levels of compliance, while at the same time suffering the pain of having to punish at all. It is precisely the response mentality in thinking about and in discussing issues of law enforcement that lies at the source of modern confusion about deterrence. Punishment that is imposed ex post cannot be a deterrent ex ante for the same offense. Hence, treated solely in a response setting, and neglecting the retributive aspects, the explicit introduction of punishment may seem arbitrary infliction of pain, action that involves disutility to persons who observe and, ultimately, select the punishment. The utility-maximizing response of the potential enforcer, as an agent for the community, may therefore be that of nonpunishment or of unduly light punishment, by comparison with that punishment which might be chosen strategically at the constitutional stage by the same community.

By saying that preferred punishment institutions should be strategically

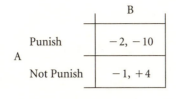

Figure 8.1

chosen at the time of constitutional decision-making and not at the postconstitutional response stage, I mean only that the basic law enforcement policy
and structure should be selected before explicit violation of law occurs, and
independently of observed violation, even in the recognition of the serious
utility losses that may, in certain cases, be borne by those who delegate the
authority to punish. In this respect, as in others already discussed, the instructions should ideally be given to an *external* agent, instructions which
should be irrevocable once made.[5]

The argument may be more carefully developed with simplified numerical illustration. Consider figure 8.1. Individual B has, we assume, already
committed a crime; he has violated a law. In a pure response setting, the
choice remaining for individual A (who is, we assume, acting as a participant
in the community's decision but is not, personally, damaged by B's crime) is
to decide whether or not B should be punished. (I shall use the simple either/
or alternatives here; more complex analysis could allow for continuous variability.) In the pure reaction context depicted in the figure, A may decide to
leave punishment undone. He will do so if he suffers utility loss in imposing
pain or penalty on another person, at least sufficient to offset the benefits
stemming from carrying out retribution.

In figure 8.1, the left-hand number in each cell represents a utility indica-
tor for A. As presented, if A confronts his punishment decision ex post, he
will refrain from taking action. To carry out punishment, to impose pain on
B, generates a higher utility loss to A than his failure to respond. Remaining
inactive in the knowledge that B is allowed to escape scot-free after having
violated law may also involve utility loss to A, but this may well be less than

5. Cf. Montesquieu, *The Spirit of Laws*, vol. 38, *Great Books of the Western World* (Chicago: Encyclopaedia Britannica, 1952), p. 35.

that which punishment embodies. The right-hand numbers are utility indicators for B. If he is punished, his utility loss may be relatively large. If he is not, he may secure utility gains over and above those already achieved in the act of law violation itself; he may experience joy in the knowledge that he has successfully exploited the "softness" of A.

As I have emphasized and as the analysis should have made clear, it is inappropriate to conceive punishment in the strict response setting depicted in figure 8.1. The individual A, here conceptualized as a participant in the community's decisions involving punishment policy, should look at the choice ex ante, that is, before law is violated. His decision should be based on predictions concerning the influence of his choice of punishment institutions on the decisions of persons, all the Bs (who will, in this instance, include A) acting under the legal system in postconstitutional stages, to abide by or to violate law. All persons are potential violators, including those who select the preferred punishment, and it is the general effect of punishment on behavior that should be relevant for the constitutional-stage strategic decision in which policy is laid down.[6]

The situation may be depicted in figure 8.2, where B's behavior is not predetermined. If A chooses to commit an agency of the community to impose punishment, after violation, and if this choice is known in advance and is believed by a potential B, this fact, in itself, may influence behavior. To the extent that it does, B may not violate law, in which case A need not suffer the utility loss involved in observing the infliction of penalty.

As before, the numbers in the cells are utility indicators, the left-hand numbers applying to A, the right-hand numbers to B. Note that, in a nonstrategic or pure response setting, there is row dominance for A. Regardless of the course of action chosen by B, the response adopted by A would be that of nonpunishment. If, however, A predicts that the punishment strategy selected

6. The argument developed here is, of course, essentially a contractarian theory of punishment, as distinct from a utilitarian theory, although there are related aspects. In a genuine contractarian theory, there is no problem raised concerning the "right" of some persons to punish others, since, in effect, individuals who find themselves in the implicit social contract that any legal order represents have presumably chosen to be punished as the law directs when they violate law. My argument seems in these respects to be close to that presented by Kant and, especially, by Hegel. On the Hegelian theory, and as related to the use made of this by Marx, see Jeffrie G. Murphy, "Marxism and Retribution," *Philosophy and Public Affairs* 2 (Spring 1973): 217–43.

	B		
	Abides by Law	Violates Law	
Punish on Law Violation	(.67) +4, +2	(.33) −2, −10	+2
Not Punish on Law Violation	(.0) +4, +2	(1.0) −1, +4	−1

A (to the left, spanning the two rows)

Figure 8.2

in advance will modify B's behavior, he may maximize his own utility by selecting the punishment alternative. Let us suppose that punishment, which we might assume to be a six-months' jail sentence, may be attached to a single violation of law, which we assume to be petty theft. Individual A, the participant in the policy decision, may choose to impose this punishment for this crime, or he may allow thieves to go free. Suppose that A predicts that an ex ante commitment to punishment will reduce by two-thirds the probability that B will commit petty theft. In two cases out of three, therefore, A's ex ante decision to impose punishment will produce a column 1 solution, one that is clearly preferable to either solution in column 2. On the other hand, if A does not select the punishment, he predicts that B will violate law in three cases out of three. If these probabilities (shown in the bracketed terms) inform A's choices, he will select punishment over the nonpunishment alternative. The expected utility for each alternative is indicated by the numbers to the right of the matrix. Individual A can expect two units of utility from choosing the punishment strategy, even if he knows that, in one out of three cases, he will suffer a two-unit utility loss.

In more general terms, A's choice will depend critically on, first, the relationship between the anticipated benefits from law-abiding behavior, from order in the community, and the anticipated utility losses consequent on the actual necessity to inflict punishment. Second, the choice will depend on the predicted influence on the behavior pattern of those subjected to the decision, the Bs. To the extent that A places a high value on order and/or is relatively indifferent to the infliction of punishment (a "hard man," who believes in retribution), he will, ceteris paribus, be more likely to select a relatively strict punishment schedule in his constitutional choice. To the extent that A considers the externalities implicit in disorder minimal, is relatively sensitive to the imposition of pain (a "soft man," who thinks all people are basically noble), and who considers himself as a potential recipient, whether as a result of law violation or error, he will tend, ceteris paribus, to choose relatively mild institutions of punishment. The predicted effects on B's behavior, impounded in "ceteris paribus" in the above statements, may, however, overwhelm the other determinants. If A predicts that the behavior of B (all the potential Bs) is highly sensitive to the penalties imposed on violations of law, the constitutional choice may rationally include a severe punishment strategy even if, otherwise, he fits the "soft man" characterization. Conversely, if the Bs are predicted to be relatively insensitive to variations in anticipated punishment, even the "hard man" may refrain from choosing a severe punishment strategy. If A predicts absolute invariance in B's behavior, there need be no strategic consideration in his choice; rules could simply not be enforced; the group would remain in Hobbesian anarchy.

The analysis may easily be generalized to allow for variation in punishment levels, allowing us to define the conditions for attaining optimally preferred or efficient institutions. As noted, an increase in the level or severity of punishment, chosen ex ante, will reduce the probability of law violation. This is the benefit side of the constitutional choice. But such an increase will also involve a higher utility loss because of the implied imposition of stiffer penalties on those who do break the law, the cost side of the ledger. For any person, A, considered as a participant in the community's choice of legal structure, the preferred or efficient level of punishment is attained when the margins are equated; that is, when an incremental increase (or decrease) in punishment generates marginal gains in behavioral order that just match the marginal losses which the more severe treatment of offenders involves, both measured in value standards of the person who makes the choice.

An additional simplifying assumption of the analysis must be modified at this point. I have implicitly discussed punishment levels, which may be conceived as involving a severity component (length of jail terms, amount of fines, physical pain, and so on) on the implicit assumption that the certainty component is exogenously determined. Characteristic of modern discussions of law enforcement, however, has been the emphasis on the effects of both of these components, certainty and severity, and on the trade-offs that are possible between them. To the extent that potential law violators predict with certainty that they will be subjected to punishment, the severity of the punishment itself may be reduced, and vice versa. The trade-off between certainty and severity introduces an interdependence between pecuniary and nonpecuniary aspects of law enforcement. Increasing the certainty of punishment for law violation may require substantial outlays on the discovery, investigation, and identification of offenders, that is, on improved policing, without substantial change in the aggregate disutility that punishment embodies. Consider an example. Suppose that improved police methods insure that five rather than two of each ten offenders are apprehended, convicted, and sentenced to jail terms of three months each. This policy may produce the same effect on the behavior of potential law violators as one that increases the jail terms from three to six months with no change in police input. The first policy alternative requires an investment of funds, and the costs in utility terms arise only because these funds must be drawn from otherwise desirable uses. The second policy alternative may be accomplished with relatively little additional resource commitments, but it generates nonpecuniary reductions in utility.[7]

THE GENERALITY OF PUNISHMENT RULES

We have discussed the punishment choice for A, treated as a participant in the selection of the basic legal rules, on the presumption that all potential violators or offenders are identical in their predicted behavioral responses to alternative punishment strategies. A major difficulty arises, however, when the number of potential violators is large and/or when predicted behavioral responses vary widely. In this case, which is descriptive of any real-world setting, the ideally preferred and efficient punishment strategy will differ over different potential offenders.

Consider the earlier numerical illustration. Suppose that the predicted response behavior of one group of potential law violators, the B_1's, is that shown in figure 8.2 above. The advance commitment to a six-months' term for petty theft will reduce by two-thirds the number of violations. As indicated, under

7. On this trade-off, along with a discussion of some of the policy implications, see Thomas Ireland, "Public Order as a Public Good."

these probabilities, the preferred strategy for A (or the group of A's participating in a collective decision) is that of punishment. If, however, there should
exist a second set of potential violators, the B_2's, which are characterized by
the pattern of response behavior depicted in figure 8.3, the preferred strategy
will be different. The discrete punishment alternative shown to be utility maximizing when applied to the enforcement of law of the B_1's will, when applied
to the B_2 group, reduce the violation of law by only one-tenth. Faced with
this array of choice alternatives, A will rationally refrain from adopting the
punishment strategy. In this instance, the utility loss which punishment itself
embodies more than counters the relatively minor utility gains secured by
the additional adherence to law that the imposition of punishment produces.

We may discuss the problem somewhat more fully with the aid of figure
8.4, I and II. Here we allow for three rather than two punishment alternatives. The model could, of course, be expanded to allow for continuous variation in the punishment set, but this extension is unnecessary for current
purposes. If the individual participant in the choice, A, considers only the
potential offenders in the B_2 group, and if his predictions about their response behavior are those summarized by the probability coefficients in figure 8.4(II), he will prefer the severe punishment strategy. However, if A considers only the potential offenders in the B_1 group, whose response behavior
is summarized by the probability coefficients in figure 8.4(I), he will prefer
the moderate punishment. The illustration clearly shows that preferred punishment varies with differences in predictions about response patterns. Note
that, in the illustration, there is no other differentiation as between the B_1
and the B_2 group. The utility indicators in the matrices are identical for the
two cases.

The constraints within which A must choose may, however, require that
the *same* punishment be imposed on all persons who break the *same* law. It
might, of course, be relatively straightforward for an external Hobbesian sovereign to impose differential punishments among different groups and, by so
doing, achieve a higher level of efficiency. Our question is the different one:
How can a community of persons, having agreed on some initial definition
of rights, agree on a set of enforcement institutions that will be tolerably efficient when behavioral response patterns are predicted to be widely different? Even if we leave aside all of the difficulties of establishing identification
of violence-prone individuals and groups, why should members of these

	B$_2$		
	Abides by Law	Violates Law	
Punish upon Law Violation	(.1) 4, 2	(.9) − 2, − 10	− 1.4
A			
Not Punish upon Violation	(.0) 4, 2	(1.0) − 1, 4	− 1

Figure 8.3

I
B$_1$

	Abide by Law	Violate Law	
Punish Severely on Violation	(.75) 4, 2	(.25) − 5, − 20	1.75
A — Punish Moderately on Violation	(.67) 4, 2	(.33) − 2, − 10	2
Not Punish	(.0) 4, 2	(1.0) − 1, 4	− 1

II
B$_2$

	Abide by Law	Violate Law	
Punish Severely on Violation	(.5) 4, 2	(.5) − 5, − 20	− .5
A — Punish Moderately on Violation	(.1) 4, 2	(.9) − 2, − 10	− 1.4
Not Punish	(.0) 4, 2	(1.0) − 1, 4	− 1

Figure 8.4

groups, at the time of the conceptual agreement, accept the imposition of differentially higher penalties? The benefits from the imposition of such penalties may accrue largely to other members of the community rather than to members of those groups that should, in some "social rationality" sense, be subjected to discriminatory punishment.

Any contractually selected discrimination in punishment seems out of the realm of possibility, regardless of the strict efficiency basis for such discrimination. As noted earlier, much of the public discussion and attitude toward punishment fails to embody the conceptual constitutional approach and, instead, tends to reflect simple ex post reaction to violations of law. In this context, there is no basis for differential treatment. In our example B_1 and B_2 violate the same law, commit the same crime. In its reaction, the community may or may not impose punishment, but there is surely no apparent basis for treating one law violator more favorably than the other. Any plausibly truthful scenario must, therefore, be constructed on the requirement that a single set of punishment institutions be applied generally to all persons in the community, even in the face of acknowledged differentials in predicted response patterns. This suggests that, for any set of institutions chosen, the sanctions will be unduly and unnecessarily repressive for some potential violators and unduly and unnecessarily permissive for others. Formal requirements for selecting the most efficient set of institutions and rules could, of course, be defined by assigning utility weights for the opportunity losses in the two directions.

Public Choice of Punishment

The formal analysis of efficient law enforcement has been developed in some detail by several modern economists, and this analysis need not be elaborated here.[8] In the elementary discussion of the preceding sections, punish-

---

8. See Gary Becker, "Crime and Punishment: An Economic Approach," *Journal of Political Economy* 76 (March/April 1968): 169–217; Gordon Tullock, *The Logic of Law* (New York: Basic Books, 1971); George Stigler, "The Optimum Enforcement of Laws," *Journal of Political Economy* 78 (May/June 1970): 526–36; Gary Becker and George Stigler, "Law Enforcement, Corruption, and the Compensation of Enforcers," mimeographed (Paper presented at Conference on Capitalism and Freedom, Charlottesville, Virginia, October 1972).

ment strategy was examined in a two-person construction, with both A and B taking on "everyman" characteristics as appropriate. Individual A, the participant in a presumed collective choice at the constitutional level, one that involves the selection of a set of institutions for punishment, can conceptually pick out a preferred option, given his own utility function, his own endowments and capacities, his predictions about the behavior of potential offenders in response to alternative punishment strategies, his predictions about the functioning of the institutions chosen, and some knowledge of the resource outlays required to implement the alternatives. His preferred solution will embody some mix between the certainty and severity components. If this were the end of it, perhaps the most difficult aspect of the punishment dilemma need never arise. In such a simple interaction, A might accept the necessity of making his choice strategically at the constitutional level and accept the implication that this choice, once made, could not be tampered with in response to expediency considerations that arise subsequently. But there are many A's in the community, including also all of the potential B's, and the selection of a set of enforcement-punishment institutions must be collective rather than individualistic. Each member of the group may reach a personal decision on his most preferred institution, but the separate individual choices must somehow be combined to produce a unique social, community, or collective outcome. All of the problems of aggregating individual orderings seem to emerge.

The set of alternative enforcement-punishment institutions that satisfy the separate personal preferences may be large indeed. In our earlier discussion of the conceptual constitutional contract, the problem of reaching general agreement was examined, especially with reference to general agreement on the quantity of law, in Chapter 7. Insofar as the first leap from anarchy takes the form of a disarmament pact, with persons agreeing to honor the rights of others, specific terms may be more readily agreed on. Tizio and Caio may accept a mutual disarmament compact in which they agree to refrain from invading each other's domain. This is not, of course, to suggest that the definition of separate individual rights emerges in some natural sense. It does suggest that, once definition is attained, the contract is more or less complete. The definition of the appropriate dividing line between those interactions subjected to formal law and those that are not was shown to be a much more difficult aspect of social contract. As we have conceptualized it, the basic constitutional contract must also include the terms under which the community may undertake collective or joint action in postconstitutional stages; that is, the basic constitutional framework must lay down the rules for making collective decision concerning the provision and financing of public goods and services. Individuals may differ among themselves over the working properties of alternative rules, and, because of this, they may optimally prefer separate structures. I have not discussed this problem as such; I have simply presumed that some general agreement on such decision rules is achieved.[9]

I have, in this chapter, argued that punishment institutions and rules should also be included as a part of the conceptual constitutional contract under which a society operates. The attainment of general agreement on a set of preferred punishment rules may, however, create more difficulties than almost any other aspect of the basic constitutional settlement. In this respect it is akin to the problem of reaching agreement on the range of law, discussed in Chapter 7. Even within the constitution-making process, some initial agreement on a decision rule may be required. Each member of the group will, presumably, have an interest in laying down some rules for punishing those who violate the basic terms. But since different members will disagree over the severity of punishment, agreement may first have to be reached on how a unique set of punishment rules can be selected. If a majority rule is chosen as the instrument, the familiar Condorcet paradox may be present. It is quite possible that separate individual orderings may not be single-peaked or single-troughed, in which case cyclical patterns may be generated.[10] Even if we disregard this prospect, the dissatisfaction of participants whose preferences are not median for the group must be acknowledged. A majoritarian decision amounts to satisfying the preferences of the median man. The selection of a set of enforcement-punishment institutions which makes the median man happy must leave others on both sides of the choice spectrum unhappy. There will be some persons who consider the median choice to be overly restrictive

9. In part, this neglect of the discussion of preferred rules for making ordinary collective decisions, and of the efficiency properties of alternative rules, stems from the earlier treatment of these questions. See James M. Buchanan and Gordon Tullock, *The Calculus of Consent.*

10. The modern seminal works on the voting paradox are Kenneth Arrow, *Social Choice and Individual Values* (New York: Wiley, 1951); and Duncan Black, *Theory of Committees and Elections* (Cambridge: Cambridge University Press, 1958).

and others who consider the median choice to be unduly permissive in its operation and effects.

As with the conceptual contractual negotiations over the range of behavioral restrictions, there must exist some means of securing general agreement on levels of punishment, provided that appropriate side payments or compensations separate from the punishment choice itself can be made. Those who intensely prefer severe punishment may, in some instances, purchase the agreement of those who prefer less severe penalties for law violation, or vice versa. Conceptually, agreement may be attained, but, practically, the choice of a set of punishment institutions presents more difficulties in attaining acceptable compromises among differing preferences than almost any other aspect of the imagined constitutional contract.

With the collective choice of an enforcement-punishment institutional structure, difficulties present themselves which do not appear in other aspects of constitutional agreement. As the analysis suggests, it is essential that the choice of punishment rules be made at the constitutional stage, where strategic effects of alternatives can be assessed and predictions made. That is to say, punishment rules must be chosen before punishment becomes necessary. To the individual participant in the constitutional choice, however, the strategic implications may not be evident. He does not feel individually responsible for the outcome that emerges from the group deliberations; the costs and benefits are diffused generally among all members of the community, and among many time-periods. The individual participant behaves as if he is purchasing a genuinely public good. He will not be motivated to invest in information about the choice alternatives.[11] To the extent, therefore, that a strategically rational approach to the selection of a set of enforcement-punishment institutions requires a more sophisticated analysis than a simple response, the collectivization of decision at the constitutional level introduces major complications. The rules for punishment that might emerge from a deliberative process may not reflect careful weighing of alternatives. The outcome may seem almost arbitrary, which, in turn, offers the temptation for

11. For a more extended discussion of these points, see my "Individual Choice in Voting and the Market," *Journal of Political Economy* 62 (August 1954): 334–43, reprinted in *Fiscal Theory and Political Economy* (Chapel Hill: University of North Carolina Press, 1960); and Gordon Tullock, "Public Decisions as Public Goods," *Journal of Political Economy* 79 (July/August 1971): 913–18.

tampering with the rules in a postconstitutional response setting. It is one thing for the analyst to suggest that community decisions about punishment should be made at the constitutional level, and that these decisions should be sophisticated in the strategic sense. It is quite another thing to suggest that the community decisions on punishment will be made in this fashion, either in terms of the levels of decision or in terms of the informational-analytical content.

Public Choice of General Rules

When both of the difficulties discussed in the two preceding sections are joined, the existence of extreme departures from individually preferred punishment strategies is not surprising. Consider an individual whose preferences and predictions lead him to hope for a much more severe set of punishment institutions than those that he observes operative in the community. This person will be dissatisfied with the punishment meted out generally to all potential law violators. But he will be even more acutely unhappy with the application of general rules to those potential violators who stand at the violation-prone end of the response spectrum. Such a person endures a double opportunity loss; the general institutions are nonpreferred, and the necessary generality in application accentuates the intensity of his dissatisfaction. The individual whose preferences and predictions are the obverse is equally frustrated by the observed operation of enforcement-punishment institutions. The set is nonpreferred in the direction of being overly repressive; liberty is sacrificed for order beyond his own personal limits of preference. And the application of the rules is also painful when those who are highly sensitive in response are subjected to the general treatment offered to everyone.

There is no escape from the conclusion that the punishment dilemma is genuine for any community that seeks to ground its legal structure on individual values. As earlier chapters have discussed, a conceptual contractual origin for the delineation of individual rights, the initial constitutional contract, can be derived. Furthermore, we can at least conceptualize a contract with some external enforcing agent (sometimes called a contract of government), with this agent being charged with the strict policing function. Such an agent must, however, be constrained in its application of punishment for law violation, and, presumably, rules or institutions embodying punishment norms must be selected by the members of the community in some quasi-constitutional setting. It is here that the dilemma emerges in its sharpest form. The genuinely democratic regime will tend to be reactive rather than strategic in its decision processes, and it will tend to renege on the punishment choices that are made in some prior stage of deliberation. The punishment institutions, as observed, will tend to reflect individuals' current motivations of retribution, justice, and compassion, rather than their rationally chosen long-term interests as embodied in quasi-permanent rules. The result can only be some structure that generates widespread dissatisfaction among members of the community, dissatisfaction which, in itself, tends to undermine the respect for rights and the enforcement of rights, respect that is essential to maintain the social capital that law, in its entirety, represents.

This much may be granted. But what is the alternative? We have discussed the possible delegation of authority for enforcement to an external agent, even if this agent is created and manned by persons who are simultaneously internal to the community. This authority may be allowed relatively free reign in locating and in identifying the violations of rights laid down in constitutional contract. But can this external enforcing authority also be empowered to make its own choices among alternative punishment strategies, independent of the preferences of citizens? There are historical examples where specialized professional classes of jurists have been allowed relatively complete powers of punishment. This avenue of escape from the dilemma, however, immediately presents another: How is the external agent to be controlled?

9. The Threat of Leviathan

Dictionaries define Leviathan as "a sea monster embodying evil." In 1651, Thomas Hobbes applied this term to the sovereign state. Three and one-quarter centuries later, we use the term only when we discuss government and political processes pejoratively, and then only when our purpose is to call attention to the dangers inherent in an expanding public sector of society. I have discussed the paradox of being governed in Chapter 6. In democracy, man considers himself simultaneously to be a participant in government (a citizen) and a subject who is forced to abide by standards of behavior that he may not have selected, including overt acquiescence in the confiscation through taxation of goods that he treats as "his own."

For late twentieth-century man, this bifurcation in his attitude toward the state is "natural" in the sense that it emerges directly from his post-Enlightenment, postsocialist cultural heritage. From our vantage point in the 1970s it is difficult to appreciate the importance of the initial change of vision which first enabled man to see himself as an independent will. I do not pose as an exegetical expert on ancient texts, but can there be much question that the conception of independent man, universalized over all persons, was largely foreign to Greek and Roman philosophy? Medieval Christianity introduces an ambivalence, in that individual salvation was stressed but almost always for the greater glory of God.[1] Only in the full emergence from the Middle Ages, only with Hobbes, Spinoza, and their contemporaries does man become possible independent of other men, of God, of state and city. In the Hobbesian jungle, the life of independent man was indeed described as poor, nasty, brutish, and short. But in Hobbes's ability to visualize, to conceptual-

1. See John Passmore, *The Perfectibility of Man* (London: Duckworth, 1970), pp. 90ff.

ize, such an existence at all lies the critical difference with earlier philosophers. Can we conceive of pre-Hobbesian anarchists?

Once independent man was set against the state, even in an argument that suggested rational bases for obedience, the potential for continuing revolution was guaranteed. The genie could not be put back into the bottle, no matter how logical the arguments of a Malmesbury philosopher. Man could now think himself into a role as king; in his mind's eye, man could now leap out of his estate or order, and some man or men would surely act out these dreams. Althusius, Spinoza, Locke, and, even more emphatically, Rousseau, commenced and continued to talk about a social contract among independent men, not a Hobbesian slave contract between men and a sovereign master. From contract among free men, all things might emerge, including basic law itself. For the first time, man seemed to be offered a prospect for jumping out of his evolutionary history. Man, in concert with his fellows, might change the very structure of social order.

The conception was as revolutionary as its consequences, the age of democratic revolution.[2] Repressed revolt, successful revolution, revolutionary terror, repressive reform, counterrevolution—these various stages in our spatially divergent modern history need not be discussed in detail here. We know that man failed to live up to the promise of his Enlightenment dreams. Hardly had some of the tyrants been overthrown and some elites vanquished, when others emerged. And once the political and social order was put up for grabs and was seen to be so, how could the economic basis of this order withstand assault? Locke's valiant efforts to erect a contractual superstructure over existing property rights were foredoomed to failure. If men, in concerted contract, are not bounded, need any limits be placed on collective action? Why need the economic order stand immune from fundamental structural rearrangements, especially when effective challenges were issued by Karl Marx? Socialism, in its varied guises, came to inform the consciousness of early twentieth-century man. The circle seemed almost complete; independent man once again seemed to have become submerged in an all-embracing collective will.

Once loosed, however, independent man could not be so readily destroyed.

2. For an excellent history, see R. R. Palmer, *The Age of Democratic Revolution*, vols. 1, 2 (Princeton: Princeton University Press, 1959, 1969).

The Soviet Union was not the future, as the Webbs had proclaimed in ignorant joy. Even in Russia, where man had scarcely attained individualized independence before communist revolution, his innate stubbornness made efficient control impossible. In the West, where men have experienced freedom, where freedom itself has a history, democratic socialism was foredoomed. Collectivized governmental attempts to do more and more have been demonstrably revealed to accomplish less and less. Man finds himself locked into an impersonal bureaucratic network that he acknowledges to be of his own making. He begins to use the term "Leviathan" in its modern connotation, yet he feels personally unable to offer effective alternatives.

This difference between prerevolutionary and modern man must be understood if the latter's predicament is to be appreciated. Modern man cannot place himself in opposition to a government that is staffed and directed by an exterior elite, by members of a wholly different order or estate. To an American patriot, there was George III. To a member of the French bourgeoisie, there was the ancien régime. To the followers of Lenin, there was the Russian aristocracy. To modern man tangled in the web of bureaucracy, there is only himself, or others of his same breed.

This is not, of course, to suggest that imperfections in democratic process are absent or that all persons possess equal power of influencing governmental policy in the modern world, and in America in particular. I am suggesting that, even if all imperfections could be removed, even if all persons were placed in positions of equal political power, the central issues facing modern man would remain. When we speak of controlling Leviathan we should be referring to controlling self-government, not some instrument manipulated by the decisions of others than ourselves. Widespread acknowledgment of this simple truth might work wonders. If men should cease and desist from their talk about and their search for evil men and commence to look instead at the institutions manned by ordinary people, wide avenues for genuine social reform might appear.

Wicksellian Unanimity

Why need there be constitutional limits or controls over the scope and range of governmental activity? In order to understand this, we may first look at the idealized model which gives to the individual full power over his destiny.

Consider a community that makes all collective decisions in accordance with a Wicksellian rule of unanimous consent. Let us further assume, this time quite unrealistically, that this rule is operative without major costs of reaching agreement. In such a model, each person is party to all collective decisions, no one of which can be taken without his express consent. How could the dynamics of such a decision model generate results that could be judged undesirable or inefficient by any one or by all of the persons in the community?

Because each person must agree positively to every decision taken, the flaw, if indeed one exists, must lie in the individual precepts for rational choice, not in the amalgamation of individual choices in producing collective outcomes. Analysis should, therefore, be concentrated on individual decision-making. Why would an individual agree to each one of a sequence of collective decisions, separately taken, only to find that the sequence generates an undesired ultimate outcome? Once the question is put in this way, numerous analogies from personal experience are suggested. Perhaps the one that is most pervasive is eating. In modern affluence, individual choice behavior in eating, on a meal-by-meal basis, often leads to obesity, a result that is judged to be undesirable. The individual arrives at this result, however, through a time sequence in which each and every eating decision seems privately rational. No overt gluttony need be involved, and no error need be present. At the moment of each specific choice of food consumption, the expected benefits exceed the expected costs.

The problem is not fully described as one of myopia in individual choice behavior, as a simple failure to take into account the future consequences of present action. Such myopia is, without doubt, one of the important bases for disappointment or regret when undesirable situations are recognized to be the result of a series of earlier choices. In this sense, all temporally related choices can be made to appear to be characterized by myopia. Consider saving and capital formation. From the vantage point of "now," a person may always wish that he had saved more and consumed less in earlier periods, and, in this vision, he may look on past behavior as having been myopic. More reasonable judgment might suggest, however, that each decision, when made, was based on some appropriately weighted calculation of costs and benefits in the "then" time setting. The decision to eat more than is dictated by the maintenance of some long-term weight standard is equivalent to a failure to save an amount sufficient to attain some long-term wealth objective. When this temporal interdependence among separate-period decisions is recognized, rational choice behavior at the "rule-making" level may internalize the interdependence through the explicit adoption of constraints on separate-period freedom of action. When he adopts a rule and insures its enforcement, the individual is exercising his freedom, at a more comprehensive planning stage of choice, only through restricting his own freedom in subsequent potential choice situations.

The person who recognizes his tendency to overeat may adopt a stringent diet. He deliberately imposes self-generated constraints on his own choice options. He locks himself into an eating pattern that he predicts to reduce the utility gains from separate-period behavior in exchange for predicted utility gains over an extended choice domain. The diet becomes the "eating constitution," the person's set of internally chosen rules that act to prevent over-indulgence. It seems clear that individuals may want to impose comparable constraints on their separate-period and separate-choice behavior in undertaking joint or collective actions, even in the idealized setting of Wicksellian unanimity. That is to say, individuals might rationally choose to operate under a set of constitutional rules for taking collective actions even if each person knows that he is empowered, personally, to veto any specific proposal that might be presented. In this setting, however, we should note that such a set of rules might be made operative by the choice behavior of a single member of the group. The determination of a single person in the community to abide by some internal constraint on the range of collective action would be effective for the whole group. Collective action would be constrained in this strictly Wicksellian setting by the mere presence of one person who chooses to adopt internal rules for his own participation in collective choices.

Majority Voting under Benefit-Cost Constraints

We move somewhat closer to reality when we drop the assumption that collective action requires unanimous consent of all participants. As suggested, under a genuine unanimity rule, individual decisions can keep government under effective controls. Things become quite different, however, once any departure from unanimity is introduced. When the costs of securing agreement are acknowledged, departures from true government by consent become necessary if the political community is to function as a collectivity. In the conceptual constitutional compact establishing this community, some set of rules for making collective or governmental decisions is selected, and these rules, once made operative, are enforceable on all members, whether or not they belong to the decisive coalition which effectively makes particular choices under the rules.

The most familiar decision rule, both in the analytical models of political process and in existing historical structures that are appropriately classified as "democratic," is that of majority voting. We may assume that some constitutional structure exists, a structure that defines individual property rights and enforces contracts among persons and, further, requires that all collective or governmental decisions secure the majority of the representatives of citizens in some legislative assembly. Even in this formulation we have, by assumption, already bypassed a significant part of the issue being discussed. At the stage of constitutional contract, when individual rights are initially defined, few persons would conceptually agree to wholly unconstrained departures from a unanimity rule for collective decision-making. The reason is, of course, that once an individual's consent is not required for a decision that will be enforced upon him, the individual holds no protection of his own nominal assignment of claims, no guarantees that his rights will not be exploited on behalf of others in the name of governmental objectives. At the same time that a collective decision rule, say that of majority voting, is adopted, procedural limits on the exercise of this rule may be incorporated into the constitutional document or understanding. Experience indicates, however, that the procedural limits incorporated in constitutional structures historically have not been very effective in curbing the appetites of majority coalitions.

Nonetheless, it will be useful for analysis to develop the argument in two stages. In the first, we assume that an economically meaningful constraint on majority decision exists. Assume that a constitutional provision requires that all proposals for public or governmental outlay satisfy a benefit-cost criterion; gross benefits must exceed gross project costs, regardless of the array of votes in the legislative assembly.

We want to look at public-goods proposals that do not benefit all members of the group sufficiently to offset fully tax-costs, but which do, nonetheless, meet the benefit-cost criterion imposed. If, for example, in a three-person group there should be only two beneficiaries of a project costing $100, and if each of these beneficiaries expects to secure a value of $51, the proposal would meet the benefit-cost criterion no matter how costs are distributed. If the costs are equally distributed among all members, say, by a general tax, the proposal would secure majority approval. The effect would be to impose net losses on the minority. The benefit-cost constraint guarantees, however, that if compensation should be required, the majority could arrange to secure minority acquiescence with appropriate side payments. Another way of saying this is to state that the benefit-cost criterion insures that all spending projects are "efficient" in the strict economic meaning of this term. Still another version, and related to the preceding section, is to say that all projects could conceptually secure unanimous approval if the costs of making side payments are ignored.

If each and every proposal for spending funds governmentally is required to meet the efficiency criterion, how could the aggregate budgetary level fail to do so? How could the overall budget be too large or too small? Since each project, considered independently, meets the efficiency test, it would seem that the test could also be met by the aggregate of all projects. As the discussion of the preceding section may suggest, however, this result need not follow when there exists interdependence among the separate decisions.

Consider, as an example, two interdependent proposals for budgetary spending, Projects I and II. In the absence of, and independent of, the other project, each of these proposals is estimated to cost $100, of which $90 is for outlay on the purchase of resource inputs, and $10 is for outlay on collection and enforcement. For each project, similarly, estimated benefits are $103. Hence, regardless of the way benefits are distributed, each proposal is economically efficient. Suppose now that Project I is approved initially under these conditions and that it is included in budgetary plans. Project II is now considered independently, but subsequent to majority approval for Project I. Direct outlay on resource inputs is again $90, as with Project I. But, because more revenues are now required in total, collection-enforcement costs are now estimated to be $12, for a total project cost of $102. Benefits are estimated to be $103; hence, the project remains apparently efficient, and we assume that Project II is also approved by a majority. In adding Project II to the budget, however, collection-enforcement costs for Project I may also have been increased, from the $10 initially estimated to the $12 estimated for Project II. The external or spillover cost that the addition of Project II generates for Project I is $2, but this was wholly left out of account in the choice-making sequence that we have outlined.

Note that, in the numerical example, aggregate benefits of the two projects ($206) exceed aggregate costs ($204). Note, however, that gross fiscal surplus is reduced below that which is attainable on the approval of only one of the two projects; the surplus falls from $3 to $2 in the process of adding Project II, which, treated independently, is equivalent to Project I. The numerical example is, of course, illustrative only, and the totals need not be taken as at all descriptive. In terms that are familiar to economists, we can say that there exists a divergence between the direct or separable costs of a single project and the genuine social costs, which must include all external or spillover effects on other projects or components in the budgetary set. When stated in these terms, economists might suggest "internalization" through simultaneous consideration of all the interrelated budgetary items. Care must be taken, however, to insure that the appropriate maximand is selected. Taken as a two-part budgetary package, both projects in the numerical example would secure approval, even if they were jointly selected. Joint benefits exceed joint costs.

The more general phenomenon that the example represents has considerable real-world relevance in terms of widely acknowledged economic effects and of observed political institutions.[3] Collection and enforcement costs are always present, and these costs increase as budget size grows, possibly disproportionately beyond certain ranges. More important, taxation necessarily modifies incentives toward the earning of taxable incomes and accumulating taxable wealth in the private economy. These effects are directly related to budgetary size, and these are genuine social costs that incremental budget-making can scarcely incorporate.

Politically, budgets are made piecemeal.[4] Different legislative committees consider budgetary components independently, and possibly divergent majority coalitions are organized in support of each component. So long as

3. For a very general and early treatment, see James M. Buchanan and Alberto di Pierro, "Pragmatic Reform and Constitutional Revolution," *Ethics* 79 (January 1969): 95–104.

4. Cf. C. E. Lindblom, "Policy Analysis," *American Economic Review* 48 (June 1958): 298–312.

benefits exceed costs, why should members of the effective supporting coalitions be concerned about spillover costs on components, past, present, or future? Political realism suggests the implausibility of achieving reforms at the level of incremental decision-making. Comprehensive budgeting, at either the executive or the legislative level or both, need not eliminate the inefficiency, as we have noted. Consider the position of a budget director or chairman of a legislative committee. By our restrictive assumption, any component must meet the overall benefit-cost constraint. But since this criterion is also satisfied for the budget in the aggregate, or may be, what incentive does this official have for reducing or eliminating particular components or line items so as to increase net fiscal surplus? Even if the official is ideally responsive to the demands of the citizenry, he will be led to incorporate too many components in the budgetary package. Consider again our two-project example. A budget director has overall coordinative responsibility; he must approve a project before it is submitted for a vote. If he eliminates one of the two projects, he incurs the displeasure of all direct beneficiaries. He pleases general taxpayers, but as we have assumed and as the real-world patterns suggest, taxes are more widely shared than the benefits. The indirect net costs that will be reduced by budgetary constraints are not likely to be sensed by the citizenry, and especially not in connection with specific budgetary choices.[5]

The inefficiencies that emerge when there exists interdependence among the separate components of a budget can be reduced only if these are predicted at some planning stage of deliberation. Because of the tendency of budget-makers and of legislative majorities to approve budgets that aggregate to sizes beyond those which maximize fiscal surplus, explicit size limits or other constraints on revenues and/or outlays may be incorporated in the fiscal constitution with the expectation that such limits will be legally enforced.[6]

---

5. It is not clear that the indirect costs should, in fact, be tied to specific choices. These costs emerge from the overall size of the budget, and are generated by all projects jointly. The problem of imputation here is identical to that involved in all joint-cost problems.

6. The discussion in this section has been limited to those interdependencies among budgetary components that tend to generate overexpansion in total spending rates unless constraints are imposed constitutionally. The facts of modern government spending should be sufficient to convince even the most skeptical observer that these are the interdependencies of importance. The analysis may, of course, be applied to interdependencies that

Majority Voting without Benefit-Cost Constraints

If we drop the arbitrary requirement that all proposals for spending publicly collected revenues meet criteria of economic efficiency, it is evident that majority-voting rules for reaching collective or group decisions will produce at least some budgetary components that are inefficient in net. Some projects that will secure majority approval will yield less in total benefits than they cost. The minority will suffer net losses from these projects, and these losses will exceed the benefits secured for members of the majority. In a regime with costless side payments, the minority could bribe the majority so as to prevent the approval of all such projects. But when the absence of effective side payments is acknowledged, the existence of inefficient spending projects can hardly be questioned.

Consider again a very simple example, a three-person group that has organized itself collectively. Taxes are equal per head, and all spending decisions are made by majority voting. Suppose that there are three potential projects to be considered, each of which costs $99, financed by a tax of $33 on each person. We assume that these projects are wholly independent and that the externality effects analyzed in the preceding section do not arise. The benefits from each project are concentrated as indicated in the following:

Person	Project I Benefits	Project II Benefits	Project III Benefits
A	$35	$35	$ 0
B	35	0	35
C	0	35	35

Under the rules that we have postulated, each of these three projects would be adopted, so long as each project is considered separately. In the process, however, each person will have paid out a total of $99 in taxes and will have received only $70 in benefits. Each person will be worse off with the three-

---

tend to reduce total spending below efficiency limits, considered in the large. This might emerge, for example, if separated budgetary components should be complementary in individual utility functions. It would surely be stretching the limits of plausibility, however, to argue that these budget-reducing interdependencies overweigh those that are budget-increasing.

project budget than he would be with no budget at all. It is clear from this example that budgets will tend to be overexpanded under simple majority voting rules if budgetary components are considered separately in the legislative deliberations, and if benefits are more concentrated than taxes.

There is, however, a difference between this and the earlier model where we assumed projects to be interdependent. In this model, which we might call one of simple majority exploitation of the minority, "internalization" in the form of comprehensive or package consideration of the whole budget may eliminate some of the inefficiency. If the three-man group in this example should be forced, by institutional-constitutional requirement, to treat projects in a bundle rather than in isolation, and if members of the group accurately measure costs and benefits, projects that are demonstrably damaging in the net for all persons will not secure approval. Alternatively, constitutional restrictions might be imposed which dictate that only spending proposals that promise *general* benefits to the whole membership of the community can be considered.[7] Historically, procedural requirements have been interpreted to dictate tax uniformity or generality, at least over broad groupings. For the benefits side, however, no fully comparable requirements have been applied. As a result, there are relatively few effective limits on the fiscal exploitation of minorities through orderly democratic procedures in the United States.[8]

7. For a detailed discussion of the United States constitutional requirements for tax uniformity and the asymmetry between the tax and spending sides of the fiscal account in this respect, see Tuerck, "Constitutional Asymmetry"; and idem, "Uniformity in Taxation."

8. As the analysis suggests there will tend to be overexpansion in the size of the public sector under the conditions postulated. Furthermore, these conditions are abstract representations of the real world. I should again emphasize, however, that the analysis, as such, is fully symmetrical. If we should postulate rules that allow nonuniformity and nongenerality in taxation while requiring that all spending projects generate benefits uniformly or generally to all citizens, majority voting would tend to produce a public sector that is relatively too small when measured against standard efficiency criteria. The asymmetry emerges from the historical record, not from the analysis. Constitutions, as they have been interpreted, do embody requirements that taxes be imposed generally. They do not embody comparable requirements on the benefits side of the ledger. This general statement is only slightly mitigated by the recognition that special loopholes in the tax structure shift the pattern in the direction of symmetry.

LOGROLLING AND MINORITY BENEFITS

The majority voting model discussed above suggests that inefficient budgetary projects may secure approval if considered separately, but that, at a minimum, the estimated value of benefits from any proposal to the members of an effective majority coalition must exceed the tax-costs borne by those members. Even this minimal constraint on budgetary inefficiency is not operative, however, when logrolling can take place among divergent minorities to produce effective majority coalitions on a subgroup of budgetary items. This procedure is familiarly known as "pork barrel" legislation in the American setting.[9]

Political Income, Bureaucratic Rents, and Franchise

To this point, the models of collective decision-making examined have not allowed for the influence of politicians, governmental employees, or bureaucrats on budgetary outcomes. Implicitly, the models have contained the assumption that voters demand publicly supplied goods and services which, once approved, are made available to final beneficiaries or consumers directly. There is no intermediation by legislative representatives and no administration by bureaucratic agencies. Such models are useful for general purposes, and especially so when budgets are relatively small. In modern democracies, however, more than one-third of the national product is organized through the governmental sector. In these settings, neglect of the influence of politicians and bureaucrats on budgetary results may severely weaken the relevance of any analysis.

POLITICIANS' PREFERENCES AND
BUDGETARY BIAS

Collective decisions are rarely made directly by voters, by those persons who pay the taxes and who are supposed to benefit from the provision of govern-

9. For an extended discussion of logrolling, along with other analysis relevant to the earlier discussion, see James M. Buchanan and Gordon Tullock, *The Calculus of Consent*.

mental goods and services. Effective political organization requires that the roles of voters be limited largely if not entirely to the selection of representatives, persons from their own ranks, who will then participate in legislative and executive decision-making. These politicians are the men who make the direct and final choices on the quantities of public goods and services and on the size of the total budget along with its composition and financing.

It is unrealistic to assume that elected officials who occupy executive and legislative positions of responsibility have no personal preferences about the overall size of the public sector, its sources of revenue, and, most important, about the particular components for public outlays. A person who is genuinely indifferent in all these respects would not be attracted to politics, either as a profession or as an avocation. Politicians are likely to be those persons who do have personal preferences about such matters and who are attracted to politics precisely because they think that, through politics, they can exercise some influence over collective outcomes. Once this basic, if simple, point is recognized, it is easy to see that budgetary results will not fully reflect voters' preferences, even of those who are members of the effective coalition that achieves victory for its own candidate or party.

Once elected, a politician has considerable freedom for choosing his own preferred position on spending or tax issues. He is constrained by voters indirectly through prospects for reelection, for long-term party support, for generalized public acclaim. But even for the politician who is highly sensitive to these indirect constraints, there remains freedom of choice over substantial ranges of the political spectrum. Within what he treats as his feasible set, the politician will choose that alternative or option which maximizes his own, not his constituents', utility. This opportunity offers one of the primary motivations to politicians. In a meaningful sense, this is "political income," and it must be reckoned as a part of the total rewards of office.[10]

---

10. This "political income" may be, but need not be, convertible directly into a monetary equivalent. Both incorruptible and corruptible politicians' behavior can be incorporated in the general model. The attractiveness of "political income" will be dependent, in part, on the compensation of politicians. At sufficiently high official salaries, persons may be attracted to politics who place relatively low values on the "political income" components.

For a general analysis of "political income" and its influence on budgets, see Robert J. Barro, "The Control of Politicians: An Economic Model," *Public Choice* 14 (Spring 1973):

The existence of opportunities for politicians to maximize personal preferences within constraints need not be of relevance to the subject matter of this chapter if the effects on budget-making could be predicted to be symmetrical or unbiased. If the "slippage" between the preferences of voters and the results emerging from the actual budgetary process should involve roughly offsetting differences on the up and down sides, no net influence on aggregate budgetary size would be exercised. Unfortunately, a unidirectional bias toward expansion in the fiscal accounts seems to be present. This direction of the political leader's preference bias involves several distinguishable elements. In the first place, those persons who place relatively high values on the ability to influence collective outcomes, and who do so in the genuinely incorruptible sense of desiring to "do good" for the whole community, are quite likely to be those who seek to accomplish their own preferred social objectives through collective or governmental means. By contrast, those persons who, ideologically, desire that the governmental role in society should be reduced to minimal levels are unlikely to be attracted to politics. Few natural anarchists or libertarians frequent capital cloakrooms.

Ideologues aside, persons may be attracted to politics because they intrinsically place high values on the power to make decisions affecting the lives of others. This characteristic is different from the first, where power to influence collective decision is instrumentally desired for the purpose of furthering social objectives. Some politicians may have very ill-defined objectives for social policy and those that they do have may seem relatively unimportant. They may seek political and/or elected office, however, because they enjoy positions of leadership and authority, positions that make it necessary for other persons actively to seek them out and solicit their assistance. This sort of politician secures utility more directly than his ideologue counterpart; his utility is increased by the emoluments of office that necessarily arise from public knowledge about the location of decision-making authority. If the list or menu for choice should be fixed in advance, the behavior of politicians of such nonideological stripe might produce results that are closer to the true preferences of voters. This correspondence would emerge from the desires to meet the demands of the largest possible number of constituents. In such

---

19–42. See also Thomas R. Ireland, "The Politician's Dilemma: What to Represent," *Public Choice* 12 (Spring 1972): 35–42.

case, no directional budgetary bias would be introduced by the necessary departures from pure democracy. When the list or menu for political choice is not predetermined, however, the directional bias toward expanded budgets again arises. The politician who secures his utility only because he chooses for and thereby pleases the largest number of constituents will find that favorable action on differentially beneficial spending projects offers more reward than favorable action reducing general tax-costs. The politician's bias, in this respect, is an additional institutional aspect of the asymmetry between the spending and taxing sides of the fiscal account. Because taxes cannot readily be lowered in a differential manner, there is a public-goods barrier which inhibits independent politician initiative toward tax reduction. By contrast, because the benefits from government spending may be differentially directed toward particular subgroups in the community, politicians are motivated to initiate the formation of coalitions that will exploit these latent demand opportunities. Given his degree of freedom to influence outcomes, the non-ideological politician's behavior will tend to generate an exaggerated version of the nonpolitician model analyzed earlier. Because of the asymmetry in the effective fiscal constitution, aggregate spending will tend to be inefficiently large even if the ultimate demands of voters-taxpayers-beneficiaries could be accurately reflected in final outcomes. The introduction of politicians as the direct decision-makers will extend the results even beyond such limits.

To this point, we have assumed implicitly that both the ideological and the nonideological politicians are incorruptible and seek no pecuniary gain from political office over and beyond formal compensation. To these two types of officials it is now necessary to add a third, that of the politician who does seek pecuniary gains from his office. The direction of budgetary bias is the same as before. The prospect for profitable bribes, kickbacks, or by-product deals is directly related to the size and complexity of total government budgets, and, more generally, of the total governmental operation in the economy. With minimal governmental intrusion into the economy, with minimal and quasi-permanent spending components, the grasping politician may have little or no opportunities for graft. However, with a complex public sector, and one that involves new and expanding spending programs, there may be numerous opportunities. In a newly enacted program, one without established guidelines and procedures, politicians may find ample sources for direct and indirect kickbacks from the producers and producing firms whose rents are enhanced by the program. Such officials will, therefore, seek continually to enlarge budgets and, especially, to introduce new and different programs. On the other hand, the potentially corrupt politician would rarely press for general budgetary reduction. The direction of bias seems apparent, again under the institutional proviso that taxes are distributed more generally than the benefits of public spending.[11]

Elected politicians may fall into either one of the three categories discussed, or a single politician may himself represent some mixture of two or all three of the types. The directional bias on budgetary size is the same for all types. Although their reasons may differ, the ideologue, the seeker after public acclaim, and the profiteer each will be motivated to expand the size and scope of the governmental sector of the economy.

BUREAUCRATIC RENTS AND FRANCHISE

Even after elected politicians make taxing and spending decisions, public goods and services do not flow automatically and directly from competitively organized suppliers outside the economy to final consumers within the economy. Governments, when authorized to do so, may purchase inputs from independent private suppliers (individuals and firms) and combine these to produce outputs. Or, alternatively, governments may purchase final outputs after these have been produced by private suppliers and distribute these to beneficiaries. In either case, and much more extensively in the former than in the latter, employees must be hired to implement the complex fiscal transaction between the ultimate taxpayer-purchaser on the one hand and the ultimate beneficiary-consumer on the other, even if, in some net accounting, these may be the same persons. Once elected officials, as representatives of the voters, decide on a quantity and a distribution of taxes, other officials (agents) must be employed to collect the revenues. Accountants must be hired to keep the books; auditors must be added to check the agents and the accountants. Inspectors must be available to search out recalcitrant taxpayers.

---

11. To the extent that tax loopholes can be opened up for the benefit of specialized subgroups, tax-side opportunities are available to potentially corrupt officials. As noted earlier, however, these departures from generality on the tax side seem relatively small by comparison with those prevalent on the expenditure side of the account.

On the spending side, budget specialists are required to maintain and present details of complex programs and to make comparative evaluations. Purchasing agents must carry out buying tasks in the framework of procedures worked out by still another layer of bureaucratic personnel. And personnel specialists are necessary to get personnel.

All of these would be needed even if no direct production of goods and services takes place within the governmental sector itself. Once direct production is attempted, massive numbers of additional employees are needed. If government produces postal services, mail clerks, postmen, and postmasters must be hired. If government produces education, administrators, teachers, supervisors, and custodians become government employees along with others who must evaluate the credentials of those who produce the services. The list can be extended almost without limit.

If taxpayers-voters, acting through their elected politicians, should be able to secure government employees externally at competitively determined wage and salary scales, the necessary existence of a bureaucratic superstructure need not itself introduce major distortion in the budgetary process. As with the enforcement problem discussed in earlier chapters, however, difficulties arise from the necessity of staffing government with persons drawn from within the political community. The sequence of budgetary outcomes tends to be biased toward overexpansion because of the potential for earning producer rents which government employment offers and because employees hold voting rights in the polity. If bureaucrats could not vote, the existence of producer rents from government employment would increase the costs of public-supplied goods and services, but this alone would not bias the results significantly. On the other hand, even if bureaucrats hold the voting franchise, no problem might arise if governmental wage and salary scales, along with tenure and promotion policies, were competitively determined. In the real world, however, governmental employees have full voting rights, *and* governmental salaries and working conditions are not settled in competitive markets.

Regardless of his interest as a demander-taxpayer or final beneficiary of a publicly provided good, a person who expects to be or is already employed by the governmental agency that provides this good will tend to favor increases and to oppose reductions in budgeted outlay. (How many medical researchers at NIH would support reductions in federal government outlays on medical research?) If he holds a voting franchise, the prospective or actual employee becomes a built-in supporter of budgetary expansion and a built-in opponent of budgetary reduction, not only for the particular component within his immediate concern but for other components as well. As students of political economy have long recognized, producer interests tend to dominate consumer interests, and the producer interests of government employees are no different from those of any other group in society. Two additional elements accentuate the effects of bureaucratic franchise on budget size. As with elected politicians, those who are attracted to governmental employment are likely to exhibit personal preferences for collective action, at least by comparison with those who are employed in the private sector. More important, because of specific producer interest that a working bureaucrat recognizes, the exercise of ultimate voting privileges is more likely to occur. Empirical evidence supports this inference; the proportion of governmental employees who vote is significantly higher than the proportion of nongovernmental employees. The result is that members of the bureaucracy can exert a disproportionate influence on electoral outcomes.

The franchising of bureaucrats need not involve serious budgetary bias when total government employment remains small. As the public sector continues to grow, however, the voting power, and hence the political power, of franchised bureaucrats cannot be neglected. In modern America, where roughly one in each five employees works for government, bureaucrats have become a major fiscal constituency, and one that politicians seeking elective office recognize and respect.[12]

This influence would be present even in an ideally working bureaucracy so long as net rents were earned in government employment. As we must recognize, however, no structure can approach the old-fashioned textbook ideal in which bureaucrats merely carry out or execute policy directives chosen for them by legislative authorities.[13] Bureaucrats, like elected politicians,

12. Much of the discussion in this section is based on a set of papers on governmental growth prepared at Virginia Polytechnic Institute and State University in 1972 and 1973. These papers are included in Thomas Borcherding, ed., *Bureaucrats and Budgets* (Duke University Press, forthcoming).

13. For a discussion which contrasts the older view with the more modern one, see Vincent Ostrom, *The Intellectual Crisis in American Public Administration* (University: University of Alabama Press, 1973).

possess varying degrees of freedom to select among alternatives. A collective decision, as made by a legislative assembly, is never sufficiently definitive to leave no scope for exercise of authority on the part of administrators of the program. Within limits, the nonelected government employee makes final decisions about government actions. Stated in a somewhat converse way, the legislature or elected executive can never exercise full control over the behavior of bureaucrats in the structural hierarchy, and any attempts to gain full control would involve prohibitive costs.[14] Within the constraints that he faces, the bureaucrat tries to maximize his own utility. He is no different from anyone else in this respect. He can hardly be expected to further some vaguely defined "public interest" unless this is consistent with his own, as he defines the latter.

Once this point, again a very simple one, is acknowledged, the influence of the bureaucracy on budgetary results can be predicted to be unidirectional. The individual who finds himself in a bureaucratic hierarchy, who knows that he earns net rents when he compares his situation with his private-sector opportunities, looks directly at the reward and penalty structure within the hierarchy. He knows that his career prospects, his chances for promotion and tenure in employment, are enhanced if the size of the distinct budgetary component with which he is associated increases. He will, therefore, exercise his own choices, whenever possible, to increase rather than to decrease project and agency budgets. There is little or no potential reward to the governmental employee who proposes to reduce or limit his own agency or bureau. Institutionally, the individual bureaucrat is motivated toward aggrandizement of his own agency.[15] And, since the effective alternatives for most governmental employees are other agencies and projects, this motivation for expansion will extend to government generally.

Democracy Unchained

The purpose of the several preceding sections was to demonstrate that even under the most favorable conditions the operation of democratic process

14. For an early recognition of this, see Gordon Tullock, *The Politics of Bureaucracy* (Washington, D.C.: Public Affairs Press, 1965).

15. For an analysis that develops that aspect of bureaucratic behavior in detail, see William A. Niskanen, *Bureaucracy and Representative Government* (Chicago: Aldine-Atherton, 1971).

may generate budgetary excesses. Democracy may become its own Leviathan unless constitutional limits are imposed and enforced. Historically, government has grown at rates that cannot possibly be long sustained. In this sense alone, modern America confronts a crisis of major proportions in the last decades of the twentieth century. In the seven decades from 1900 to 1970, total government spending in real terms increased forty times over, attaining a share of one-third in national product. These basic facts are familiar and available for all to see. The point of emphasis is that this growth has occurred, almost exclusively, within the predictable workings of orderly democratic procedures.[16]

The authors of the United States Constitution, the Founding Fathers, did not foresee the necessity or need of controlling the growth of self-government, at least specifically, nor have these aspects been treated in traditional political discourse. The limits or constraints on governmental arms and agencies have been primarily discussed in terms of maintaining democratic procedures. Rulers have been subjected to laws because of a predicted proclivity to extend their own powers beyond procedural limits, at the presumed expense of the citizenry. But implicit in much of the discussion has been the notion that, to the extent that democratic process works, there is no need for limits. The system of checks and balances, ultimately derivative from Montesquieu, has rarely been interpreted to have as one of its objectives the limiting of the growth of the government. The excesses of the 1960s created widespread public disillusionment about the ability of government, as a process, to accomplish specific social objectives. But, before the 1960s, the checks and balances that were present in the United States constitutional structure were far more likely to be criticized for inhibiting the extent of governmental action than for their inability to accomplish an effective limitation on this action. In this respect, the 1970s and beyond present a new and different challenge. Can modern man, in Western democratic society, invent or capture sufficient control over his own destiny so as to impose constraints on his own government,

---

16. Major wars have exerted an influence on this rate of public-sector growth, and the displacement effects of such emergencies have, no doubt, contributed to the acceleration. See A. T. Peacock and Jack Wiseman, *Growth of Public Expenditures in the United Kingdom* (New York: National Bureau of Economic Research, 1961).

The veritable explosion of the late 1960s and early 1970s cannot, however, readily be explained under the Peacock-Wiseman thesis. The Viet Nam war was not the major causal influence in this explosion.

constraints that will prevent the transformation into the genuine Hobbesian sovereign?

Beyond Constitutional Boundaries

In earlier chapters, we found it useful to make a sharp conceptual distinction between the productive state and the protective state, and the dual functioning of government in these two conceptually different roles was noted. The productive state is, ideally, the embodiment of postconstitutional contract among citizens having as its objective the provision of jointly shared goods and services, as demanded by the citizens. The discussion of Leviathan in this chapter has been wholly concerned with this part or side of government, measured appropriately by the size of the governmental budget. The analysis has shown that budgetary excess will emerge from democratic process, even if overt exploitation is avoided. To the extent that majoritarian democracy uses governmental process to modify the basic structure of individual rights, which are presumably defined in the legal structure, there is an encroachment on the domain of the protective state. Dominant coalitions in legislative bodies may take it on themselves to change "the law," the basic constitutional structure, defined in a real and not a nominal sense. To the extent that the protective state acquiesces in this constitutional excess, the social structure moves toward "constitutional anarchy" in which individual rights are subject to the whims of politicians.

There is, however, an equally if not more significant overstepping of constitutional boundaries when the agencies of government that properly belong to the protective state, and to this state only, begin to act in putative contractual capacities, at both constitutional and postconstitutional stages. A modern treatment of Leviathan would be seriously incomplete if these possible excesses were not discussed. The protective state has as its essential and only role the enforcement of individual rights as defined in constitutional contract. This state is law embodied, and its role is one of enforcing rights to property, to exchanges of property, and of policing the simple and complex exchange processes among contracting free men. In the game analogy that we have used several times before, the protective state is the umpire or referee, and, as such, its task is conceptually limited to enforcing agreed-on rules.

Few who observe the far-flung operation of the executive arm of the United States government along with the ubiquitousness of the federal judiciary could interpret the activities of either of these institutions as falling within meaningful restrictions of the enforcer. Ideally, these institutions may be umpires in the social game; actually, these institutions modify and change the basic structure of rights without consent of citizens. They assume the authority to rewrite the basic constitutional contract, to change "the law" at their own will. At yet other interfaces, these institutions take on legislative roles and effectively displace representative assemblies in making decisions on "public good"—decisions which can in no way be derived from individual evaluations in some quasi-contractual setting. Democracy can generate quite enough of its own excesses even if decision-makers adhere strictly to constitutional norms for behavior. When these norms are themselves subjected to arbitrary and unpredictable change, by decision-makers who are not representative of the citizenry, the omnivorousness of the state becomes much more threatening.

It is more difficult to measure the growth of Leviathan in these dimensions than in the quantifiable budgetary dimensions of the productive state. There is a complementary relationship here, but the two are conceptually independent. An interfering federal judiciary, along with an irresponsible executive, could exist even when budget sizes remain relatively small. Conversely, as noted, relatively large budgets might be administered responsibly with a judicial system that embodies nonarbitrary decision-making. Historically, we observe a conjunction—relatively large and growing budgets along with increasingly irresponsible interpretations of law. Essentially the same philosophical orientation informs both extensions of governmental powers. Burgeoning budgets are an outgrowth of the American liberal tradition which assigns to government the instrumental role in creating the "good society." The arrogance of the administrative and, particularly, the judicial elite in changing basic law by fiat arises from the same source. If the "good society" can first be defined, and, second, produced by governmental action, then men finding themselves in positions of discretionary power, whether in legislative, executive, or judicial roles, are placed under some moral obligation to move society toward the defined ideal.

There is a fundamental philosophical confusion here, one that must be removed if Leviathan is to be contained. A "good society" defined independent of the choices of its members, *all* members, is contradictory with a social order derived from individual values. In the postconstitutional stage of contract, those outcomes are "good" that emerge from the choices of men, in both the private and the public sector. The "goodness" of an outcome is evaluated on procedural criteria applied to the means of its attainment and not on substantive criteria intrinsic to such outcome. The politician, who represents the citizenry, however crudely and imperfectly, seeks to attain consensus, to find acceptable compromises among conflicting individual and group demands. He is not engaged in a search for some one "true" judgment, and he is not properly behaving if he seeks to further some well-defined ideal drawn from the brains of his academic mentors. The judge is in a distinctly different position. He does seek "truth," not compromise. But he seeks truth only in the limits of constitutional structure. He looks for, and finds, "the law." He does not make new rules. To the extent that he tries deliberately to modify the basic constitutional contract so as to make it conform to his independently defined ideals, he errs in his whole understanding of his social function, even more than the elected politician who seeks the liberal grail.

False philosophical precepts that are so pervasively held cannot be readily overthrown. If our Leviathan is to be controlled, politicians and judges must come to have respect for limits. Their continued efforts to use assigned authority to impose naively formulated constructs of social order must produce a decline in their own standing. If leaders have no sense of limits, what must be expected of those who are limited by their ukases? If judges lose respect for law, why must citizens respect judges? If personal rights are subjected to arbitrary confiscation at the hands of the state, why must individuals refrain from questioning the legitimacy of government?

Leviathan may maintain itself by force; the Hobbesian sovereign may be the only future. But alternative futures may be described and dreamed, and government may not yet be wholly out of hand. From current disillusionment can come constructive consensus on a new structure of checks and balances.

10. Beyond Pragmatism
Prospects for Constitutional Revolution

The ethical problem of social change seems to me to have been seriously if not fatally misconceived in the age of liberalism. It must be viewed in terms of *social*-ethical self-legislation, which involves a creative process at a still "higher" (and intellectually more elusive) level than that of individual self-legislation. It is a matter of social choice, and must rest on the conception of society as a real unit, a moral community in the literal sense. It is intellectually impossible to believe that the individual can have any influence to speak of, or especially any predictable influence, on the course of history. But it seems to me that to regard this as an ethical difficulty involves a complete misconception of the social-moral problem or that of the individual as a member of a society striving for moral progress as a society. I find it impossible to give meaning to an ethical obligation on the part of the individual to improve society.

The disposition of an individual, under liberalism, to take upon himself such a responsibility seems to be an exhibition of intellectual and *moral* conceit. It is sheer love of power and self-aggrandizement; it is *un*-ethical. Ethical-social change must come about through a genuine moral consensus among individuals meeting on a level of genuine equality and mutuality and not with any one in the role of cause and the rest in that of effect, of one as the "potter" and others as "clay."

—Frank H. Knight,
"Intellectual Confusion on Morals and Economics"

The analysis of this book is intended to be relevant for America's third century, for the emerging issues that challenge the viability of traditional institutions of social order. Despite disclaimers to the contrary, the American constitutional structure is in disarray. It is time for the social scientist or social philosopher to go beyond the manipulation of elegant but ultimately irrelevant models. He must ask the question: What sort of social order can man create for himself at this stage in his history?

There are two distinct approaches that may be taken in answering this question. The first involves basic structural diagnosis, which is perhaps the best descriptive appellation for my own efforts in this book. The existing as well as the possible institutions for human choice must be analyzed in terms of criteria for promoting "improvement," defined largely by potential agreement and independent of advance description. The second approach involves description of the "good society" independent of either that which exists or the means through which attainment might be secured.

Despite the urging of several critics, I have not gone beyond the restrictions imposed by the first approach. I have not tried to present in detail my own private proposals for constitutional reform; I do not offer a description of the "good society," even on my own terms. In part my reluctance is based on comparative advantage. As I noted earlier, many social philosophers seem willing to essay the second of the two tasks suggested, with neither recognition of nor interest in the first. This concentration, in its turn, often promotes intellectual and moral arrogance. An attempt to describe the social good in detail seems to carry with it an implied willingness to impose this good, independent of observed or prospective agreement among persons. By contrast, my natural proclivity as an economist is to place ultimate value on process or procedure, and by implication to define as "good" that which emerges from agreement among free men, independent of intrinsic evaluation of the outcome itself.

The social philosopher who takes either of these two roles must reject the pragmatism that has characterized the American mind-set on social policy reforms. The time has come to move beyond this, to think about and to make an attempt at reconstruction of the basic constitutional order itself. My analysis suggests that there are structural flaws in the sociopolitical system which can scarcely be remedied by superficial tampering. Acceptance of this, as diagnosis, becomes a necessary starting point in the search for alternatives. I am convinced that the social interrelationships that emerge from continued pragmatic and incremental situational response, informed by no philosophical precepts, is neither sustainable nor worthy of man's best efforts. History need not be a random walk in sociopolitical space, and I have no faith in the efficacy of social evolutionary process. The institutions that survive and prosper need not be those that maximize man's potential. Evolution may produce social dilemma as readily as social paradise.[1]

"Dilemma" is explicitly used here in order to draw attention to an interaction that has been exhaustively analyzed in modern game theory. In its most familiar setting, the "prisoners' dilemma," the independent utility-maximizing behavior on the part of each party generates results that are desired by neither party, results that can, with behavioral coordination, be changed to the benefit of all parties within the interaction. In the terminology of economic theory, the results of independent behavior are nonoptimal or inefficient in the Pareto sense; changes can be made which will improve the lot of some without harming anyone.

The generality and ubiquitousness of the social dilemma force concentration on a dual decision process. As we have noted, even an isolated Crusoe may find it helpful to adopt and abide by rules that constrain his choice behavior. In a social setting, the duality is essential. Men must choose mutually agreeable rules for behavior, while retaining for themselves alternatives for choice within these rules. Recognition of the distinction between what I have called constitutional and postconstitutional contract is an elementary but necessary first step toward escape from the social dilemma that confronts man in the Hobbesian jungle, whether this be in its pristine form or in its more sophisticated modern variants.

The costs of rules, when the alternative is their absence, are measured in the losses that are anticipated to occur because of the defined inability to re-

---

1. My basic criticism of F. A. Hayek's profound interpretation of modern history and his diagnoses for improvement is directed at his apparent belief or faith that social evolution will, in fact, insure the survival of efficient institutional forms. Hayek is so distrustful of man's explicit attempts at reforming institutions that he accepts uncritically the evolutionary alternative. We may share much of Hayek's skepticism about social and institutional reform, however, without elevating the evolutionary process to an ideal role. Reform may, indeed, be difficult, but this is no argument that its alternative is ideal. See F. A. Hayek, *Law, Legislation, and Liberty,* vol. 1, *Rules and Order,* and his *Studies in Philosophy, Politics, and Economics.*

For a general discussion of individual interaction where social dilemma characterizes the results, see Gordon Tullock, *The Social Dilemma* (forthcoming).

spond to situations in a strictly short-term utility-maximizing manner.[2] These costs may be dominated by the promised benefits of stability which will allow for planning at the moment when rules are chosen. Once adopted, however, adherence to the rules involves a different choice and a different cost. Because utility is maximized through unilateral violation of existing rules, adherence or obedience to the terms of contract cannot be secured costlessly. This applies to all members of the social group, not just to those who are observed to be the most likely violators. This suggests the necessity of some enforcement structure.[3]

Almost inadvertently, the discussion points toward the derivation of a logical basis for constitutional contract, a basis which involves the demonstration that all members of a community secure gains when rights are defined, when rules imposing behavioral limits are settled, and when enforcement institutions are established. On this, however, no quarrel should arise; even the ardent romantic revolutionary would prefer almost any order when the alternative is pristine Hobbesian jungle. The problem worthy of attention is quite different. Given an existing constitutional-legal order, as it is actually enforced and respected, how can changes be made so as to improve the positions of all or substantially all members of the social group? History produces an evolving status quo, and predictions can be made about alternative futures. If we do not like the particular set of alternatives that seem promised by nonrevolutionary situational response, we are obliged to examine basic structural improvements.

This is the definitional basis for the term "constitutional revolution," which may appear to be internally contradictory. I refer to basic, nonincremental changes in the structural order of the community, changes in the complex set of rules that enable men to live with one another, changes that are sufficiently dramatic to warrant the label "revolutionary." At the same time, how-

2. Costs must always be tied to the specific choice that is made. The costs of one set of rules from among alternative sets are measured differently from the costs of rules, generally, when the alternative is an absence of rules. On problems in defining opportunity costs, see my *Cost and Choice.*

3. In this book I have deliberately avoided discussion of the ethical-moral arguments for adherence to rules, for law-abiding. These arguments have been the subject of renewed interest since the widespread civil disobedience of the 1960s. For an analysis which relates these arguments to type of government, see Peter Singer, *Democracy and Disobedience* (Oxford: Clarendon Press, 1973).

ever, it is useful to restrict discussion to "constitutional" limits, by which I mean that structural changes should be those upon which all members in the community might conceptually agree. Little, if any, improvement in the lot of modern man is promised by imposition of new rules by some men on other men. Nonconstitutional revolution invites counterrevolution in a continuing zero- or negative-sum power sequence.

If there exist potential structural changes in legal order which might command acceptance by all members of the society, the status quo represents a social dilemma in the strict game-theoretic terminology. Even if we consider ourselves far removed from the genuine Hobbesian jungle, where life is brutish and short, the status quo contains within it elements or features that are in principle equivalent. Life in the here and now may be more brutish than need be, and certainly more nasty. If after examination and analysis, no such potential for change exists, the legal-constitutional order that we observe must be judged to be Pareto optimal, despite the possible presence of discontent among specific members in the body politic.

A central hypothesis of this book is that basic constitutional reform, even revolution, may be needed. The existing legal order may have lost its claim to efficiency, or, in a somewhat different sense, to legitimacy. At the very least, it seems to be time that genuine constitutional change be considered seriously.

Institutional-Constitutional Change and Pragmatic Policy Response

The distinction between institutional-constitutional reform and the enactment or adoption of specific policy correctives for blatantly unsatisfactory situations as they emerge must be understood first by working scholars, then by politicians and by the citizenry. Pragmatism has been hailed with approbation as the American behavioral characteristic. When something has gone wrong, our response is to fix it up with baling wire and to go on about our business. This baling-wire syndrome presumes, however, that the underlying structure or mechanism is sound and itself not in need of repair or replacement. But, eventually, baling-wire repairs fail, and more fundamental change becomes necessary. When such a stage is reached, continuation of the established response pattern may create more problems than it resolves.

"Politics," by which I mean governmental action, notably federal governmental action, has been the social analogue to baling wire. The identification of a "social need," whether this be real or manufactured, has come to suggest, almost simultaneously, a federal program. Social progress has been measured by the quantity of legislation, and our assemblies are deemed to be political failures when new programs are lacking. Properly interpreted, the succession of New Deal, Fair Deal, New Frontier, Great Society, and New Federalism formats represents the pragmatic and essentially nonideological working of American democratic process. Little or no attention has been paid to the possible interlinkage of program with program, to the ability of the underlying structural system to sustain the growing pressures put upon it, to the questions of aggregate size and scope for political activity.

There have been ideological supports for the pragmatist policy directions, but these have not really informed the attitudes of practicing politicians or their constituents. Even without John Dewey, and perhaps even without either Marxian or non-Marxian socialism, the American policy history might have been much the same. The faith in politics exhibited by twentieth-century man, at least until the 1960s, stems ultimately from his loss of faith in God, accompanied by an ignorance about the effective working of organizational alternatives. Eighteenth- and early nineteenth-century men seem to have possessed greater wisdom, but skepticism is suggested even here. Perhaps their judgments were based on a closer observation of governments, and their negative attitudes may have reflected not so much a faith in the nongovernmental alternative as their rejection of statist attempts at "solution."

There is, nonetheless, a fundamental difference between the approach taken by the philosophers of the eighteenth century and that which I have referred to as the pragmatic or incremental political response to issues that emerge. The difference is methodological, in that the earlier emphasis was on structural or institutional change, not on the particulars of programs. Adam Smith sought to free the economy from the fetters of mercantilist controls; he did not propose that the specific goals of policy be laid down in advance. He did not attack the failures of governmental instruments in piecemeal, pragmatic fashion; he attacked in a far more comprehensive and constitutional sense. He tried to demonstrate that, by removing effective governmental restrictions on trade, results would emerge that would be judged better by all concerned. Precisely because of this comprehensiveness, this concentration on structural-institutional change, Adam Smith deservedly won acclaim as the father of political economy. He and his compatriots proposed genuine "constitutional revolution," and their proposals were, in large part, adopted over the course of a half-century.

The triumph of laissez-faire was achieved because intellectual and political leaders came to accept a new *principle* for social order, a principle that enabled them to rise above the narrow and short-sighted pragmatic vision that must accompany analytical ignorance. The principle was that of ordered anarchy: a regime described by well-defined individual rights and by freedom of and enforcement of voluntary contracts. An understanding of this principle enabled man to conceptualize a social process that was orderly and efficient *without* the detailed direction of a centralized decision-maker, *without* a necessary major role for governmental action beyond that of the strictly protective state. The importance of conversion to a new organizing principle cannot be overemphasized. It was this conversion that facilitated what can only be judged as a genuine constitutional revolution in Britain. Adam Smith and his colleagues could not have been successful had they chosen to attack the previously existing order on a pragmatic, policy-by-policy basis. The shift in vision was essential, the shift that established new benchmarks against which departures might be measured.

Socialist critics were successful in identifying particular flaws in the conceptually ideal order of laissez-faire, as well as in its practicable counterparts. These critics did not, however, offer an alternative organizing principle that was even remotely comparable in intellectual appeal. Marxian doctrine is characterized by an absence of analytical description of society "after the revolution." Later attempts to model the working of socialist order amounted to a translation of laissez-faire precepts, almost in a literal sense. In practice, regimes organized under socialist rubrics are acknowledged to be bureaucratic monstrosities.

Because of the negative impact on the laissez-faire principle exercised by socialist ideas, however, the pragmatically generated erosion of the minimal government principle achieved intellectual-ideological respectability. The central organizing principle that dominated early nineteenth-century thinking, one that embodied a vision of viable society with minimal government direction, was gradually undermined in particularistic stages. Failures were first identified and acknowledged by intellectually honest men. Following this, corrections were proposed, corrections that almost always took the institutional form of governmental action. Intellectual controversy and political debate shifted away from concentration on alternative principles for social organization and toward specific policy choices in a situational context. Social scientists and/or social philosophers abandoned attempts to examine large-scale institutional differences, and they came to look upon their own functional roles as particularistic critics of the existing structure. Welfare economics, in its twentieth-century gloss, became a theory of *market* failure.

It should not have been at all surprising that this setting proved to be highly conducive to very rapid growth in the size and scope of the public or governmental sector. Governmental correctives to presumed particular flaws in the operation of markets were considered piecemeal and independent one from the other. More important, these correctives were presumed to work ideally once they were introduced. Because there existed no principle or vision of the process of governmental operation, the naive presumption was made that intention was equivalent to result. Program was piled on top of program, with little or no attention being paid to the effects of such aggregation on the supporting structure, on the principle of constitutional-legal order itself.[4]

By the middle of the twentieth century, American pragmatism seemed to reign supreme, and there was almost no talk about fundamental revolutionary change, either in the academy or in the streets.

Confusion and Challenge

This pattern changed dramatically and unpredictably in the 1960s. There were several causal factors. Scholars in the academic groves commenced, as early as the late 1940s and early 1950s, to advance simplified theories or mod-

---

4. The disciplinary split of the older "political economy" into the separate modern disciplines of "economics" and "political science" was partially responsible for the intellectual confusion that developed. Economists, in the large, tended to remain positive analysts, at least in their examination of market or exchange processes. Political scientists, by contrast, tended to remain normative in their treatment of governmental processes. As a result, the social choice between organizational alternatives was often informed by a comparison between an actual institution on the one hand and an ideal one on the other. On this point, see David B. Johnson, "Meade, Bees, and Externalities," *Journal of Law and Economics* 16 (April 1973): 35–52.

els of democratic process, models that must have given pause to those who thought seriously of implementing socialist ideals. Governmental action which emerged from majoritarian institutions, held to be the essence of democracy, need not produce "public good." And perhaps even more damaging was the intellectually formidable proof that such action need not itself be internally consistent.[5] Furthermore, it came to be recognized that governmental programs, once enacted, were necessarily administered by bureaucratic personnel, and theories of behavior were developed on the elementary presumption that bureaucrats are ordinary men.[6] Conceptually, the base was laid for the emergence of theories of *government* failure that are on all fours with the more familiar theories of market failure.

These essentially intellectual developments were accompanied and overshadowed in public consciousness by accumulating evidence that governmental nostrums do not effect miracles. By a sequence of events, collective decision-makers were led to enact programs which found their origins, not in the demands of citizens, but in the brains of academicians and the slogans of politicians. Unfortunately, many citizens, and some politicians, expected more results than the institutional structure could possibly deliver. "New Frontier" slogans were too hurriedly translated into "Great Society" realities, precisely at a time when the public began to lose its tolerance for governmental wastage. Citizen reaction was acerbated by an activist judiciary, whose behavior indicated widespread departures from any protective-state limits, departures that were seen as such by the public at large. These legislative and

5. Although the ideas here, as elsewhere, have roots in earlier discourse, the modern revolution in thinking about political choice in democracy stems from the works of Kenneth Arrow and Duncan Black. Arrow, *Social Choice and Individual Values,* and Black, *Theory of Committees and Elections.* Both works had been foreshadowed in papers published earlier. My own interest in collective choice theory was indicated in papers published in 1950 and 1954, all of which are reprinted in my book *Fiscal Theory and Political Economy.* In another work, published in 1957, Anthony Downs analyzed political parties in a manner analogous to the analysis of profit-maximizing firms. See his *An Economic Theory of Democracy* (New York: Harper and Row, 1957).

6. As with the theories of collective choice, modern theories of bureaucracy have antecedents in the traditional literature. But the modern shift in bureaucratic paradigm can be attributed to a few basic works. See Tullock, *The Politics of Bureaucracy;* Anthony Downs, *Inside Bureaucracy* (Boston: Little, Brown, 1967); Niskanen, *Bureaucracy and Representative Government.* For a contrast between the newer conception and the traditional one, see Ostrom, *The Intellectual Crisis in American Public Administration.*

judicial excesses were more than matched by the independence exerted by the executive branch of the United States government in foreign affairs, notably in the Viet Nam involvement. The observed failures, at all levels of the federal government, combined to foster an antigovernmental attitude that was perhaps unique in American history.

The implications for policy were, however, clouded by the accompanying behavioral revolution of the 1960s, itself motivated in part by the same forces. As governmental failures came to be more widely acknowledged, personal respect for "law" deteriorated. Politics and politicians became more blatantly profit-seeking, and pressures for governmental handouts accelerated. As the federal courts were seen to "make" law in their own idealized image, by natural extension individuals came to think of their own private criteria for discriminating between "good" and "bad" law. Initially motivated by wholly admirable precepts for achieving racial justice, unlawful demonstrations were mounted against the operation of "bad laws" generally, demonstrations that were condoned ex post by judicial failure to enforce existing legal norms. The limited manpower needs for a limited war guaranteed that conscription could be and would be judged to be unjust and highly discriminatory. Protest came to be the order of the day in the late years of the decade. Venerable institutions that had long survived by adherence to unwritten behavioral rules, workable ordered anarchies such as universities, proved to be exceedingly vulnerable to disruption once voluntary respect for the rules broke down. An inability and an unwillingness to defend established "rights" could mean only that there was a genuine shift in the basic structure of control.

These confusions of the 1960s were compounded as the nonprotesting citizenry called for "law and order," overlooking the governmental origins of the turmoil. The law-abiding citizen failed to understand his own plight. He observed apparent erosion in public capital; he read about and sometimes suffered from rising crime rates; he saw behavioral changes that he considered to represent losses of personal respect and tolerance. He demanded "law and order," which meant increased rather than decreased collectivization of society. He was, in this stance, trying to evoke response on the part of the protective state, the external enforcer, and he was asking that this state reestablish the apparent claims embodied in constitutional contract.

The state cannot, however, wave some magic wand and produce instant improvements. If individual rights are in some disarray, better and more effective enforcement requires more investigation and more severe punishment for offenders. But here the punishment dilemma emerges. The selfsame citizen who demands enforcement may be quite unwilling to allow for the increased severity or certainty of punishment that efficient enforcement may require. The state responds by moving along those dimensions of adjustment which generate minimal feedbacks. It hires more policemen, and keeps punishment levels stationary or declining. It responds to prison riots by rewarding the inmates with better facilities. The costs are borne by the general taxpayer and the size of government grows.

The citizen responds to George Wallace's attacks on the bureaucratic superstructure. He rejects claims of legitimacy on the part of agents of the state, and he senses increasing insecurity against governmental domination. At the same time, however, he is quite unwilling to yield up his own share in the special benefits that he thinks only government can provide. The American suburbanite who is most vehement in his opposition to cross-city bussing of his children to publicly financed schools is unwilling even to question the right of the collectivity to levy taxes, coercively, on all families in order to finance the schooling of children for some families (and, in the process, to subsidize the production of more children in an overcrowded world).

Intellectual Bankruptcy

In sociopolitical matters, the 1970s can be described as an era of intellectual bankruptcy. Theoretical welfare economists continue to develop sophisticated demonstrations of market failures; public choice theorists, who have been charged with dabbling in "welfare politics," match the welfare economists with their own demonstrations of governmental failures. The theorems of the economists are put to alleged practical usage in the discussion of pollution-environmental issues that occupies policy debates. The "solutions" that are proposed, however, involve widening the sphere of bureaucratic control rather than shrinking it. The libertarians are scarcely preferred over their liberal counterparts. They score effectively when they point to the analytically demonstrable and empirically verified flaws in the collectivist alternatives. Positively, however, they can suggest little other than a shift of organizational structure toward the marketplace. Both liberals and libertarians alike presume implicitly that their task is to offer advice to some nonexistent but benevolent wisdom that will accept rational argument.

The facts are different. Both markets and governments fail, and there is no such benevolent wisdom. The man of the 1970s is trapped in his own dilemma. He recognizes that the "grand alternatives," laissez-faire and socialism, are moribund, and that revival is not to be predicted.[7] What modern man does not recognize, in either an intellectual or an intuitive sense, is that the pragmatic alternative is equally suspect, and that viable social order may be seriously threatened by long-continued failure to consider his situation systematically and nonincrementally. In this as in other aspects of his life, modern man seems to be in need of sociopolitical "conversion" to a new conception of society. Without such a conversion, the constitutional revolution that may be necessary for survival cannot take place.

In this respect at least, the modern radical revolutionaries may be correct; improvement may well require changes in the system, not in the personnel that man it and not through peripheral adjustments. But if both markets and governments fail, what is the organizational alternative? Throughout the ages men have dreamed of character ideals descriptive of the person who acts out of love for others or duty toward his fellow men. There is a role for ethics in social order. It is, however, extremely dangerous to generalize ideally personal behavior into the basis for social organization, taking the route of William Godwin and other romantic anarchists. Regardless of the organizing principle, the larger the proportion of "good" men in the community, the "better" should be the community, provided the terms are defined in accordance with individualistic precepts. But it is folly to expect *all* men to be behaviorally transformed. Yet this becomes the minimal requirement for an acceptably orderly society without organization.

Social order may be imposed by a despotic regime, through either an individual ruler or through an elite ruling group. Despotism may be the only organizational alternative to the political structure that we observe. In which

---

7. Dahl and Lindblom suggested that the era of the grand alternatives (the term is theirs) is over, and their argument supports the efficacy of pragmatist alternatives. See R. A. Dahl and C. E. Lindblom, *Politics, Economics, and Welfare* (New York: Harper and Row, 1953).

case, those who claim no special rights to rule had best judge existing institutions in a different light. This would amount to a counsel of despair, however, and there may be alternatives worthy of consideration.

The Contractarian Revival

It is in this respect that the modern contractarian revival, stimulated largely by the publication of John Rawls's book, *A Theory of Justice* (1971), is highly encouraging. In this work, Rawls made no attempt to lay down precepts or principles of justice on the basis of any externally derived ethical norms, utilitarian or otherwise. Instead, he advanced the individualistic conception of "justice as fairness." Those principles are just which emerge from the unanimous agreement of men participating in a setting where each places himself behind a veil of ignorance concerning his own position in postcontractual sequence. No man counts for more than any other, and no precepts for justice are defined independently of this conceptualized contractual setting. Unfortunately, in my view, Rawls went further than this and attempted to identify those precepts that might be predicted to emerge. In this extension, Rawls was, perhaps, responding to the pressures of critics who demand specific reform proposals. And, predictably, it is this aspect of his work that is drawing attention away from his more basic contribution, which is the relationship of justice to the outcome of the contractual *process* itself.

My efforts in this book are simultaneously more and less ambitious than those of Rawls, or some of my own earlier works.[8] Rawls is content to discuss the emergence of potential agreement on principles of justice from an idealized contractual setting within which men are led to behave as moral equals. He does not discuss the critically important bridge between such an idealized setting and that within which any discussion of basic structural rearrangement might, in fact, take place. In this respect, my approach is more ambitious. I have tried to examine the prospects for genuine contractual renegotiation among persons who are not equals at the stage of deliberation and

8. In *The Calculus of Consent,* Gordon Tullock and I examined the structure of collective decision-making rules in a setting that is more closely related to that used by Rawls. We asked the question: What sort of political decision structure might be predicted to emerge from a constitutional setting within which individual participants are uncertain about their own positions in postconstitutional sequences?

who are not artificially made to behave as if they are, either through general adherence to internal ethical norms or through the introduction of uncertainty about postcontract positions. It is for this reason that the return to the conceptual emergence of contract from Hobbesian anarchy has been necessary to develop my argument.

In another respect that has been noted, however, my efforts are much less ambitious than those of Rawls. He identifies the principles of justice that he predicts to emerge from his idealized contractual setting. Although perhaps this was not Rawls's specific intent, these principles may become the basis of proposals for specific institutional changes, which may then be debated in the pragmatically oriented arena of day-to-day politics. I take no such step. I do not try to identify either the "limits of liberty" or the set of principles that might be used to define such limits.

The "principles" that might be said to be implied in this book are that the multidimensional trade-off between liberty and law should be recognized, that the interdependence among different laws as they constrain individual liberties should be reckoned with, that continued misunderstanding and confusion above the separate constitutional and postconstitutional stages of collective action leads to disaster. The reform that I seek lies first of all in attitudes, in ways of thinking about social interaction, about political institutions, about law and liberty. If men will only commence to think in contractarian terms, if they will think of the state in the roles as defined, and if they will recognize individual rights as existent in the status quo, I should not at all be insistent on particulars. It is as if a less ambitious John Rawls might have limited his concern to ways that men think about justice.

Political and Public Philosophy

The contractarian revival suggests that there may be widespread agreement among scholars that a renewed discussion of basic problems of social order is desirable. To the extent that this revival continues, the groundwork may be laid for a rebirth of political and legal philosophy in our institutions of higher learning. To the extent that contractarian precepts emerge victorious in this discourse, the ways of thinking that I have called for here may come into being. The trade-offs between law and liberty may be recognized, and the dual role played by the state more fully understood, along with some appreciation

for the problem of keeping collective action within limits. General acceptance by working scholars is perhaps a necessary prelude to acceptance of
such ideas by a frustrated public.

The emergence of a modified public philosophy in this respect should not
be beyond the bounds of hope. Both the ideas and the events of the preceding decades have created a potentially receptive attitude in the ordinary man.
He has lost his faith in government as it operates, but he remains unwilling
to jettison the governmental crutch. He searches silently for a philosophy
that might offer him some reconciliation and that might partially restore his
social faith.

If this were all there is to it, reform of basic constitutional structure might
be, relatively speaking, an easy task. Judges would cease legislating and stick
to adjudicating conflicts, enforcing laws, and imposing punishments. Legis-
lators would cease using the political mechanism to make uncompensated
transfers of rights among individuals and groups. Citizens would not seek
private profits, individually or in groups, from resort to the governmental
sector, and they would refrain from supporting political entrepreneurs who
promise to deliver such profits. Those who observe and discuss governmental
processes, be they journalists or professors, would cease measuring social
progress by the amount of legislation enacted, by the sheer size of the budget
account. Individual liberty, as an independent value, is inversely correlated
with these familiar scalars, and this would be given its proper place among
other social values in the attitudinal revolution which I am suggesting here.
Individuals would recognize that government, the state, is ultimately subject
to their own control. They would no longer accept, implicitly, the positivist
view that the state, and only the state, can define and redefine individual
rights, and, by inference, its own. Democracy remains conceptually possible
only if individuals view government in the consent paradigm.

Individual Rights in Democracy

On cursory examination, the attitudinal shift that I have outlined seems to
be in accord with straightforward laissez-faire precepts. The orthodox libertarian would find no apparent difficulty in associating himself with the position suggested. When the level of discussion is brought back one stage,
however, a new set of issues emerge which have been glossed over in the tra-

ditional conceptions. Too often, the libertarian, like his socialist counterpart, discusses reforms under the "as if" assumption that he is simply advising some benevolent despot who will lay down the proposed changes, with little or no reference to the consent of participating parties. With this political presupposition, it becomes relatively easy for the market-oriented libertarian to neglect any analysis of the existing distribution of rights and claims among persons. But unless these rights and claims are first identified and agreed on, what do the terms used above mean? What is an uncompensated transfer? What qualifies as profit-seeking through the use of the political mechanism?

Once such questions as these are raised, elements of the social dilemma come to light that are too readily ignored when we remain at the level of philosophy. Practical operational significance can be placed on the precepts only when a major condition is fulfilled: the agreement of all members of the social group on the assignment of individual rights that exists in the status quo. So long as there is continuing disagreement on just who has the right to do what with what and to do what to whom, the attitudinal shift suggested above may remain operationally empty.

A necessary step in the process of genuine constitutional revolution is a *consensual redefinition* of individual rights and claims. Many of the interventions of government have emerged precisely because of ambiguities in the definition of individual rights. The central issue here concerns the reconciliation of nominally expressed claims by individuals to private property, to human as well as nonhuman capital, and the equalitarian distribution of the "public property rights" through the voting franchise. Whether treated as value or as fact, modern democracy incorporates universal adult suffrage. From this elementary base, several questions arise. How can the poor man (with "poor" defined in terms of private-property claims) exert his putative claims to the wealth nominally held by the rich man except through exercise of his voting franchise? Acknowledging this, how can the rich man (or the libertarian philosopher) expect the poor man to accept any new constitutional order that severely restricts the scope for fiscal transfers among groups? Consensual support for such restriction could scarcely be predicted to be forthcoming. This need not, however, suggest that all attempts at renegotiation of the basic constitutional structure should be abandoned before they commence. There may well exist potential gains-from-trade for all participants, but the existing as well as the prospective distribution of rights and claims must inform the bargaining process. The rich man, who may sense the vulnerability of his nominal claims in the existing state of affairs and who may, at the same time, desire that the range of collective or state action be restricted, can potentially agree on a once-and-for-all or quasi-permanent transfer of wealth to the poor man, a transfer made in exchange for the latter's agreement to a genuinely new constitution that will overtly limit governmentally directed fiscal transfers.

Consider a highly simplified two-person example. A rich man, A, nominally owns an asset that yields $100,000 in annual income, which is taxed at 50 percent, leaving a post-tax income of $50,000. A poor man, B, owns no assets, and earns $5,000 annually from his labor services. The "government" (here treated as exogenous) collects taxes exclusively from the rich man, for a total revenue of $50,000, which it uses for a variety of projects, with varying degrees of efficiency. The benefits accrue in such a manner as to provide the rich man with a benefit value of $10,000, and the poor man with a benefit value of $20,000. Can the "social contract" be renegotiated with gains to both parties? Suppose that the rich man offers to transfer to the poor man one-third of his asset, with a gross income of $33,333, in exchange for the latter's agreement to reduce the size of the governmental budget to zero. The rich man, under this arrangement, retains a new real income of $66,667, higher than he retained under the previous arrangement ($60,000). The poor man, B, secures a real income of $38,333 (own earnings plus governmental benefits), higher than he secured under the other arrangement ($25,000). Both parties are made better off under the postulated terms of the new contract.[9]

Potential agreement might be secured even if the present value of claims is not increased in a strictly measurable sense. If the rich man, A, anticipates onerous tax burdens in the future, even if these do not currently exist, he may agree to the sort of rearrangement suggested. Or, more dramatically, if

9. Some implications of treating voting franchises as property rights valued by individuals were examined in my paper "The Political Economy of the Welfare State," Research Paper No. 808231-1-8 (Center for Study of Public Choice, Virginia Polytechnic Institute and State University, June 1972). This paper was prepared for the Conference on Capitalism and Freedom in honor of Professor Milton Friedman, held in Charlottesville, Virginia, in October 1972. The paper will be published in the volume of proceedings of the conference, edited by Richard Selden.

either or both parties fear nonconstitutional revolution, during which all claims are abrogated, agreement may well be forthcoming on terms that do not seem mutually beneficial under direct measurements. There seems little doubt that, at least conceptually, distributional aspects of the renegotiation can be settled.[10]

The Creation of Rights

Assume that the problems of income and wealth distribution among persons could be satisfactorily settled in a renegotiated constitutional contract, one that would redefine individual rights and reduce the scope for collectively determined coercive activity. Would this basic step be sufficient to allow for the implementation of laissez-faire principles? If property rights should be redefined so that distributional results are acceptable to all participants, would the operations of private markets, with minimal collective enforcement of contracts, be sufficient to insure efficient outcomes, to remove the social dilemma? A negative answer is immediately suggested with reference to the many problems summarized under the rubrics: congestion, pollution, environmental quality. Here the issues are specifically not distributional, or at least not exclusively or predominantly so. The alleged failures of existing social arrangements in many of these situations cannot legitimately be attributed to markets or to government, if we think of these as alternative processes of postconstitutional contracting. The social dilemma reflected in apparent results here stems from incomplete constitutional agreement, from first-stage failure to define and to limit individual rights. Resolution of this dilemma lies not in any explicit redistribution of rights among persons, not in some reshuffling of claims, but in the *creation* of newly defined rights in areas where none now exist, at least none that can offer a basis for predictability and exchange. In essence, congestion and pollution describe settings analogous to that generalized in Hobbes's model of anarchy. Individuals find

10. Under any legal-constitutional order that defines individual rights, there must be a relationship to the expected structure of individual claims in the "natural equilibrium" of genuine anarchy. As the latter distribution shifts, the relative strengths of claims under existing legal order may shift, giving rise to potential ranges of agreement for constitutional redefinition. For extended discussion, see *Explorations in the Theory of Anarchy,* ed. Tullock.

themselves in conflict over the use of scarce resources, with results that are desired by no one because there is no agreed-on and enforced set of rights. The constitutional revolution suggested involves mutual agreement on those restrictions on behavior that are required to achieve tolerably efficient outcomes.

To the extent that there is mutuality of gain in prospect, agreement should be conceptually attainable. The status quo provides a reasonable base from which limitations can be measured. "Congestion on the common" can be eliminated by guaranteeing to each participant a level of well-being at least as high as that which he secures in the dilemma of commonality. Improvement is precisely analogous to that which is achieved through the mutual disarmament contract which first enables man to leap from the brutish dilemma of Hobbes.

Idealized constitutional revolution here would require that limits be placed on behavior with respect to *all* scarce resources, whether this be in the form of assigning individual ownership titles or of imposing restrictive behavioral limits under common titles. Much of the dilemma summarized under the pollution rubric finds its origins in the presumption made by the founders of our constitutional-legal order that certain resources were in permanent abundance. Growth and technological advance have converted once-free resources into scarce resources, but existing property assignments have failed to keep pace. The resulting dilemma was predictable. This alone suggests that genuine constitutional change must take place as population grows, as technology develops, and as demand shifts through time.

Conclusion

The alternative that falls between anarchy on the one hand and Leviathan on the other must be articulated, analyzed, and, finally, made into models amenable to public comprehension. As an organizing principle, laissez-faire is too closely associated with the rights of property in the historically determined status quo, defined in nominal independence of the contingency claims represented in modern democracy. Socialism is the throughway to Leviathan. The failure of these two grand alternatives need not, however, dispel all of the Enlightenment dreams. The vision of the eighteenth-century philosophers which enabled them to describe a social order that did not require the centralized direction of man over man may yet stir excitement. *Free relations among free men*—this precept of ordered anarchy can emerge as principle when successfully renegotiated social contract puts "mine and thine" in a newly defined structural arrangement and when the Leviathan that threatens is placed within new limits.

Selected Bibliography

Aaron, H., and McGuire, M. "Public Goods and Income Distribution." *Econometrica* 38 (November 1970): 907–20.

Acton, Lord. *Essays in Freedom and Power.* Glencoe, Illinois: The Free Press, 1948.

Alchian, A. A., and Kessel, R. "Competition, Monopoly, and the Pursuit of Money." In *Aspects of Labor Economics* (New York: National Bureau of Economic Research, 1962), pp. 157–75.

Aristotle. *Politics.* Translated by H. Rackham. Cambridge: Harvard University Press, 1967.

Aron, Raymond. *The Opium of the Intellectuals.* Translated by Terence Kilmartin. New York: Norton, 1962.

Arrow, Kenneth J. *Social Choice and Individual Values.* New York: Wiley, 1951.

Avineri, Shlomo. *Hegel's Theory of the Modern State.* Cambridge: Cambridge University Press, 1972.

Barro, Robert J. "The Control of Politicians: An Economic Model." *Public Choice* 14 (Spring 1973): 19–42.

Baumol, William J. *Welfare Economics and the Theory of the State.* Cambridge: Harvard University Press, 1952; rev. ed., 1965.

Becker, Carl L. *The Heavenly City of the Eighteenth-Century Philosophers.* New Haven: Yale University Press, 1932.

Becker, Gary. "Crime and Punishment: An Economic Approach." *Journal of Political Economy* 76 (March/April 1968): 169–217.

Becker, Gary, and Stigler, George J. "Law Enforcement, Corruption, and the Compensation of Enforcers." Mimeographed paper presented at Conference on Capitalism and Freedom, Charlottesville, Virginia, October 1972.

Bell, Daniel. "Meritocracy and Equality." *Public Interest* 29 (Fall 1972): 29–68.

Benn, S. I., and Peters, R. S. *The Principles of Political Thought.* New York: The Free Press, 1959.

Bernholz, Peter. *Grundlagen der Politischen Ökonomie,* vol. 1. Tübingen: J. C. B. Mohr, 1972.

Black, Duncan. *Theory of Committees and Elections.* Cambridge: Cambridge University Press, 1958.

Borcherding, Thomas, ed. *Bureaucrats and Budgets: The Sources of Government Growth.* Durham, North Carolina: Duke University Press, forthcoming.

Breit, William H. "Income Redistribution and Efficiency Norms." Paper presented at Urban Institute Conference on Income Redistribution, Washington, D.C., 1972. Forthcoming in conference proceedings volume.

Brennan, Geoffrey. "Pareto Desirable Redistribution: The Non-Altruistic Dimension." *Public Choice* 14 (Spring 1973): 43–68.

Brittan, Samuel. "A Rebirth of Political Economy? The End of Some Fashionable Myths." *Encounter,* May 1973, 54–65.

Buchanan, James M. *The Bases for Collective Action.* New York: General Learning Press, 1971.

———. "A Behavioral Theory of Pollution." *Western Economic Journal* 6 (December 1968): 347–58.

———. *Cost and Choice: An Inquiry in Economic Theory.* Chicago: Markham Publishing Company, 1969.

———. *The Demand and Supply of Public Goods.* Chicago: Rand McNally, 1968.

———. "An Economic Theory of Clubs." *Economica* 32 (February 1965): 1–14.

———. "Equality as Fact and Norm." *Ethics* 81 (April 1971): 228–40.

———. "Ethical Rules, Expected Values, and Large Numbers." *Ethics* 76 (October 1965): 1–13.

———. "Externality in Tax Response." *Southern Economic Journal* 32 (July 1966): 35–42.

———. *Fiscal Theory and Political Economy.* Chapel Hill: University of North Carolina Press, 1960.

———. "The Political Economy of the Welfare State." Research Paper No. 808231-1-8. Center for Study of Public Choice, Virginia Polytechnic Institute and State University, June 1972.

———. "Politics, Property, and the Law: An Alternative Interpretation of Miller *et al.* v. Schoene." *Journal of Law and Economics* 15 (October 1972): 439–52.

———. *Public Finance in Democratic Process: Fiscal Institutions and Individual Choice.* Chapel Hill: University of North Carolina Press, 1967.

———. "Public Goods and Public Bads." In *Financing the Metropolis.* Edited by John P. Crecine. Vol. 4, Urban Affairs Annual Review. Beverly Hills: Sage Publications, 1970, pp. 51–72.

———. "The Samaritan's Dilemma." In *Altruism, Morality, and Economic Theory.* Edited by Edmund S. Phelps. Russell Sage Foundation, forthcoming.

————. "What Should Economists Do?" *Southern Economic Journal* 30 (January 1964): 213–22.

Buchanan, James M., and Devletoglou, Nicos E. *Academia in Anarchy: An Economic Diagnosis.* New York: Basic Books, 1970.

Buchanan, James M., and di Pierro, Alberto. "Pragmatic Reform and Constitutional Revolution." *Ethics* 79 (January 1969): 95–104.

Buchanan, James M., and Flowers, Marilyn. "An Analytical Setting for a Taxpayers' Revolution." *Western Economic Journal* 7 (December 1969): 349–59.

Buchanan, James M., and Tullock, Gordon. *The Calculus of Consent: Logical Foundations of Constitutional Democracy.* Ann Arbor: University of Michigan Press, 1962.

Bush, Winston. "Individual Welfare in Anarchy." In *Explorations in the Theory of Anarchy.* Edited by Gordon Tullock. Blacksburg, Virginia: Center for Study of Public Choice, 1972, pp. 5–18.

Bush, Winston, and Mayer, Lawrence S. "Some Implications of Anarchy for the Distribution of Property." Mimeographed paper. Center for Study of Public Choice, Virginia Polytechnic Institute and State University, Blacksburg, Virginia, 1973.

Charnovitz, Diane Windy "The Economics of Etiquette and Customs: The Theory of Property Rights as Applied to Rules of Behavior." M.A. thesis, University of Virginia, Charlottesville, Virginia, 1972.

Cheung, S. "Private Property Rights and Sharecropping." *Journal of Political Economy* 76 (December 1963): 1107–22.

Dahl, R. A., and Lindblom, C. E. *Politics, Economics, and Welfare.* New York: Harper and Row, 1953.

Demsetz, Harold. "The Exchange and Enforcement of Property Rights." *Journal of Law and Economics* 7 (October 1964): 11–26.

————. "Toward a Theory of Property Rights." *American Economic Review* 57 (May 1964): 347–59.

————. "Wealth Distribution and the Ownership of Rights." *Journal of Legal Studies* 1 (June 1972): 223–32.

Downs, Anthony. *An Economic Theory of Democracy.* New York: Harper and Row, 1957.

————. *Inside Bureaucracy.* Boston: Little, Brown, 1967.

Ely, Richard T. *Property and Contract in Their Relations to the Distribution of Wealth.* Vols. 1, 2. New York: Macmillan, 1914.

Friedman, David. *The Machinery of Freedom.* New York: Harper and Row, 1973.

Furubotn, Eirik G. "Economic Organization and Welfare Distribution." *Swedish Journal of Economics* 4 (1971): 409–16.

Furubotn, Eirik G., and Pejovich, S. "Property Rights and Economic Theory: A Survey of Recent Literature." *Journal of Economic Literature* 10 (December 1972): 1137–62.

Gough, J. W. *The Social Contract.* 2d ed. Oxford: Oxford University Press, 1957.

Guerin, Daniel. *Anarchism.* With an introduction by Noam Chomsky. Translated by Mark Klopper. New York: Monthly Review Press, 1970.

Hacker, Andrew. "Getting Used to Mugging." *New York Review of Books,* 19 April 1973.

Hall, John C. *Rousseau: An Introduction to His Political Philosophy.* London: Macmillan, 1973.

Hayek, F. A. *Law, Legislation, and Liberty.* Vol. 1, *Rules and Order.* Chicago: University of Chicago Press, 1973.

———. *Studies in Philosophy, Politics, and Economics.* London: Routledge and Kegan Paul, 1967.

Hearn, William E. *The Government of England.* London: Longmans Green, 1867.

Hobbes, Thomas. *Leviathan.* London: J. M. Dent, Everymans Library, 1943.

———. *Man and Citizen.* New York: Doubleday, Anchor Books, 1972.

Hobhouse, L. T. *Liberalism.* London: Oxford University Press, 1964.

Hochman, Harold M., and Rodgers, James D. "Pareto Optimal Redistribution." *American Economic Review* 59 (September 1969): 542–57.

The Holy Bible. King James Version.

Hume, David. *A Treatise of Human Nature.* Edited by L. A. Selby-Bigge. Oxford: Clarendon Press, 1960.

Hutt, W. H. *A Plan for Reconstruction.* London: Kegan Paul, 1943.

Ireland, Thomas R. "The Politician's Dilemma: What to Represent." *Public Choice* 12 (Spring 1972): 35–42.

———. "Public Order as a Public Good." Typescript. Chicago: Loyola University, 1968.

Johnson, David B. "Meade, Bees, and Externalities." *Journal of Law and Economics* 16 (April 1972): 35–52.

Kaufmann, Walter. *Without Guilt and Justice.* New York: Peter H. Wyden, 1973.

Kedourie, Elie. "The Lure of Revolutionary Revolution." *Encounter,* July 1972, 45–50.

Knight, Frank H. "Intellectual Confusion on Morals and Economics." *International Journal of Ethics* (January 1935).

———. *Intelligence and Democratic Action.* Cambridge: Harvard University Press, 1960.

Kristol, Irving. *On the Democratic Idea in America.* New York: Harper and Row, 1972.

Leoni, Bruno. *Freedom and the Law.* Princeton: Van Nostrand, 1961.

Lindblom, C. E. "Policy Analysis." *American Economic Review* 48 (June 1958): 298–312.

Locke, John. *Second Treatise of Civil Government.* Chicago: Henry Regnery, Gateway Edition, 1955.

Luce, Duncan, and Raiffa, Howard. *Games and Decisions.* New York: John Wiley and Sons, 1957.

Maine, Henry S. *Ancient Law.* Boston: Beacon Press, 1963.

Maitland, F. W. *The Constitutional History of England.* Cambridge: Cambridge University Press, 1961.

Martin, Donald L. "The Economics of Jury Conscription." *Journal of Political Economy* 80 (July/August 1972): 680–702.

McGuire, M., and Aaron, H. "Efficiency and Equity in the Optimal Supply of a Public Good." *Review of Economics and Statistics* 51 (February 1969): 31–39.

McIntosh, Donald. *The Foundations of Human Society.* Chicago: University of Chicago Press, 1969.

McKean, Roland N. "Divergencies between Individual and Total Cost within Government." *American Economic Review* 54 (May 1964): 243–49.

———. "The Economics of Trust, Altruism, and Corporate Responsibility." In *Altruism, Morality, and Economic Theory.* Edited by E. S. Phelps. New York: Russell Sage Foundation, 1973.

———. *Public Spending.* New York: McGraw-Hill, 1968.

Michelman, Frank I. "Property, Utility, and Fairness: Comments on the Ethical Foundations of 'Just Compensation' Law." *Harvard Law Review* 80 (April 1967): 1165–1257.

Montesquieu. *The Spirit of Laws.* Vol. 38, *Great Books of the Western World.* Chicago: Encyclopaedia Britannica, 1952.

Moss, Laurence. "Private Property Anarchism: An American Variant." Paper presented at Southern Economic Association meeting in Washington, D.C., November 1972.

Moynihan, Daniel P. "An Address to the Entering Class at Harvard, 1972." *Commentary* 54 (December 1972): 55–60.

Mueller, Dennis. "Achieving a Just Polity." *American Economic Review* 44 (May 1974): 147–52.

Murphy, Jeffrie G. "Marxism and Retribution." *Philosophy and Public Affairs* 2 (Spring 1973): 217–43.

Musgrave, R. A. "Comment." *American Economic Review* 60 (December 1970): 991–93.

———. *The Theory of Public Finance.* New York: McGraw-Hill, 1959.

Musgrave, R. A., and Peacock, A. T., eds. *Classics in the Theory of Public Finance*. London: Macmillan, 1958.

Niskanen, William A. *Bureaucracy and Representative Government*. Chicago: Aldine-Atherton, 1971.

North, Douglass C., and Thomas, Robert Paul. *The Rise of the Western World: A New Economic History*. Cambridge: Cambridge University Press, 1973.

Nozick, Robert. "Distributive Justice." *Philosophy and Public Affairs* 3 (Fall 1973): 45–126.

Oates, Wallace E. *Fiscal Federalism*. New York: Harcourt Brace Jovanovich, 1972.

Olson, Mancur. *The Logic of Collective Action*. Cambridge: Harvard University Press, 1965.

——. "Some Historic Variations in Property Institutions." Typescript. University of Maryland, 1967.

Ostrom, Vincent. *The Intellectual Crisis in American Public Administration*. University: University of Alabama Press, 1973.

Palmer, R. R. *The Age of Democratic Revolution*. Vols. 1, 2. Princeton: Princeton University Press, 1959, 1969.

Passmore, John. *The Perfectibility of Man*. London: Duckworth, 1970.

Peacock, A. T., and Wiseman, Jack. *Growth of Public Expenditures in the United Kingdom*. New York: National Bureau of Economic Research, 1961.

Peel, J. D. Y. *Herbert Spencer: The Evaluation of a Sociologist*. London: Heinemann, 1971.

Pejovich, S. "Towards an Economic Theory of the Creation and Specification of Property Rights." *Review of Social Economy* 30 (September 1972): 309–25.

Plott, Charles R., and Meyer, Robert A. "The Technology of Public Goods, Externalities, and the Exclusion Principle." California Institute of Technology, Social Science Working Paper No. 15, February 1973.

Polanyi, Michael. *The Logic of Liberty*. Chicago: University of Chicago Press, 1951.

Polinsky, A. Mitchell. "Probabilistic Compensation Criteria." *Quarterly Journal of Economics* 86 (August 1972): 407–25.

Posner, Richard A. "Killing or Wounding to Protect a Property Interest." *Journal of Law and Economics* 14 (April 1971): 201–32.

Pound, Roscoe. *Law and Morals*. Chapel Hill: University of North Carolina Press, 1962.

Rae, Douglas W. "The Limits of Consensual Decision." Mimeographed paper presented at Public Choice Society Conference, College Park, Maryland, March 1973.

Rawls, John. *A Theory of Justice*. Cambridge: Harvard University Press, 1971.

Riker, William H. "Public Safety as a Public Good." In *Is Law Dead?* Edited by E. V. Rostow. New York: Simon and Schuster, 1971, pp. 379–85.

Riker, William H., and Ordeshook, Peter C. *An Introduction to Positive Political Theory.* Englewood Cliffs: Prentice Hall, 1973.

Roberts, Paul Craig. *Alienation and the Soviet Economy.* Albuquerque: University of New Mexico Press, 1973.

———. "An Organizational Model of the Market." *Public Choice* 10 (Spring 1971): 81–92.

Rothbard, Murray. *For a New Liberty.* New York: Macmillan, 1973.

Rousseau, J. J. *A Discourse on the Origin of Inequality.* Vol. 38, *Great Books of the Western World.* Chicago: Encyclopaedia Britannica, 1952, pp. 319–66.

———. *A Discourse on Political Economy.* Vol. 38, *Great Books of the Western World.* Chicago: Encyclopaedia Britannica, 1952, pp. 367–85.

———. *The Social Contract.* Vol. 38, *Great Books of the Western World.* Chicago: Encyclopaedia Britannica, 1952, pp. 387–439.

de Ruggiero, Guido. *The History of European Liberalism.* Translated by R. G. Collingwood. Boston: Beacon Press, 1959.

Russell, Bertrand. *Authority and the Individual.* New York: AMS Press, 1968.

Samuels, Warren J. "In Defense of a Positive Approach to Government as an Economic Variable." *Journal of Law and Economics* 15 (October 1972): 453–60.

———. "Interrelations between Legal and Economic Processes." *Journal of Law and Economics* 14 (October 1971): 435–50.

———. "Welfare Economics, Power, and Property." In *Perspectives of Property.* Edited by G. Wunderlich and W. L. Gibson, Jr. State College: Institute for Land and Water Resources, Pennsylvania State University, 1972, pp. 61–146.

Samuelson, Paul A. "The Pure Theory of Public Expenditure." *Review of Economics and Statistics* 36 (November 1954): 387–89.

Schelling, Thomas C. "The Ecology of Micromotives." *Public Interest* 75 (Fall 1971): 59–98.

———. "Hockey Helmets, Concealed Weapons, and Daylight Saving." Discussion Paper No. 9, Public Policy Program, John F. Kennedy School of Government, Harvard University, July 1972.

———. *The Strategy of Conflict.* Cambridge: Harvard University Press, 1960.

Schlatter, Richard B. *Private Property: The History of an Idea.* New Brunswick: Rutgers University Press, 1951.

Singer, Peter. *Democracy and Disobedience.* Oxford: Clarendon Press, 1973.

Smith, Adam. *The Wealth of Nations.* New York: Modern Library, 1937.

Southern, R. W. *The Making of the Middle Ages.* New Haven: Yale University Press, 1953.

Sowell, Thomas. "Violence and the Payoff Society." *University of Chicago Magazine,* November/December 1971, 2–8.

Stigler, George J. "The Optimum Enforcement of Laws." *Journal of Political Economy* 78 (May/June 1970): 526–36.

Taylor, Gordon Rattray. "A New View of the Brain." *Encounter,* February 1971, 25–37.

Taylor, Richard. *Freedom, Anarchy, and the Law.* Englewood Cliffs: Prentice-Hall, 1973.

Thompson, Earl. "The Taxation of Wealth and the Wealthy." Los Angeles: UCLA Working Paper, February 1972.

Tuerck, David. "Constitutional Asymmetry." *Papers on Non-Market Decision Making* 2 (1967) (now *Public Choice*).

———. "Uniformity in Taxation; Discrimination in Benefits: An Essay in Law and Economics." Ph.D. diss., University of Virginia, 1966.

Tullock, Gordon. "The Charity of the Uncharitable." *Western Economic Journal* 9 (December 1971): 379–92.

———. *The Logic of Law.* New York: Basic Books, 1971.

———. "The Paradox of Revolution." *Public Choice* 11 (Fall 1971): 89–100.

———. *The Politics of Bureaucracy.* Washington, D.C.: Public Affairs Press, 1965.

———. "Public Decisions as Public Goods." *Journal of Political Economy* 79 (July/August 1971): 913–18.

———. *The Social Dilemma,* forthcoming.

Tullock, Gordon, ed. *Explorations in the Theory of Anarchy.* Blacksburg, Virginia: Center for Study of Public Choice, 1972.

van den Haag, Ernest. *Political Violence and Civil Disobedience.* New York: Harper Torchbooks, 1972.

von Mises, Ludwig. *Human Action: A Treatise on Economics.* New Haven: Yale University Press, 1949.

Wagner, Richard E. *The Fiscal Organizations of American Federalism.* Chicago: Markham Publishing Company, 1971.

Wicksell, Knut. *Finanztheoretische Untersuchungen.* Jena: Gustav Fischer, 1896.

Wildavsky, Aaron. "Government and the People." *Commentary* 56 (August 1973): 25–32.

Wunderlich, Gene, and Gibson, W. L., Jr., eds. *Perspectives of Property.* State College: Institute for Research on Land and Water Resources, Pennsylvania State University, 1972.

Index

This book is set in Minion, a typeface designed by Robert Slimbach specifically for digital typesetting. Released by Adobe in 1989, it is a versatile neohumanist face that shows the influence of Slimbach's own calligraphy.

This book is printed on paper that is acid-free and meets the requirements of the American National Standard for Permanence of Paper for Printed Library Materials, z39.48-1992. ⊛

Book design by Louise OFarrell, Gainesville, Fla.
Typography by Impressions Book and Journal Services, Inc., Madison, Wisc.
Printed and bound by Worzalla Publishing Company, Stevens Point, Wisc.